This book is hugely timely and import
point out, as coaches and leaders, we r
world one person at a time. This era cal

approach, and for those willing to step up, this rich and wise book will be the ideal
companion to help them do so.

Liz Hall, coach and editor of Coaching at Work and author of *Mindful Coaching* (Kogan Page), and *Coach the team* (Penguin), UK

Hawkins and Turner masterfully challenge us as coaches and leaders to engage in a necessary revolution to become 'future-fit' for the ever-growing complexities of the 21st century. Shifting our focus from the individual to the wider ecology, cultivating a system view and regularly disrupting ourselves with an eye to the longer view in these most formidable times. This book is truly a tour de force and must read for all of us!

Pam McLean, PhD, CEO Hudson Institute of Coaching, USA;
Author, *Self as Coach, Self as Leader* & *Completely Revised Handbook of Coaching*

It is time to question everything we thought we knew about coaching. The future of coaching lies not in one narrow cultural or philosophical domain but in diverse responses to complexity, in the aspirations of new generations, in wider social impact and in coach-AI partnerships. Peter and Eve capture this challenge admirably.

Professor David Clutterbuck, David Clutterbuck Partnership, UK

As our profession takes shape, and evolves, coaches' pursuit of Excellence and Mastery – and the wider systems that we serve – needs to stay *relevant* so that we create the biggest ripples, or collective impact, within both business and society. The authors of *Systemic Coaching* convey this beautifully, as an essential read for any practitioner or leader coach, looking to find greater meaning in their work.

Katherine Tulpa, Group CEO, Chair & Co-founder,
Association for Coaching; and Executive Director, Wisdom8, UK

This is truly a book for our age. Hawkins and Turner deliver a rich and insightful exploration of the systemic coaching model, emphasising that coaching is not just for the highly privileged few, but for the benefit of all. They highlight the collective change which is needed in our approach towards coaching, and the need to respond to the future in a more informed, compassionate and conscious way. We all need to take responsibility for our place in the world and for our ecological crisis. Applying the 'Ecological Awareness Model' to coaching will be crucial in coming years. As Hawkins and Turner rightly point out, the ecological dimension is present in every coaching session, overtly or covertly, consciously or unconsciously.

Clive Mann, Executive Coach working with senior leaders and
their teams, Managing Director of Ridler & Co and Author of the
Ridler Report, UK

Hawkins and Turner's *Systemic Coaching* powerfully addresses what continues to be, sadly, a consistent failing in the coaching industry. All too often we find coaches trapped in the vacuum of the individual, blind to organisational and market system dynamics. This malaise renders a lot of coaching into nothing more than a fancy counselling session, for ten times the price. However, when coaching is delivered systemically, in the way that Hawkins and Turner beautifully elucidate in this book, it has the potential to be one of the most profound value creating interventions available in the business world of today. This is a must read. Every coach should have a copy on their bookshelf with dog ears and margin notes.

Dr Marc Kahn, Global Head of HR & OD, Investec Plc, and Visiting Professor of People, Organisation and Strategy Practices, Middlesex University, London, UK

A tour de force! Essential reading for every OD consultant, HR specialist, coach and supervisor! It addresses *the* issue of our time, liberating coaching from the shackles of individual development to integrate the wider organisational, eco and ethical system in which we all exist.

Tony Worgan, Head of BBC Coaching and Mentoring, BBC Leadership & Personal Development, UK

Coaching was once the domain of the privileged few, or perhaps reserved as a tool to be used for remedial cases. However, both the coaching industry and organisations have matured and now coaching is increasingly seen as way of achieving substantial and sustained change. As coaches, we are arguably uniquely placed to influence organisational thinking – to pierce the organisational conscience. Without doubt, coaching is a force for good, and this book, 'Systemic Coaching' challenges us all to be an even greater force for good. Whether you are an Individual, team coach or a supervisor, through the themes explored, through the well thought through questions asked together with the case studies, the book holds up a challenging mirror to our practices. Like any well-placed coaching questions, they are designed to make us sit up and think. Many coaches work as individuals or in small practices, perhaps ploughing a lonely furrow, maybe wondering if they are actually making a difference. I was delighted therefore to read in the final chapter about the 'call to action' and for each of us to 'raise our game'. We often encourage our coachees to dream big, to imagine what might be possible, and so on. Well, just imagine what kind of paradigm shift we could achieve by collectively rising to the challenge of the 'call to action'.

Tim Dench, Head of Coaching & Mentoring, Euroclear, UK

This book offers a blueprint for the next stage in the evolution of coaching. It blends a call to coaches for deeper personal development with an expansion of Peter's highly regarded systemic approach to include an ecological commitment. May it inspire you to join the necessary revolution.

Dr David Drake, CEO, Moment Institute, founder of narrative coaching, USA

Systemic Coaching: Delivering Value Beyond the Individual takes coaching to a whole new level. It challenges coaches to raise their game further by focusing on the positive difference they are and could be making in the human and more-than-human world. I highly recommend this to coaches, mentors, supervisors and leaders.

Dr Marshall Goldsmith, World-renowned business educator, coach and author, USA

This splendid new book from master coaches Peter Hawkins and Eve Turner is a major contribution to the growing field of New Generation Coaching: coaches committed to partnering with leaders in service to a better world. Clearly structured, addressing their theme of systemic coaching from every angle, and offering a rich range of examples, case studies and guidelines, the authors pull no punches. They address the key questions we need to ask ourselves at this critical juncture in the planet's history and in the development of coaching: What and who is coaching for in the face of our huge, complex global challenges? How can coaches help organisations become 'future fit' in an interdependent, volatile and uncertain world? How might coaches work together with leaders to develop an eco-systemic vision and multi-stakeholder perspective? What does it take to deliver coaching value beyond the individual? This is a riveting read and a landmark publication that should be in every coach's library.

Hetty Einzig, author of *The Future of Coaching: vision, responsibility and leadership in transforming times*, UK

Systemic Coaching breaks open the box of traditional coaching to show us a new vision and role for the profession. Hawkins and Turner then lay out the tools, models and method to make it real. From a place of passion and purpose they challenge all coaches to see more, be more and do more for individuals, teams, organizations and the planet. This book will shift your horizon and enrich your work.

Phillip Sandahl, coauthor of *Teams Unleashed: How to release the power and human potential of work teams,* and *Co-Active Coaching: The proven framework for transformative conversations at work and in life*, USA

A profound and essential read for anyone who is engaged in and with the field of coaching. The book highlights the importance of coaching becoming increasingly aware of the social, ecological and political changes in order to peer and partner with clients beyond the individual or the team. Having worked in a global matrix organisation for many years I believe this is critical for the future, as is the point the book makes on redistributive coaching and echo empathy, brilliant!

Claire Davey, Former Head of Coaching & Leadership Development, Deloitte UK; Director at CDPerformance Ltd, UK

This challenging book shows how organisations today face some daunting challenges in their quests to be successful, including the rapid evolution of technology, the disintermediation of industries and an ever more pressing need to learn and adapt. Also how those coaches who desire to contribute to the ongoing, unceasing transformation of society must embrace the same challenges, viewing them as opportunities rather than threats. The role of the future coach will evolve, as organisations re-insource the functions of the traditional coach. The future coach will be adept at working with groups and teams. If it is to be useful, the coaching industry will move beyond the current narrative around coaching competencies and its desire to become a profession. Instead it will focus on learning how to navigate change in a complex world and will invite thought leaders from other disciplines and domains to engage in dialogue. The authors show how coaches can reinvent themselves and provide many practical insights, case examples and approaches to help us coaches on our way. All coaches who want to be 'future-fit' need to read it.

Dr Paul Lawrence, Centre for Coaching in Organisations, Lecturer in Coaching at Sydney Business School (UoW), Sydney, Australia

Not a book for the shelf, but a book for every day – on each page there is something that will resonate with thoughtful Coaches, Supervisors or OD Practitioners who are ready to stretch and embrace systemic coaching. This book will challenge your thinking and transform your practise.

Dr Colleen Harding, Head of Organisational Development, Bournemouth University, UK

Hawkins and Turner offer provocative new thinking for a complacent world. If you want to be challenged about your coaching practice and how you deliver value to individuals and organisations this book is a great place to start your thinking journey to develop Horizon 3 thinking about the future of coaching.

Jonathan Passmore, Director Henley Centre for Coaching, UK

Oxford Saïd Business School and Meyler Campbell recently announced the Ignite partnership, to help leaders tackle the existential challenges almost all sectors face: this book opens up many of the issues faced by those working systemically and is warmly welcomed.

Anne Scoular, Founder Meyler Campbell and Associate Scholar, Oxford Saïd Business School's Ignite Programme, UK

Systemic Coaching is a must read for all coaches in training as well for experienced, mentors, coaches, and coach supervisors who are committed to use system thinking in their work and be prepared to meet the future needs of our societies. The authors, through a dialogical approach, invite readers to a reflective space that provides an extraordinary learning opportunity and challenge them to think beyond traditional frameworks. They create awareness of the critical role of the coaches, not only at supporting leaders to be prepared for the future but also their ethical responsibility of revolutionizing the coaching practice to meet these needs.

Dr Damian Goldvarg, MCC, CSP, ESIA. President, The Goldvarg Consulting Group, Inc. International Coach Federation Global Past President (2013–2014), USA

This book is a passionate and persuasive appeal for the coaching community to keep the needs of the whole world rather than one person in front of us in the core of our philosophy. In the current state of the world, the values that the authors advocate are incredibly important for all of us, not only for coaches. At the same time, I recall that after one of the author's presentations a coach from the audience thanked him for reminding about such importance. I wish we knew why such a reminder is needed and why we forget! I suspect that the answer to this question brings us back to the individual and how they face what is happening within and around them.

Professor Tatiana Bachkirova, Director of the International Centre for Coaching and Mentoring Studies, Oxford Brookes University, UK

Peter Hawkins and Eve Turner have co-authored a tour de force of Systemic Coaching. The approach goes beyond coaching as we know it and highlights the importance of looking at the whole picture. This comprehensive book is thorough and covers everything a trainee or experienced coach will need to know about the theory and practice of Systematic Coaching. It's great to see that the authors have included an exciting chapter on Eco-systemic coaching.

Professor Stephen Palmer, University of Wales, Trinity Saint David, UK

The central challenge of coaching has always been: who is it for: the person or the organisation they work for? At last, we have a clear-sighted view of where the answers lie. Hawkins and Turner understand the delicate and complex interplay between people and place and skilfully, wisely disentangle it. At its best, coaching makes organisations and the individuals in them smarter, braver, more alert and farsighted. It's a lofty goal and never achieved without effort. But this book gets you started in the right place: knowing the ultimate destination.

Margaret Heffernan, CEO and author, *Wilful Blindness*, UK

How fortunate we are to benefit from Peter's wisdom on systemic coaching. It is a very profound and future-fit philosophy. It reinvents the traditional approach in individual coaching, team coaching and organizational coaching. Leaders can make breakthrough once their view shifts from ME to WE with stakeholder engaging into coaching process. Coaches can make larger impact to the world with ecological mindset and the grounded process, methods and tools introduced in this book.

Karen Wu, CEO, Co-wisdom Coaching Center, China

Time to think again about coaching and our contract as coaches with the wider world, with this journey into the future, providing inspiration and challenge in equal measure. Warmly recommended.

Erik de Haan, Director of Ashridge Centre for Coaching and Professor of Organisation Development, UK

A book of awakening. Peter and Eve provoke us to redefine what success means in tomorrow's world. They trigger our minds in search for the true meaning of "win-win-win" that we as leaders of our era should envision for the next generation and beyond. This book marvellously paves the way to lead traditional coaching mindset and leadership beings to go beyond single individual or organization level to the larger whole of the planet that we ought to take responsibility for. A must read for all coaches and leaders.

Deana Peng, Executive Coach, Presence, Japan

With Peter as our guide and working with the principles and ideas outlined in this book, we have co-created a leadership development programme for our law firm partners. Taking a systemic approach, exploring future-back and outside-in perspectives, building collaborations and networks and empowering individuals to design and lead their own learning has created a real shift in our culture. More open. More collaborative, More innovation. More stretch in development.

Trevor Comyn, Director of Knowledge, Learning and Development and **Rachel Donath**, Head of Learning and Development Team at Mills & Reeve, UK

In the years that I have known Peter, he is nothing if not thought-provoking. Peter has a unique ability, a prescience almost, to glimpse into future possibilities while connecting it to the present. And so it is with this new book with Eve Turner. Together, they provoke us with persuasive clarity, the challenges facing coaching in the future, spur us to a call for action and journey alongside us by sharing their research and experiences, together with illustrative case studies, tools, practical tips and a way forwards that is both compelling and inspiring. The warning signs are there -- that the practice of coaching needs to change to be fit-for-purpose for the challenges of the future. This book aptly sounds the warning not in a foreboding way but with optimism and vision. It is a powerfully informative and empowering book!

Paul Lim, Managing Consultant, Phoenix Leadership Consulting, Singapore

We're almost daily alerted to the turbulent times of the digital age and influence of AI demanding rather than attracting change. Similarly, coaching has necessarily moved beyond the narrow margins of its origins in individual development. In a dynamic world with an ecologically threatened environment coaching must necessarily mature to survive, thrive and serve the constantly changing needs of all stakeholders. Coaching can contribute to the value chain of disrupters easing the transition into work that is yet to be named and supporting the reversal of inherited eco-disasters.

Systemic Coaching: *Delivering Value Beyond the Individual* succinctly names just what this text delivers. The combination of chapters takes you on a progressive journey transporting coaching and coach supervision to be future-fit for tomorrow's anticipated world of work. Refinements for practice combine with persuasive reasoning for co-creating synergistic systemic applications that strengthen coaching's contribution ultimately for the benefit of society. The appendix of multi-cultural case studies from around the globe adds a further level of vibrancy to an already abundantly rich text.

Dr Lise Lewis, EMCC International Special Ambassador, UK

This is a seminal book setting the ground for the next stage of coaching and coach training for future generations of coaches. Thoroughly researched it builds on the work of those "fellow travelers" who have developed aspects of Systemic Coaching. It addresses the ethical issues and doesn't shy away of challenging coaching on the environmental responsibility to the wider system.

John Leary-Joyce, Founder & Chair AoEC, co-author of *Systemic Team Coaching*, UK

"This is a radical, comprehensive, wide-ranging and pioneering investigation of individual and team systemic coaching. Peter Hawkins and Eve Turner argue that to think and be systemic, it is essential to bring in the challenges that come 'future-back' and 'outside-in'. *Systemic Coaching* covers the breadth and depth of systemic coaching, from individual, executive, leadership, team and group coaching. It encompasses the matching and evaluation of coaches, systemic questions for client contracting and multi-party as well as multi-regional contracting. *Systemic Coaching* is accessible, scholarly and evidence based.

Hawkins and Turner take a strategic look at coaching to help determine the role that coaching can play in an organization. This moves us away from individual and ad hoc coaching that does not satisfy what an organisation, its future and wider stakeholders will need from an integrated coaching intervention. The Authors' original approach takes an innovative look at what coaching can effectively achieve for the organization, all its members, customers and stakeholders over a period of time that will impact the behaviour and performance of all stakeholders and so benefit the health of the organisation.

What is made very clear is the importance of relationships. 'In systemic coaching, as with any form of coaching, collaboration is the foundation of the working partnership and the heart of an effective contracting relationship'. In this book, the practitioner will find a wide range of activities, processes, methods and case studies to use in individual and team coaching and in building collaborative relationships. There is an overview about how to supervise coaches, ethical considerations for coaching and supervision, and criteria for systemic coach training. The authors introduce the idea of *eco-systemic team coaching* which sees the team as "co-evolving in dynamic relationship with its ever-changing eco-system".

What is different about this book, is that it asks the reader to take part in developing a comprehensive look at systemic coaching. Asking and answering questions is a role played by the reader as Hawkins and Turner deepen and widen their lens on every aspect of systemic coaching. This book is suitable not just for practitioners, but also for leaders who need to "develop We-Q" (collective and collaborative intelligence), and who wish to understand the nuts and bolts of an integrated systemic coaching approach that will help transform their organisational culture, behaviour and performance. It is a must read for anyone who wants coaching to make an impact on every aspect of an organisation's success.

Sunny Stout-Rostron, DProf, Faculty, University of Stellenbosch
School of Business, Cape Town, South Africa

This book is exactly what coaching, and more to the point, what our world needs right now. Hawkins and Turner have produced an inspiring wake up call for coaching, leaders and organisations alike. They ask us to see the world from a bigger systems perspective and begin to take concrete action from that perspective. Some years ago I argued that coaching in the 21st century needed perspectives that incorporated much wider system boundaries, longer temporal frames and perspectives that really paid attention to the processes and interconnections that operate across the whole system. Hawkins and Turner have done this with thoughtfulness, practicality and excellence. This book should not be in every leader's and every coaches library – it should be on their desks, dog-eared and falling apart with use.

Michael Cavanagh, Deputy Director, Coaching Psychology
Unit, University of Sydney

Systemic Coaching

Hawkins and Turner argue that coaching needs to step up to deliver value to all the stakeholders of the coachee, including those they lead, colleagues, investors, customers, partners, their local community and also the wider ecology. *Systemic Coaching* contains key chapters on how to contract in various settings, how to work relationally and dialogically, how to expand our own and others' ecological awareness, how to get greater value from supervision, work with systemic ethics and expand our impact. While illustrating why a new model of coaching is necessary, Hawkins and Turner also provide the tools and approaches that coaches and clients need to deliver this greater impact, accompanied by real-life case examples and interviews from the authors and other leading coaches and leaders globally.

Systemic Coaching will be an invaluable resource for coaches in practice and in training, mentors, coach supervisors, consultants in leadership development and HR and L&D professionals and leaders.

Peter Hawkins, Ph.D., is founder and Chairman of Renewal Associates and Professor of Leadership at Henley Business School. He is a leading consultant, writer and researcher in leadership and leadership development and an international thought leader and best-selling author in systemic coaching, systemic team coaching and leadership.

Eve Turner combines research and writing with a busy coaching and supervision practice. A fellow at Henley Business School and the University of Southampton, she received the 2018 EMCC and Coaching at Work awards for Supervision, the Coaching at Work 2019 and 2015 Best Article/Series awards and the 2015 EMCC Coaching Award.

Systemic Coaching

Delivering Value Beyond the Individual

Peter Hawkins and Eve Turner

LONDON AND NEW YORK

First published 2020
by Routledge
2 Park Square, Milton Park, Abingdon, Oxon OX14 4RN

and by Routledge
52 Vanderbilt Avenue, New York, NY 10017

Routledge is an imprint of the Taylor & Francis Group, an informa business

British Library Cataloguing-in-Publication Data
A catalogue record for this book is available from the British
Library

Library of Congress Cataloging-in-Publication Data
A catalog record for this book has been requested

ISBN: 978-1-138-32248-6 (hbk)
ISBN: 978-1-138-32249-3 (pbk)
ISBN: 978-0-429-45203-1 (ebk)

Typeset in Times New Roman
by Apex CoVantage, LLC

To my grandchildren, Nancy, Charlie, Freddie, Iris and Florence – on behalf of my generation I apologise for the many challenges in the world we are leaving your generation, and may you find many great coaches and mentors who can support you in making a beneficial difference in the world. (PH)

To some amazing women in my life, especially my beloved late sister Anne Lyon whose generosity, selflessness and love connected our family globally. And to Nancy Kline, for helping me become truly attentive. To my many fellow travellers, including two Peters in my life (husband and co-author), for support, learning and challenge – thank you. (ET)

Contents

Figures

Tables

Preface

Ma (間)

The space between
Creates the frame,
To see the heavens
Peeping through.
So we can realise
We are three
Not Two.
  Peter Hawkins,
  Kyoto, April 2019

The Japanese concept of Ma is the space between and can be roughly translated as "gap", "space", "pause" or "the space between two structural parts". It is used in Japanese gardening, music and dance. It can also be applied to the 'pause' in work created by the coaching session, and also to the space between the coach and coachee, which if held appropriately allows the 'space for grace' for attending to the third implicit in every dyad.

In this book we are both celebrating the enormous contribution that coaching has made to individual leaders and managers, privileged enough to receive it over the last 40–50 years, as well as arguing that the mid 21st century requires a radical shift in all aspects of coaching and calling for a major paradigm change. In doing this we want to be clear that what we describe as the 'new' approach to coaching, for some readers will not be that new. We appreciate there are many fellow travellers and creators of this 'new' approach, many of whom we have learnt from and drawn upon. For many others, there will be some familiar elements, but much that is different. For some this will be a challenging text, as it has been for us at times (!), that takes you out of your comfort zone and current ways of thinking and framing your work, and invites you to reflect on yourself and your work from new perspectives. We encourage you to stay with the challenge, neither agreeing with us or rejecting our offerings, but seeing how they can dialogue with your own experience and thinking and create something new.

We do not think we have all the answers to what is required. What we have done is to go out and explore as much of the world of coaching as we can encompass, through interviews and dialogues and supervision with coaches and leaders from many parts of the world and from diverse backgrounds, approaches and trainings. We have also looked at much of the recently published literature, reports and research on coaching. There is a great deal of it, and so we have been inevitably selective, particularly looking for the green shoots of new approaches that focus beyond the individual and create value for the organization and stakeholders. We have also explored the parallel transformations that are going on in the worlds of leadership, leadership development, organizational thinking, approaches to teams, teaming and team development, psychology, psychotherapy and counselling. Further out we have looked at many other approaches to studying the necessary paradigm shifts in human ways of knowing (epistemology) and being (ontology), from philosophical, scientific, neuro-scientific, relational, systemic and ecological and spiritual schools.

Our hope is that we have managed to integrate the findings from all these many explorations, in an accessible way, and provide some pointers to the direction we believe coaching should go next. We hope this book is not seen as us trying to be summative, but rather opening up new dialogues with, and explorations by, others and merely providing a new springboard for further dialogues. Indeed, the book has brought dialogue between the two authors who have not necessarily always agreed but have made the disagreements productive!

We have an enormous debt of gratitude not only to the many people who have contributed directly to this book, through interviews, writing case studies and writing their own papers, research and books which have informed our work; but also, to the many contributions from all our other stakeholders, and there are many. We start with our clients, individuals, teams and organizations, who have trusted us to work with them and provided constant new challenges and learning. We are grateful to our trainees, who have pushed our thinking by asking challenging questions and making acute observations; readers of our other books and articles, who have showed what they found helpful and challenged what they disagreed with us, thus moving on our thinking; our friends and families who have provided the psychological containers for our maturation and the love that sustains us. Not least we look to our children and grandchildren (in Peter's case) who remind us by their very presence, of our accountability to future generations.

Acknowledgements

This book has matured over many years. Eve, having received some of her training by Peter in coach supervision, approached him in 2014 about supporting her research in how coaches carried out multi-stakeholder contracting. Through this research both of us became convinced that multi-stakeholder contracting was an underdeveloped aspect of coaching and deserved to be developed further. Peter was also being approached by coaches asking him to develop what he had done to make team coaching more systemic into the field of individual coaching. Both of us became committed to the need to have a new coaching book that focussed on how coaching could, in the 21st century, deliver value beyond the privileged individual coachee, to make a much bigger impact for the coachee's organization, their stakeholders and the wider world, including the-more-than-human ecology.

Many people have been influential in writing this book, to whom we owe a great gratitude. Over the years we have been blessed with great teachers and trainers, supervisors and spiritual teachers, and continue to learn and be supervised by people who keep our learning deepening and maturing.

Then there are our friends who have been so generous in reading and commenting on early drafts of this book, particularly Michaela von Britzke and Judy Ryde, who have carefully gone through each chapter and made it more readable.

Fiona Benton and Julie Jeffery have been extremely patient and generous in helping us sort out computers when they tried our patience, the permissions for quotes, the bibliography and manuscript and so much more. This book could not have been written without you, thank you. We are also grateful to our illustrator Jasmine Angell for her excellent cover design.

A particular thank you needs to go to all our coachees and the teams and organizations we both have worked with. We have learned from each and every one; and to our editing team at Routledge for their continuing support and enthusiasm: Susannah Frearson, Autumn Spalding and Heather Evans.

Finally, we need to thank our partners and wider families who have been both patient and highly supportive as we have spent many hours completing this book.

Contributors

Authors

Peter Hawkins is an international thought leader in systemic coaching, systemic team coaching and coaching supervision as well as leadership and organizational development and has taught in over 50 countries. He is Professor of Leadership at Henley Business School, Chairman of Renewal Associates and Honorary President of both the Association of Professional Executive Coaching and Supervision and the Academy of Executive Coaching. He is author of many best-selling books including *Leadership Team Coaching* (3rd edition 2017, Kogan Page); *Leadership Team Coaching in Practice* (2nd edition 2018, Kogan Page); *Creating a Coaching Culture* (McGraw Hill, 2012); *Coaching, Mentoring and Organizational Consultancy: Supervision and Development* (with Nick Smith, 2nd edition 2013, McGraw Hill); *Wise Fools Guide to Leadership* (O Books, 2006); *Integrative Psychotherapy in Theory and Practice* (with Judy Ryde Jessica Kingsley 2020); and *Supervision in the Helping Professions* (4th edition, 2012, McGraw Hill). Peter's work centres on the necessary shift in human consciousness to face the human and ecological challenges of our times.

Eve Turner researches and writes on a range of subjects including supervision, ethics and contracting in coaching with articles, co-authored book chapters and her first co-edited book *The Heart of Coaching Supervision – Working with Reflection and Self-Care* (2019, Routledge). A fellow at Henley Business School and the University of Southampton, Eve is an active volunteer within the profession. In 2016 she set up and leads the Global Supervisors' Network, a unique, free-of-charge, participative personal and professional development network for supervisors worldwide working in coaching, mentoring and consultancy that also supports research and writing: www.eve-turner.com/global-supervisors-network. An accredited master executive coach and supervisor, Eve has won several awards, including two EMCC European awards, the 2018 Supervision and the 2015 Coaching Awards, two from *Coaching at Work* magazine including the 2018 Contributions to Coaching Supervision Award and received the BPS Special Group in Coaching Psychology's 2008 award for a distinguished research project.

Contributors

Preeti D'mello leads Leadership Development and Diversity at Tata Consultancy Services and her 30-year career spans several industries and sectors. A leadership coach and an expert in positive organizational development and change, her education includes a master's in positive OD from Case Western University; adult development, the science of positive &coaching psychology at Harvard University and leadership maturity coaching. Preeti is an integral practitioner who brings together east and west approaches to development and spiritual integration, working with integral yoga and Buddhism drawing on polarity thinking, Zen, coaching, gestalt, and positive and constructive developmental psychology.

Corine Hines is a senior practitioner coach certified with the EMCC, systemic team coach and co-director of Spring Leadership Ltd. For nearly ten years Corine has been working with leaders and teams at the sharp end of coaching transformations in businesses ranging from £300M+ to less than £100K. Helping teams and individuals manage personal change and growth, each in their own unique circumstances, has allowed her to bring a wealth of experience to everyone with whom she works. Corine puts creating stakeholder value and always achieving return on expectation at the heart of how she works.

Giles Hutchins is a thought leader, executive coach, keynote speaker and C-Suite adviser on regenerative leadership– leadership aligned with living-systems thinking and being. He has been working at the nexus of business, living systems, eco-systemic thinking and regenerative leadership consciousness for over a decade and is author of the books *Regenerative Leadership* (2019), *Future Fit* (2016), *The Illusion of Separation* (2014) and *The Nature of Business* (2012). He is Chair of The Future Fit Leadership Academy (see www.ffla.co).

David Jarrett is an executive team coach for senior teams. He runs Orchard House Partners which specifically developed Orchard House as a special team development venue to create unique experiences for teams and leaders that give them time to think, connect with nature and consider their role in the ecosystems they are part of or leading. Teams use 150 acres of land including SSSI Wildwood, Commercial Cider Orchard, horse stud and re-wilding spaces. David includes the horses to provide equine facilitated coaching. Previously he was a partner in one of the Big 4 consultancy firms and CEO of Bath Consultancy Group.

Ingela Camba Ludlow is a PCC coach and supervisor with a master's in psychoanalytic psychotherapy. Ingela has more than 20 years of business experience and 15 years working in human development, training and coaching. Based in Mexico, she has partnered with clients in various countries in Latin America as well as the US, Canada and Singapore. Ingela embraces and prioritizes sustainable projects as the key answer to reconcile human civilization with nature.

Sarah McKinnon has 20 years of experience of developing leaders and in leading cultural change in complex and diverse organizations around the world, working both in-house and in consultancy across a wide range of sectors. Sustainability leadership in individuals and organizations has been a specialism for over ten years. Shifting thinking by integrating experience of the natural world, with the information and motivation to have a positive impact, she runs programmes from Borneo to Brazil. Sarah is an experienced coach and team coach, a developer of in-house coaching capability and has recently started supervision training.

Dr Josie McLean began her career in the finance and automotive industries as a corporate strategic planner having initial qualifications as a financial analyst. Her fascination with strategy, process, people and change led her to explore coaching. In 1999 Josie founded her coaching business and now specializes in guiding the development of leaders and organizations to equip them to cope with and lead through increasing changing and complex challenges, including organizational cultural evolution. Josie has expertise in organizational sustainability, complex adaptive systems, adaptive leadership, emergent change, and organizational culture. She continues to publish in these areas.

Dr Michel Moral spent most of his career in an international environment as a manager and executive. Since 2003 he has been a coach, a supervisor (ESIA) and a supervisor's trainer (ESQA). He has published ten books on coaching and supervision. He explores new domains of coaching and supervision such as organizational coaching and its supervision, supervision of coaching with horses, supervision of "win or die" situations, supervision of coaching for collective intelligence, etc. Michel likes challenges and research.

David Matthew Prior works in leadership development with over 20 years of experience in executive coaching. Credentialed as a master certified coach (ICF) and board certified coach (CCE), David is an instructor, coaching supervisor and examiner in the Columbia University Coaching Certification Programme. An MBA in international business, David has coached 1,000 executives in 30 countries, trained 5,000 executive coaches and created results for more than 100 organizations. His multilingual (English, Spanish, French) skillset has benefited a global clientele and been applied within varied cultural landscapes.

Ram S Ramanathan, an accredited master coach with ICF, EMCC and BCC, co-founded Coacharya in 2013, which has graduated over 600 credentialed coaches, of whom 27 are MCC coaches. A coach who has long CEO and serial entrepreneur stints, with deep interest in spirituality, Ram integrates Eastern wisdom with Western sciences to coach corporate leaders in their transformational leadership journey of 'Mindless Barefoot Leadership'. Ram and his wife are Singapore citizens with permanent residence in Bangalore, India with their dog, spending part of the year with their grandchildren in US.

Nick Smith is an APECS–accredited executive coach and an EMCC–accredited supervisor. He has over 20 years of experience as a leadership and organizational change consultant and was the lead consultant on setting up and running the international project for the client in his case study. The project is still ongoing. Nick trains supervisors and has co-authored various contributions to both supervision and coaching practice with his long-time colleague Peter Hawkins. His book on transformational coaching is published in 2020.

Tammy Turner is a master certified coach with the ICF and CEO of Turner International. Since 2001, Tammy has worked globally with key industry and government decision makers, leveraging her previous executive background in information and communications technology to catalyze change. As one of the most experienced leadership and team coaches in Australasia, she has been a contributing author to numerous articles and textbooks on coaching and the power of collaborative leadership to create learning organizations.

Barbara Walsh is Managing Director of Metaco, based in South Africa. As a master systemic team and executive coach, she works locally and internationally with leadership teams to achieve far-reaching organizational results. She has an MSc in coaching and behavioural change through Henley Business School in the UK and is registered as a master HR practitioner: learning and development with the South African Board of People Practices.

Julie Zhang is an executive coach and facilitator with around 20 years of leadership experience in global financial services, electronics manufacturing and management consulting. Certified by ICF as an ACC with over 900 coaching hours, she is passionate about helping leaders and organizations grow towards realizing their unlimited potential. Julie has an MBA from China Europe International Business School and is based in Shanghai, China, working in both Mandarin Chinese and English.

Chapter 1

The need for a new approach to coaching

Coaching by its nature is relational and dialogic, where two or more people discover new meaning and co-create new thinking and ways of being and doing in the world between them. This book also needs to be dialogic, for as Marshal McLuhan (1964) famously said: "The medium is the message" – or to put it another way: what we say and how we say it need to be congruent and aligned.

So, let us, authors and reader, start in dialogue. We invite you to consider some opening questions that are central to how a systemic coaching conversation needs to begin. Perhaps you can imagine you are coming to meet the two of us and we begin by asking:

- Please tell us, what is most important to know about you?
- What are you most passionate about – what really matters to you?
- What is your work and whom does your work serve? Please list all your current and future stakeholders (those that may benefit directly or indirectly from the work you do).
- If we could invite five to ten representatives of your current and future stakeholders into this imaginary dialogue and ask them what they would like you to learn from reading this book and dialoguing with the two authors, what might be some of their answers? What questions would they like you to ask while you are here, so they can benefit and get value from you reading this book? Please write down their names and list the questions they would bring and the learnings they would benefit from.
- Now what are the questions and new learnings you want to engage with while reading this book – that will ensure that you and your future life and work, as well as your stakeholders, gain maximum value from the time you spend with us?

We cannot promise to answer all those questions – and anyway, even if we could, that would not fit the nature of a dialogue –but we can promise that by you holding those potential learnings and questions in mind the dialogue will be richer and the learning more valuable.

In the first section of this book and in this chapter, we will address our starting question: why do we believe that coaching needs a revolution in its theory and practice? In Chapter 2 we will explore how the needs of our clients are rapidly changing. In chapter 3 we will explore the 'What': what is Systemic Coaching? We will provide a working definition and outline how it builds on other recent developments in thinking about coaching. Having established the 'Why' and the 'What', in Chapters 4, 5, 6 and 7 we will go on to the 'How'. In Chapter 4 we will explore what organizations can do to deliver more value from the coaching they manage. In Chapter 5 we discuss the importance of multi-stakeholder contracting. In Chapter 6 we present the maps of the coaching journey that we have found helpful at the organizational engagement and individual client engagement levels and for the process of an individual coaching session. Then in Chapter 7, we will describe the tools and approaches that are particularly useful and possibly necessary for this journey.

We start by sharing some of our own questions that led us to enter this dialogical exploration.

1. How can coaching help avoid business and organizational catastrophe?

It was early in 2009 I (Peter) gave a keynote lecture to a coaching conference in the U.K. I asked the question: "What were the coaches doing while the banks were burning?" I had been perturbed to discover that Lehman Brothers, Royal Bank of Scotland and many other leading financial companies that had crashed in the financial crisis of 2008–2009 had spent a large amount of time and money on coaching. This had clearly failed to contribute sufficiently to developing leaders able to prevent their organization from failing spectacularly and which created high human cost. Having raised the question, someone at the back of the room raised his hand and said: "It is obvious what the coaches were doing!" I responded that it was not obvious to me, and could he enlighten us? He replied: "They were sending in their invoices quickly!" Many of the others in the hall burst into laughter and I too started to laugh and then gasped with shock. What was this saying about the profession of coaching? We began to ask: how can coaching help organizations overcome what our colleague Margaret Heffernan (2011) calls "Wilful Blindness" and help them have the learning crisis before they have the catastrophic commercial crisis?

In Hawkins (2011a) I asked the hypothetical question: what team coaching would the UK cabinet of Tony Blair have needed for the cabinet team to have been strong enough to create the right dialogical and collaborative inquiry before deciding to invade Iraq? I am referring to a team dialogue that could have explored all the potential scenarios, whether or not there were weapons of mass destruction, all the possible actions, as well as the intended and unintended consequences of each etc. Such a team dialogue could have possibly stopped the war in Iraq or at least slowed down the rush to allow time to consider possible future scenarios and plan how the post-war situation was going to be managed.

2. How can coaching deliver value beyond the individual development?

The next Damascus road experience for me (Peter) about coaching was when I was working with the regional government of Cape Town in South Africa. They had been developing a holistic 'Coaching Culture Strategy' and I had been asked to run a large workshop including not only the coaches and those managing coaching for the South African government, but many of the stakeholders of the coaching scene, including senior leaders, middle and frontline managers; those working in local businesses, hospitals, schools and universities; local taxpayers and service users. I asked those in charge of managing coaching to present their 'Coaching Culture Strategy' and suggested that every so often they stop and receive feedback from the various stakeholders speaking from their place in the wider ecosystem. I even had three people role play 'our collective grandchildren' and give feedback from the future generations who would be affected by decisions and actions taken now.

Suddenly one of the young black frontline managers got up and said:

> It sounds like the people with the big offices, big cars, big pay-checks, now get the big coaches. I think this is very expensive personal development for the already very highly privileged.

I felt this comment as a punch to my stomach. Again, I thought "what an indictment of our profession and is this what I am spending so much time and effort on, just to provide expensive personal development for the already highly privileged?" I began to question how much coaching was creating positive benefit for the wider human family and the 'more-than-human world' (Abrahms, 1996) – whether coaches were just feeding western individualistic narcissism and self-absorption, which may be part of the root causes of many 21st-century human problems.

Marc Khan, Group HR director of the international bank Investec, said when we interviewed him for this book:

> If executive coaches only do a form of counselling at work or one-on-one skills training, then they should only charge the much lower rates for counsellors and trainers. If they want to charge the much higher fees that business coaching demands, then they need to be delivering demonstrable value to the business.

3. How can coaching deliver demonstrable value to the individual, their team, the organization and the organization's stakeholders?

In training workshops and supervision groups we have run and presentations we have given, many coaches have told us that they believe if the individual grows and develops, then automatically their team, organization and the organization's stakeholders benefit. We believe that this is a complacent and very questionable assumption that perhaps reflects a lack of systemic focus in training and understanding of contemporary leadership. A fundamental question is "who is the client?" and the answer is not either the one or the other. We have come to believe that the assumption that all development starts with the individual, and that learning always happens inside individuals, is part of a pervasive Western post-enlightenment cultural belief system. This serving of material advancement in the last 250 years has also brought a dangerous shadow side in its wake (Hawkins, 2017b; Ryde, Seto and Goldvarg, 2019).

4. To deliver value to the individual, their team, the organization and their stakeholders, how does coaching need to be set up and contracted?

One of the limiting factors that has led to coaching being so individual centric has been the lack of sophistication in how executive coaching has been contracted. In 2014 we carried out global research on multi-stakeholder contracting (Turner and Hawkins, 2016), which raised some of the challenges and issues coaches experienced in addressing the needs of the coachee's team and organization when contracting for the individual's coaching. This book has in a large part been inspired by addressing the questions that emerged from that joint research. How coaching can be set up and focussed through effective multi-stakeholder contracting will be addressed in Chapter 5.

5. How do we evaluate the value created by coaching for the individual, their team, the organization and the organization's stakeholders?

In the early years of business coaching there was a lack of quality research on both the process and the outcomes of coaching, and the coaching industry rapidly rose on a tide of enthusiasm and belief in the coaching of individuals. In the last ten years there has been a marked change with a large growth in research, fuelled by academic centres for coaching being established, with master and doctoral programmes and academic research staff. However, much of the research has focussed on the 'inputs' to the coaching process, what the coach does, the nature of the relationship, and the coaching interventions. Far less research has focussed on the more important, but harder to research, aspects of coaching. These include

- The outputs – the new learning and development the coachee takes from the coaching, including new competencies, capabilities and capacities they can apply at work.
- The outcomes – what the coachee does differently at work as a result of the coaching – how they engage their teams, customers and stakeholders; how they manage meetings, organize their work and utilize other new capabilities.

- Value creation – this refers to the value that is created by new behaviour and actions of the coachee for their team, their wider function in the organization and for all the stakeholders. The stakeholders include customers, suppliers and partners, investors, employees, communities where the organization operates and the 'more than human world' of the ecological environment.

In Chapter 12 we will address the importance of linking all four aspects of evaluating coaching in ways that show the connections between the inputs, outputs, outcomes and value creation.

6. How does supervision make a difference to the quality of systemic coaching and the value created for all parties?

Given the nature of systemic coaching, which includes being aware of the many wider contexts beyond the individual and being able to reflect on the coaching relationship of which you are part, we strongly believe that it is impossible to do quality systemic coaching without engaging in systemic supervision. In Chapter 10 we will describe the nature of systemic supervision, drawing on vignettes of supervision and their impact on the coaching process that follows.

7. Why we need to wake up to the future

In training sessions, we often hear from our students – "you cannot predict the future, so why worry about it?" We respond by emphasizing that the future is already here. Somewhere in the world, often unnoticed, are the early shoots and signs of what will become foreground in the very near future. When IBM were world leaders in mainframe computers, they were so successful that they did not notice two young people working away in a garage, inventing new personal computers and operating systems, until it was nearly too late to respond.

In 'Three Horizon Thinking', Bill Sharpe (2013) writes about the great acceleration of change we are all currently living through and how we need to constantly think in three time horizons. Horizon one is constituted by the immediate issues of 'business as usual', such as attending to the next coaching client, running our coaching business, winning new work etc. Horizon two is innovating for tomorrow, the need to constantly upgrade our skills, stay abreast of new developments, and create and introduce new methods and approaches. Horizon three is future foresight, noticing what is coming from over the horizon that may fundamentally require us not just to upgrade our current game or approach, but to radically change it.

We invite you to stop at this point and write down for yourself what percentage of your work time in the last month you have spent on each of the three horizons, with the total adding up to 100 percent. Now consider how you think you should be allocating your work time in a year from now and write down a new list of the three percentages. Now look at the difference between the two sets of figures and ask yourself, what do you need to do to move from the first set of figures to the second group? How are you going to make that change?

Bill Sharpe argues that in today's world of exponential change, we can no longer afford to work in the order horizon one then two then three but instead must move from horizon one to the future foresight of horizon three, and do our horizon two innovation out of horizon three awareness so we are innovating to play tomorrow's game, not just to become better and better at yesterday's game.

8. How has coaching had such a meteoric rise and become so successful? How does coaching need to disrupt itself to meet the challenges of the next 30 years?

Executive coaching has had a meteoric rise since the late 1970s and early 1980s when it came to prominence (partly driven by Tim Galwey's 1975 book, *The Inner Game of Tennis*. It now has an estimated 53,300 professional practitioners in an industry valued at $2.356 billion (ICF, 2016). In that time coaching has achieved a great deal. When we started on the coaching path in the 1970s and 1980s, many of us had an IQ (intelligence quotient) that was several times more developed than our EQ (emotional quotient). Coaching has played a big part in helping many leaders and managers to develop their emotional intelligence and their ability to relate better to others, both in work and more widely.

Coaching has become the most popular and most appreciated form of leadership development and has taken leadership development out of the classroom study of historic case studies and refocussed on the individual, addressing current and future challenges in individual or group action learning. It has built on the work of Reg Revans and the whole development of 'action learning' and challenge-based syndicate learning advanced at Henley Business School in the 1950s and 1960s.

Coaching has become a key ingredient of many leadership development programmes and there is wide evidence that coachees positively report the benefits of coaching, including growth in personal awareness and insight into their key relationships (De Meuse, Dai and Lee, 2009: 121; Wasylyshyn, 2003). Some studies show that managers of those who receive coaching indicate mainly positive improvements in these coachees' performance (De Meuse et al, 2009: 119; Luthans and Peterson, 2003).

Soske and Conger argue that despite the exponential growth in, and expenditure on, leadership development programmes there are critical shortcomings. One reason, they believe, is the failure to recognize that "the exercise of leadership in organizations is not an individual act . . . the complexity, interconnectedness, and transparency of today's organizations means that no individual can get much accomplished alone. The nature of most challenges and opportunities is systemic" (2010: 242–243). Their concern is that leadership development can become separated from the business rather than being an "in situ practice" (2010: 243). Eve was involved in the BBC's leadership development programme in the early 2000s and leaders consistently rated most highly the key benefits of the coaching element that ran alongside the formal, taught programme. Particularly the senior leaders wanted more coaching and action learning and fewer taught sessions.

There is a lot of evidence that individual clients appreciate and positively rate their coaches and report that they find coaching helpful. We are also mindful that benefits may be felt elsewhere, such as with family and friends as we firmly believe that everything is connected. However, there is far less evidence that individual coaching delivers value beyond the individual and contributes benefit to those the coachee leads, their team, their colleagues, the wider organization and the many stakeholders of their organization.

9. How does coaching need to disrupt itself to meet the challenges of the next 30 years?

The influential American coach Marshall Goldsmith used the book title *What got us here, won't get you there* in 2008, where he showed the importance of unlearning the ways of our previous success and the need to reinvent ourselves for changing roles and changing times.

Peter Diamandis, the founder of Singularity University in Silicon Valley, says that in today's world of exponential change, every organization and profession has the choice of whether to disrupt itself or be disrupted. We also know that it is harder for organizations that are riding on the waves of success to see both how the world of tomorrow needs different things compared to the customers of today and that there is a need to notice small innovative competitors who are creating the new market. Recent history is full of examples of how market leaders such as Olivetti in typewriters and Kodak in photography failed to take on board the impact of external disruption to their industry. Our perspective is that coaching also rides the waves of its own success and positive appreciation from its clients and is failing to radically challenge and disrupt itself, so that it is future fit for the changing challenges of the 21st century.

We see too little evidence that coaching is being bold enough in challenging itself to ask the questions about how the mid-21st century will require coaching to be radically different from the current approaches that grew out of the late 20th century. Many people have pointed out that it is harder to radically change when and while you are being successful. Success can easily bring complacency and arrogance in its wake. Coaching conferences and publications can easily be filled with inward-looking presentations of past successes and rarely invite disruption from critical CEOs, or young millennials capable of challenging the comfortable assumptions of the community. We will argue in this book that to think and be systemic, it is essential to bring in the challenges that come 'future-back' and 'outside-in'. We insist that in today's world, coaching as a practice and a profession must be much more self-challenging and prepared to confront its clients, as highlighted by Blakey and Day (2012).

10. What are some of the disrupters that face the coaching profession?

As we contemplate the future horizon and look at the weak signals of the future that are already out there in today's world, we are aware of several key disrupters that we believe will accelerate and grow in magnitude in the very near future. You might like to take time to consider which of these will have an impact on your work, and which are the disruptive trends you are aware of.

a)   **Coaching being re-insourced** – First to internal coaches and then to leaders and line managers. Many years ago, I (Peter) described coaching as "a way of outsourcing difficult conversations." If a manager had a difficulty with somebody reporting to them, rather than deal with the difficulty themselves, often they would ring up the Human Resources department and ask for help. When the HR professional decided they did not want to confront or deal with this person, they would call an external coach and offer coaching to this individual! Since that time there has been a great development of internal coaches (Hawkins, 2012; St John-Brooks, 2014). Some of them are full-time coaches who are internally employed by the organization or other employees who have gone through an internal coach training programme and subsequently spend part of their working week coaching staff from other parts of the organization. Indeed, this is how Eve began her coaching career, working as an internal coach alongside her role as a BBC leader.

  More recently there has been a large increase in leaders and managers learning coaching skills, either as part of more general leadership and management development programmes, or as a specific training (Hawkins, 2012). They are encouraged to use these skills in coaching their own staff. More recently still we have seen the introduction of training leaders in team coaching approaches, so they can grow the collective capacity of their team (Hawkins, 2018, chapter 16). This development has been recognized by one of the professional bodies, the Association for Coaching (AC), introducing accreditation for being a "Recognized Leader as Coach" (2019, online). They write: "Our belief is that coaching skills are an essential leadership tool. The AC is working to help organizations benefit from a coaching culture and enable their leaders and managers to develop and empower their teams through a coaching approach."

b)   **Fewer clients** – All the large companies interviewed in our leadership research (Hawkins, 2017c) said they anticipated employing far fewer people in the next ten years as a result of digitalization, robotics, artificial intelligence (AI) and outsourcing. With fewer employees and more of them being coached internally, there will inevitably be a decrease in the number of external coaches employed by large companies.

c) **Coaching by artificial intelligence**– AI is an area advancing at a breathtaking pace. Every day brings more articles, more advances, more uses for AI. There has been a recent upsurge in the development and use of digital online learning and the growth of digital coaching applications. Already we are witnessing digital systems that have integrated a vast range of the coaching world's best questions; other computer systems can read the mood and emotions of the caller and adjust their tonality to match them and show artificial empathy. If coaches are just trained in asking good questions that enable the independent thinking of the coachee, digital systems will soon be able to replicate this offering at a much cheaper rate and more accessibly. It is important that we learn to view AI and digitalization as a partner in our coaching efforts, rather than as a threat that is going to replace us. Peter is working closely with Saberr (www.saberr.com/), who have developed a team coaching bot that utilizes the five disciplines of systemic coaching (Hawkins, 2017a) and a panel of trained global systemic team coaches, so that the AI system can support the team coaching and sustain the work between the team coaches' visits. Also, having used the team coaching bot with the senior team of an organization, the members of that team can use the coaching bot to support them in coaching their own team. In this way the digital and AI systems don't replace the coach or team coach but expand their ripple effect and influence.

d) **Coaching on demand** – In our research with millennial future leaders (Hawkins, 2017c), we heard that because they had grown up in a world of instant and regular contact via social media, whether by Facebook, Snapchat, WhatsApp or other applications, they were reluctant to wait to address what they perceive as an urgent learning need, until their next monthly coaching session. For them this makes no cultural sense. Some of them said to us: "Why wouldn't I just send my issue out to all my friends or peers, and get immediate feedback and response? Why wait?" In response to this cultural change, some coaching providers have established coaching-on-demand services, where there is always an online or on-call coach ready to help those who have an instant need.

e) **Peer coaching** – Linked to the preceding two disrupters is the fact that the up-coming generations are more ready to go to their peer group for help than previous generations who were much less transparent about their personal world and wanted the private confidential space of the confessional or coaching closet. In Chapter 9 we will explore systemic group coaching and how group coaching can be supported to morph into peer group coaching.

f) **Self-coaching** – As more and more managers and leaders are trained in emotional intelligence and coaching skills and undertake workshops in mindfulness, they are much better equipped to coach themselves. Their ability to manage structured "time-in" (Rooke, Siegel, Poelmans and Payne, 2012) and develop their awareness and internal witness, to self-reflect, has significantly grown.

There are probably other key disrupters that coaching needs to focus on; perhaps you can add those you are aware of and the implications for your practice? There are also the external disruptors in the wider systems that coaching operates within and we will look at these both in the next chapter and Chapter 8 where we address the great challenge of ecological degradation and the disruption it will cause.

Conclusion

In many parts of the world there is still a growing need to train more external and internal coaches, managers and leaders in coaching skills. However, we question whether in North America and Western Europe we are still training more traditional coaches (we define what we mean by this in Chapter 3), than will be needed in the coming period.

We believe that it is important for all coach trainings not just to teach the past models, approaches and skills of coaching, but also to engage in horizon three future foresight on the potential disrupters to the coaching profession. Not only do we believe it is important for all coaches and coaching students to focus on the internal disrupters, but also to develop foresight on how the world of our clients, the managers and leaders of tomorrow, is exponentially changing; how tomorrow's client may have radically different needs than today's. This is what we will turn to in the next chapter.

Chapter 2

A necessary revolution in coaching

> *"I've got lots of coaches who can coach (individuals), lots of consultants who can work with individual parts of the system, but all my challenges lie in the connections."*
>
> – CEO interviewed for *Tomorrow's Leadership and the Necessary Revolution in Today's Leadership* (Hawkins, 2017c)

Introduction

Having explored the potential internal disrupters in the previous chapter, in this chapter we want to engage you in exploring the following questions:

- What different challenges will coaching clients be facing in the future?
- How does coaching have to change to enable our clients to address these challenges?
- What sort of change is required for coaching to fully realize its potential and create the maximum benefit for future individuals, their teams, the organizations they are part of, and the wider ecosystem?
- What does coaching need to do to become 'future-fit' and enable leaders, teams and organizations to be 'future-fit' and make a positive contribution to the world of tomorrow?

In the previous chapter we described some of our 'wake up' experiences when we realized that the coaching we were currently doing was not delivering all the value that it could. We would invite you to stop before rushing into this chapter and reflect on times when you have had moments of waking up to question what your coaching (or supervising) was achieving, either the coaching you were delivering as a coach, buying as an organizational buyer of coaching, or receiving as a coachee. What new challenges and questions did these moments open up for you?

Please capture these questions here and hold them alongside the questions we are carrying into the dialogue of this chapter, so we can discover how our joint questions connect and speak to each other.

The 21st-century challenges

In 2016–2017, Peter led a global research project through Henley Business School to explore *Tomorrow's Leadership and the Necessary Revolution in Today's Leadership Development* (Hawkins, 2017c).

The research addressed four key questions:

1   How will the leadership needed for tomorrow's organizations be different from today's leadership?
2   What development is needed for tomorrow's leadership?
3   How suitable is current best practice for developing tomorrow's leadership?
4   What more needs to be done?

To address these issues, we set out a broad and ambitious research approach to combine depth and breadth, qualitative and quantitative research, and input from many sectors and geographies.

Our basic design was based on the triangulation of various data sources.

Firstly, we decided to interview the following people individually:

- The CEO (or another executive team member),
- The HR director or head of leadership development, and
- A young millennial leader of the future that the company considered a potential executive leader within 10 years.

We carried out interviews with 40 different companies from different sectors, as well as organizations from the public and not-for-profit (or 'for benefit') sector, drawn from diverse parts of the globe. We were interested in how each of these groups was seeing both the challenges for tomorrow's leadership and what they thought was needed from leadership development today. We also wanted to discover what could be generatively created by interconnecting their different perspectives.

The second triangulation was to take the three most recent and comprehensive surveys we could find on the perspectives of CEOs, HR directors and millennials and carry out a 'survey of surveys', comparing and contrasting what each found and relating these three different perspectives.

In the third triangulation we interviewed several key 'thought leaders' individually and held a two-day inquiry group with some of these and other thought leaders before comparing these dialogues with what was emerging from our extensive literature review of published books, papers, articles and blogs.

One CEO of a global technology business told us how "Leadership for big companies and leadership for small companies is converging." We were concerned that much of our current data was generated from large companies and we wanted to also look at what was happening in the high-tech, internet and data-driven 'exponential organizations' (Ismail, 2014) that were moving at incredible speed from start-up to multi-billion-dollar global businesses. So, we reviewed the research done by Ismail (2014) and Diamandis and Kotler (2014) at the Singularity University and research on 'unicorn companies' by Lee (2013).

We also thought there was a lack of representation from China, so we explored case studies of both Haier and Xiaomi, two very successful Chinese companies, as well as interviewing leaders from the Chinese division of Thermo Fisher, a large American biotech company.

The fourth and final triangulation was to look across these diverse data sources and the three different triangulations to draw tentative hypotheses, conclusions and guidance for moving forward.

The first research outcome was based on the many responses to the question, "what do you see as the 3–5 biggest challenges for your organization over the next 3–5 years?" In order of priority the challenges identified were:

1   Unceasing and accelerating transformation;
2   The technological and digital revolution;
3   Disintermediation and 'Uber-ization';
4   The hollowing out of organizations and the growing complexity of the stakeholder world;
5   Globalization;
6   Climate change;
7   The need to learn and adapt faster.

These challenges are not separate; they are all interconnected. Each one is driving and being driven by all the others. They each bring opportunities as well as threats.

1. Unceasing and accelerating transformation

In 2008, Thomas Friedman wrote a ground-breaking book – *Hot, Flat, and Crowded*. It detailed how the world was facing global warming ('hot'), knowledge was becoming available everywhere and to everyone through the internet ('flat'), and the world's population was growing exponentially ('crowded') – more than trebling from 2.4 billion in 1950 to 7.7 billion in 2019 (World Population Clock, 2019).

Friedman later in 2012 discussed how much had changed in the seven years since he wrote his original book *The World Is Flat*: "Twitter was a sound. The Cloud was in the sky. 4G was a parking place. LinkedIn was a prison. Applications were something you sent to college. And for most people, Skype was a typo." He argues this has taken the world from connected to hyper-connected, which brings both opportunities and challenges.

It is estimated that human beings discovered as much in the first 14 years of the 21st century as it took our predecessors the whole of the 20th century to discover, and that we will now discover more in seven years than the previous 14.

Cairo and Dotlich sum it up:

> The fundamental challenge of leadership today is not how to solve problems
> so that they go away, but how to manage ongoing dilemmas or paradoxes that
> have no long-term solution: achieving short-term goals without sacrificing
> investment in the future; ensuring cost efficiencies do not inhibit innovation;
> focusing relentlessly on performance while still creating an environment in
> which people feel valued; or leading a global organization from the center
> without losing touch with local markets. Managing these types of inherently
> ambiguous issues will require stamina, resilience, and the ability to live with-
> out real closure.
>
> (Cairo and Dotlich, 2010: 288–289)

2. The technological and digital revolution

Leaders saw the digital revolution as bringing many significant challenges. Some
frequently mentioned ones are:

"Having the capacity and the skills to cope with Big Data."
"We have more and more data, but do we have the skills to really use it
well?"
"The technology is changing jobs faster than we are able to upskill the work-force
to work in the new ways."

Large companies have created zero growth in employment in the last
20 years, whereas the massive increase in employment has come from 'start-
ups'; small companies, individual freelancing; and the not for profit or 'for
benefit' sector.

Klaus Schwab, founder of the World Economic Forum, also points out that
"The fourth great Industrial Revolution . . . is characterised by a fusion of tech-
nologies that is blurring the lines between the physical, digital, and biological
spheres" (Schwab, 2016). Revolutions in the digital world, artificial intelligence,
virtual reality and 'presencing' through mixed reality, robotics and biotechnology
will come together to change the workplace in as-yet unimaginable ways and at
accelerating speeds.

As one leader in our research pointed out:

> Technology is enabling both the rise of mega-corporations like Amazon,
> Google, HP with immense power, while also enabling communities to shape
> their own destinies through the use of participatory and collaborative tech-
> nologies. Understanding the role of a business leader in this increasingly digi-
> tized context and how we best connect as people/authentic leaders amid this
> dynamic is important.

3. Disintermediation and 'Uberization'

One significant aspect of this technological revolution that many CEOs were keen to talk about was the threat of being 'Uberized'. This was shorthand used by several leaders to describe the threat of their whole industry being 'disintermediated' by a whole new mode of operating. The term refers to the way in which Uber and its imitators and competitors have been able to radically transform the global taxi industry by removing a whole intermediate part of a value chain. In the case of hire cars, this involves removal of the taxi company by having an internet-based system for customers to directly find the nearest freelance driver and book direct. Airbnb allowing homeowners to directly let their rooms as an alternative to hotels, and Amazon allowing writers to self-publish and reach large audiences are other examples of disintermediation.

It is no longer sensible for organizations to strategically focus only on how to become number one in their sector, because the industry in which they are operating could be radically and suddenly dismembered. Any strategic intent also needs to have built-in agility.

As one CEO said: "the new competition will not come from where it is currently happening or where we are currently focussing."

A CEO that we interviewed from the insurance industry spoke of the impact that Amazon could have on radically transforming how insurance is made available, due to both their ease of access to large numbers of global customers and the amount of data they have on those customers to apply logarithmic analysis of insurance risk.

4. The hollowing out of organizations and the growing complexity of the stakeholder world

Here are two quotes that illustrate many themes that were echoed by many interviewees.

> Leaders of tomorrow need to be brilliant collaborators and brilliant impresarios that spot and create partnering and cross-hatching possibilities with other agencies. Partnerships today are lumbering, slow and paranoid.
>
> Margaret Heffernan, best-selling author, serial entrepreneur and past CEO

> The ability to get things done through networks is a huge necessary leadership competence.
>
> Interviewed CEO of a global technology company

The most radical tipping point that has emerged from the research is that the whole paradigm of how we think about leadership needs to change to cope with the world of tomorrow. Many of the CEOs interviewed were concerned about what one of them described as:

> The hollowing out of the organization, through a mixture of digitalization, robotics and off-shoring, radically reduces the number of people we have on the pay-roll.

As Ismail from the Singularity University puts it: "Anything predictable has been or will be automated by AI and robots, leaving the human worker to handle exceptional situations" (2014: 139).

Many leaders also described the growing number, diversity and complexity of the groups and organizations they needed to partner with for their company to be successful. They were not just in the supply chain or the 'outsourced support functions'. The critical stakeholders who needed to be effectively partnered included customers, distributors, local community groups, pressure groups and, significantly, competitors.

The 'Leaders of Tomorrow' will have fewer people to vertically manage and many more people they need to partner with, both within their organization and outside. Laloux talks of the need to shift to what he terms "Teal" organizations that emphasize wholeness and connectedness in relation to others. He argues that those who make this transition "can accept . . . that there is an evolution in consciousness, that there is a momentum in evolution toward every more complex and refined ways of dealing with the world" (2014: 43).

5. Globalization

Many of the leaders who were interviewed were leading global companies and they spoke eloquently of the challenges of leading across countries, cultures, different business contexts and time zones. They mentioned the enormous challenge to develop enough leaders who can relate effectively across different cultures and stakeholder groups. Ghemawat had reported similar findings in 2012: "Of senior executives, 76 percent believe their organizations need to develop global-leadership capabilities, but only 7 percent think they are currently doing so very effectively." (Ghemawat, 2012)

But those leaders leading companies operating primarily within one country were also emphasizing the need for a global outlook.

"Whatever business you are in, customers can benchmark what you are doing with the best in the world."
"Our customers are informed globally so we need to be."
"Innovation can come from anywhere in the world, so we need to be globally connected and globally alert."

Another aspect of the digital revolution, discussed earlier, is that even locally based businesses need to think globally, as their competition can be based anywhere in the world. The local cinema competes with Netflix and Amazon, the local hotel with Airbnb, the local garage with remote computer car servicing, and the local hospital with patients going abroad for cheaper treatments. Coaches also now operate in a global marketplace, with executives being coached virtually from the other side of the world, and coaches receiving virtual supervision at a distance.

6. Climate change

One of the conundrums that has emerged in the research is that a large majority of the chief executives and HR directors interviewed did not mention climate change in their top three to five challenges that organizations will have to deal with in the next 20 years; yet when prompted they would all say 'yes, of course' climate change will have a major impact on the world in which we operate – an impact that could be devastating.

There were a few exceptions, mostly from those selected for their pioneering and innovative approach. For example, a global CEO of a manufacturing company talked about re-visioning their company mission: "taking the company beyond 'zero emissions for 2020' into a future of net positive . . . 'climate take-back' – how our company can contribute to reversing the impact of climate change and bring carbon home."

The majority of millennials spoke of climate change as one of the most significant challenges organizations and leaders will face, prompting a major turn in thinking about the way we do business: "changing business models from linear to circular economies and the impact this will have on business and leadership."

This could reflect a generational difference in awareness; however, all the older thought leaders mentioned it as one of the most critical challenges. We concluded that for senior executives it is more likely that this critical issue is drowned out by the pressure of urgent current issues, which are more 'front of mind'. George Marshall's 2014 book *Don't Even Think About It: Why Our Brains Are Wired to Ignore Climate Change* suggests our brains are wired to privilege the current and short-term issues and screen out issues with greater long-term consequences, as well as issues that involve potential loss. The immediate will trump the important. He quotes how 85 percent of people interviewed in the UK think climate change will be a major challenge for future generations, but very few included it in the top three issues that they think the government should be addressing. We experience the same phenomena happening in much of the executive coaching we come across through supervision and research, where climate change is rarely mentioned or addressed and even when it is it is drowned out by the more immediate and local issues of the day.

Yet the best scientific evidence that we could find suggests that the critical time for addressing climate change is in the next few years. "To stabilize global temperature, global emissions must peak within the next five [to] ten years and then decline rapidly every year after that" (Roberts, 2012). The International Energy Association has calculated that every year of delay adds $500 billion to the investment required between 2010 and 2030. "Earth Overshoot Day" – the day when we have used more from nature than our planet can renew in a year – moved to 29th July in 2019, compared to 29th September in 1999. We are now using 1.7 of the Earth's resources compared to 1.4 Earths 20 years earlier (Earth Overshoot Day, 2019).

In December 2018, Sir David Attenborough, now in his 90s, while taking the People's Seat at the United Nations–sponsored climate talks in Katowice, Poland, gave the following call to action:

> Right now, we are facing a man-made disaster of global scale. Our greatest threat in thousands of years. Climate change.
> If we don't take action, the collapse of our civilizations and the extinction of much of the natural world is on the horizon.

Four years earlier the pioneering Canadian writer Naomi Klein (2014) gave her call to action about climate change in her book *This Changes Everything*, but still we as a species seem deaf, dumb and blind to these calls. Josie McLean (2017: 17) believes that we can only solve the problems of our planet if we effect a paradigm shift, "distinguished by a change from seeing and working with parts of the problem (such as economic growth or climate change) to understanding the whole and the relationships between the parts." But she also notes, "it appears that the human family are in a state of perpetual denial, unable or unwilling to implement the actions that we know are needed" (McLean, 2017: 16). In her doctoral thesis she links sustainability, change management and leadership within organizations.

As Laloux recognizes, "No one can be made to evolve in consciousness, even with the best of intentions – a hard truth for coaches and consultants, who wish they could help organizational leaders adopt a more complex worldview by the power of conviction" (2014: 39–40).

7. The need to learn and adapt faster

Many of the leaders talked, on the one hand, of the need for their organization to learn and adapt faster to the accelerating speed of change in the world around them while, on the other hand, they shared that they had little time to stand back from everyday pressing demands and reflect on the patterns of what was happening in their organization, in their business ecosystem and in the wider world. They also lacked the space to take a wider view, both in space and time, and to practice 'strategic foresight'.

One international chief executive said:

> Leaders face a learning crisis when they move from leading one size of group to a larger group. This happens at around 15 people, 50, 100, 200 and 1,000. As you progress you need to eat your own children – what made you successful at one stage will not make you successful at the next.

Another CEO said: "You cannot rely on your MBA – it will help you get to step one, but you will have to find ways of learning steps 2–10 yourself." Kelly (2016) talks about how the speed of technological change, with shorter innovation shelf life, means that we will need to become 'perpetual newbies' and will need to get used to being struggling beginners.

The most common words used when asked about the leaders of tomorrow were 'flexible' and 'adaptable'.

Yet nearly all senior leaders reported they did not have enough time or adequate support structures to keep learning. Some talked about the value of having a coach or mentor, or good non-executives who act as sounding boards. However, several commented on not being challenged enough, even by their coach or mentor, to accelerate their learning and development. This is a sentiment echoed by Blakey and Day (2012) in their book *Challenging Coaching* who show ways that coaches can increase the amount and effectiveness of their challenge. As one CEO put it: "Unless CEOs are constantly shifting what they think and how they think they will have a limited shelf life."

Many of the leaders talked, on the one hand, of the need for their organization to learn and adapt faster to the accelerating speed of change in the world around them while, on the other hand, they shared that they had little time to stand back from everyday pressing demands and reflect on the patterns of what was happening in their organization, in their business ecosystem and in the wider world. They also lacked the space to take a wider view, both in space and time, and to practice 'strategic foresight'.

Reg Revans, the founder of action learning, gave us the simple formula 'L ≥ EC'. This is the Darwinian law of organizational survival – that learning must equal (or be greater than) the rate that the environment is changing, otherwise it is on the road to extinction.

Many chief executives talked about the need for leaders to regularly reinvent themselves. They have to unlearn what has made them successful at one level of leadership in order to discover how to be a new leader at another level of leadership.

We believe that this research poses several important critical challenges for the whole coaching profession:

1   How do coaches raise the level of challenge in coaching while staying true to the core principles of coaching and without 'knowing better or knowing first'?
2   How does coaching not get trapped in the overwhelming demand to focus on current issues in ways that drives out the critical importance to create space to focus on the challenges that are coming over the horizon at such great speed?
3   How does coaching deliver value beyond the individual to the growing complexity of stakeholders that the coachee needs to partner with?

Conclusion

In this chapter we have explored the necessary revolution in coaching for it to be 'future-fit' and how the many challenges facing leaders and managers in today's fast-changing world require them to be learning and developing in new ways, and this in turn requires coaching to step up its practice. These are some of the critical areas we believe 'future-fit coaches' will need to do (please add additional ones you believe will be important):

- Listen deeply to not only the story of the coachee but also what is communicated through them verbally and non-verbally by the team dynamics of the teams they belong to, the culture of their organization and the wider zeitgeist they are part of.
- Enter the coaching session with an open mind, open heart and open will, and be fully present and fluidly responsive to what emerges and what is necessary for learning to happen at all levels.
- Contract with both the individual coachee and the wider systems that the coachee serves and is responsible to and for.
- Regularly review the emerging nature of the coaching and how it is serving and creating value for the coachee and the wider systems they serve.
- Be able to reflect on their coaching work, both live in the coaching and also through a disciplined supervision practice, seeing not only the many layered systemic levels of the coach, but the relational systems they co-create with the coachee and with the organization etc.
- Partake in coaching evaluation that understands the connections between the learning inputs, outputs, outcomes and value creation.
- Achieve this in a way that attends to an ever-changing ethical challenges and complexity.
- ? (please add your additions)

How to develop these capabilities and capacities and how to deploy them will be the focus of the remaining chapters.

Chapter 3

What is systemic coaching?

Introduction

In the first two chapters we examined why we believed that coaching needs to change in response to the changing needs of our clients. We now turn to what systemic coaching is.

We invite you to consider for a moment your responses to these questions, which we will then explore with you in the following pages.

- When we work within an organization (with an individual or group/team) as a coach, mentor, supervisor or consultant, who do we consider to be the client?
- Which systems do we need to consider when we do coaching?
- What do you consider to be systemic coaching?
- How might systemic coaching differ from, and build on, traditional coaching?
- What role does 'impact on others' have in your judgement of the success of coaching?
- What other questions do you have about systemic coaching?
- You might like to make a few notes before reading on and reflect on them alongside our questions as we continue our dialogue.

At a recent coaching conference looking at the future of coaching there was much interest in the whole area of systemic coaching and systemic team coaching, but many reported that they were not clear about what these terms meant. Others thought they were clear but demonstrated that their clarity was very different from the clarity of others. We were all speaking English, but many of us were speaking different conceptual languages, while possibly the wise or shy were remaining silent! One participant said: "I always work systemically because I always hold in mind the wider system out there." I (Peter) provocatively replied: "Anyone who talks about 'The System', is not thinking systemically? Systems are not things."

On reflection I do not think that was a kind or helpful response, but it did wake us up to the need for ways of clarifying different systems and systemic lenses and to develop some shared language for thinking, perceiving and dialoguing systemi-cally. This is what we will attempt to do in this chapter.

The shifting paradigm

Coaching is slowly waking up to a fundamental paradigm shift that is happening in science, philosophy, religion, psychology and organizational science and leader-ship development. This paradigm shift began with quantum physics (Heisenberg, 1958; Bohr, 1934) nearly a hundred years ago and gradually spread to chemistry (von Bertalanffy, 1928; Prigogine and Stengers 1984) and the natural sciences in the 1930s and 1940s. It was mainly after the second world war in the late 1940s, 50s and 60s that it first spread into the human sciences (Bateson, 1972; Capra, 1996, 2002; Capra and Luisi, 2014; Maturana and Varela, 1998), later to the vari-ous approaches to understanding organizations as living systems (Morgan, 1986; Hutchins, 2012, 2016; Boulton and Allen, 2015) and even later to understanding individual psychology, learning and adult and leadership development (Hawkins, 2017c; Bunker, Hall and Kram, 2010).

Capra and Luisi argue that the first principle for systemic understanding is interdependence, that "The behaviour of every living member of the ecosystem depends on the behaviour of many others" (2016: 353).

Individual coaching has grown out of the fields of counselling, psychology and psychotherapy, and to a large extent adopted now-outdated notions of psychother-apy and counselling that were prevalent in the period 1960–1990. These included the belief in the importance of staying objective while trying to 'objectively' understand and enable their patient or client to achieve better health and a fuller life. In this paradigm, health, thinking, learning and development are all located internally within the client. The counsellor, psychologist or coach attempts to be an objective outsider and applies well-developed tools and methods to enable the client's development.

Existential (May, 1961, 1969; Laing, 1965, 1967), humanistic (Perls, 1968; Maslow, 1968; Rogers, 1951), inter-subjective (Stolorow and Atwood, 1992; Stolorow, Atwood and Orange, 2002) and integrative (Hawkins and Ryde, 2020) psychotherapies have all questioned and moved on from these traditional approaches. They have recognized, like the quantum physicists before them, that you can never know something, let alone somebody, objectively. Firstly, you only know them in how they show up within the social and culturally defined con-text in which you meet them. Secondly, how you turn up, verbally, non-verbally, emotionally etc. will affect how they feel and behave and what they say and do. Thirdly, your perception of them happens through the lenses of your own rich and dense subjectivity. All knowledge of another is fundamentally inter-subjective. Many of us in the helping professions make grand sweeping statements about the nature of the other person, rather than humbly accept that all we know is how they respond to us within the specific social and cultural context in which we meet them, filtered through our own perceptions.

The beginnings of systemic coaching

Only recently has coaching begun to question many of its own assumptions and the bedrock paradigm that these are built upon.

One of the first to do this was Mary Beth O'Neil (2000) in her book *Executive Coaching: Coaching with Backbone and Heart*. O'Neill advocates a systems perspective so that "we resist identifying one element or person in a system as the root cause of a problem"(2000: 42); she suggests instead that we can pay attention to the whole with bifocal vision. Nowadays we might evolve this to describe what we name varifocal vision to emphasize the many parties that are relevant to systemic coaching, mentoring and supervision, not just the organization. This could, for example, include the sector, the country, our planet, and also our family and our friends.

Rimanoczy and Brown also reiterate this idea in 2008 when they say that "in order to better understand and tackle individual and organizational issues, we have to take into account the different systems and contexts that mutually influence one another and effect these issues" (2008: 189).

In 2011 Anne Scoular, writing about business coaching, was very clear about the need for coaches to understand the wider context of coaching practice. Her concern is that some coaches, "usually former therapists . . . maintain that the 'client' to whom they have primary and sole responsibility is the person sitting in front of them" (2011: 65). She strongly disagrees, believing "this is wrong: ethically, and indeed legally, if the coach is contracted with the organization, then the organization is the client" (2011: 65). She argues that the "real client is not the person sitting in front of you, it's the organization paying the bill" (2011: 64) and when: "working in organizations there is the need to understand the context and contract well in the shifting political sands of organizational life" (2011: 65).

She offers 11 key questions (2011: 66), which include

- Who are the key stakeholders?
- What is the need of the organizational client?
- How does it relate to their current or future business needs and drivers?
- What are likely to be the coaching issues from their point of view?
- Are the organization's and individual's goals in alignment?

Huffington takes a more nuanced approach as to who the client is. She describes dual listening: to the individual in the organization and to the organization in the individual (2006: 44). She argues that the important thing is not to get "stuck in one circle of context" (2006: 45). In describing the "organization-in-the-mind" Huffington refers to two ways in which the organization is present in the coaching space: "as an internal reality, or an internal object in the mind of the client and as an external reality independent of the coach and client" (2006: 49). This second way it is present she describes as "the third party in the wings" (2006: 65).

In 2011 and 2012 Peter wrote several books and papers outlining aspects of systemic coaching. This began with *Leadership Team Coaching* (Hawkins, 2011a), showing how coaching teams needed to be grounded in a systemic team coaching approach, that not only focussed on the process of the team but also on the purpose and collective tasks of the team and not only on what was going on inside the team, but also on how the team engaged the many systems it was nested within and which it needed to engage. In the third edition of this book (Hawkins, 2017a), Peter expanded the approach to include a fourth level of team coaching 'eco-systemic team coaching', to recognize that systemic team coaching needs to go beyond the team and its relation to the wider organization, and even beyond creating value for the organization's stakeholders, to relating to how the organization is working with others in partnerships and networks to create value for the wider business ecosystem and also the wider environmental ecology upon which we are all dependent.

This fourth level is in line with the work of the many pioneering businesses that are members of the B team – that focus on 'beyond business as usual'. It includes very successful businesses like Unilever and Virgin Group. These ideas were extended into the realm of systemic coaching supervision (Hawkins, 2011b) and ways of *Creating a Coaching Culture* (Hawkins, 2012), showing ways of liberating coaching from the confidential closet of the individual one-to-one engagement, to become a way of all parts of any organization learning and developing, both within the parts and between the parts, both within the whole organization and between organizations.

In 2014, Marc Khan in South Africa wrote *Coaching on the Axis,* placing coaching as a relational engagement located at the meeting place of individual and organizational learning and development, facing both ways, seeing both the organization and the individual as equal clients. He advocates an approach that

> positions coaching in a way that promotes the success of the organization as a whole, as opposed to just that of the individual being coached. It does this by systemically bringing personal, interpersonal and organizational realities into an improved state of relationship through the coaching dialogue.
>
> (2014: 55)

In 2017 Hetty Einzig in the UK, in her book *The Future of Coaching – Vision, Leadership and Responsibility in a Transforming World* argues for a 'Next Generation Coaching' based on four pillars:

1   **Partnership**, coach and client working collaboratively in partnership: "If we understand everything to be interdependent then the question is not just how to be a leader in the world but how to create together leadership for the world" (2017: 7).
2   **Systemicity**, seeing everything as interconnected and interdependent, embracing complexity.

3   **Purpose**, helping "leaders discover not only their authentic self but also their contribution to the wider picture" (2017: 46).

4   **Spirituality**, "working with, through and beyond the individual towards a greater good: of the organization and of the society it serves" (2017: 47).

This growing interest in systemic work was followed in 2018 by Paul Lawrence and Allen Moore. Writing in Australia, their book *Coaching in Three Dimensions* shows in very clear and illustrated ways the difference between three approaches, which they term:

- **traditional coaching**: "helping coachees think things through for themselves. They see themselves as outside agents and don't often encounter others in the client organization. The best traditional coaches are great listeners, able to empathize and see the world through their coachee's eyes."
- **dialogic coaching**: coaches . . . see themselves as agents in the coaching process . . . co-creators of whatever insights and intentions emerge from the interaction. They are aware of their own role in the reflective process and the extent to which their own listening enables or inhibits divergent thinking.
- **systemic coaching**: coaches are not only comfortable working with dialogue but are also able to work with patterns of dialogue. They understand that change takes place every day in the client organization. Systemic coaches take a view of the function of the organization as a whole.

(Lawrence and Moore, 2018: 9–10).

While they recognize that all three approaches have some benefits, they clearly show that when a coach is delivering coaching in a business or organizational context, to deliver value to all systemic levels one needs to combine a dialogic and systemic approach.

Another fellow traveller on this journey to more systemic coaching and to delivering coaching beyond the individual is Marshall Goldsmith, one of the most celebrated and prolific coaches alive in the world today. In his recent work with Sal Silvester, *Stakeholder Centered Coaching* (2018), they lay out some important principles for their approach "Success isn't determined by the leader being coached, but by the people impacted by the coaching" (p. 17).

They describe three differentiators between Stakeholder Centered Coaching (SCC) approach and other coaching methodologies as:

1   The stakeholder emphasis.

2   The emphasis on feedforward – the provision of ideas and suggestions for the future and the shift of focus from the past to the future.

3   The focus on both behaviour change and perception change.

Systemic coaching would share all of these differentiators. The difference between our two approaches would be more in the process. The steps in stakeholder centred coaching are:

1   Leader identifies a clear development goal.
2   "Leaders go public with their goals" – they declare their development goal with carefully selected stakeholders and ask for feedback and feedforward.
3   They develop an online action plan shared with the key stakeholders.
4   "Leaders follow-up on a monthly basis with their stakeholders" – to "support change and help close the perception gap".
5   The leader modifies their action plan for the coming month based on the stakeholders' feedforward.
6   The leader formally measures results with mini surveys of stakeholders, measuring progress on a scale of −3 through +3, 0 represents no change.

Marshall Goldsmith and his associates provide training in this approach around the world. They suggest that to carry out this stakeholder centred coaching process, coaches need the following skills.

1   To help the leader determine their goals.
2   To help leaders rehearse interactions (similar to enabling fast-forward rehearsals in transformational coaching (Hawkins and Smith, 2013, 2018).
3   To help the leader create an action plan.
4   The ability to reinforce positive change.
5   Conduct after action assessments to help leaders from their assessments based on four key questions:

    a)   What did you intend in the last 30 days?
    b)   What actually happened?
    c)   What did you learn? Or are you learning?
    d)   What are your next steps?

6   The ability to tell stories to create teachable moments.

Our approach shares much in common with this approach, particularly the focus on:

- Stakeholder involvement in the whole coaching process.
- What we have termed 'future-back' and 'outside-in' inquiry.
- The importance of rehearsing new behaviours.
- Following the action learning cycle right through new thinking, rehearsing, new action and then an after-action review to learn from what happened, leading to the next cycle of new thinking.
- Assessing and evaluating coaching impact throughout the process, including a representative(s) of the system, too, perhaps at the midpoint, not only at the end.

The difference would be:

- Our approach is far less structured and more open ended. We take a broader and more nuanced approach to setting goals, in line with that outlined by David, Clutterbuck and Megginson (2013) in their book *Beyond Goals*.
- Where SCC focuses on setting goals at the beginning of the process that can then be informed and built on by stakeholders, our approach asks the coach and coachee constantly to discover the work that needs to be done in service of the wider systemic world, informed by regular stakeholder dialogue and engagement.
- We spend more time helping the coachee (or supervisee) stand back from their surface situations and discover their patterns of behaviour, emotional triggers, and fundamental assumptions and beliefs and then rework their 'self and other' narratives.

Despite these differences we are clearly travelling in a similar direction.

Integrating the various approaches

We view all these authors as fellow travellers and comrades in bringing new paradigm systemic thinking to revolutionize the value business and executive coaching can create for much-needed future-fit organizations and for a sustainable world.

All these authors distinguish between various levels of coaching. Several of the authors point out that this is not arguing hierarchically, later levels are not necessarily better than the former, but they are more inclusive; i.e. Level IV includes all the other levels, but Level I does not include the wider levels beyond it; each level has a wider perspective than the ones preceding it.

The levels can be summarized as:

I   Traditional individual centred coaching attempts to objectively focus on enabling the individual or team as a separate entity to develop itself using tried and tested methods.

II   Relational, dialogic and inter-subjective coaching recognizes that the coach is an engaged partner in a collaborative inquiry with the coachee.

III   Systemic coaching recognizes that learning and development happens not inside the individual but in dynamic engagement with the wider systems they are part of and relate with; it reflects that we are part of communities and cultures that shape our language, ways of being, thinking and doing.

IV   As yet there is very little written about the fourth level of eco-systemic and ecological coaching, but we will address this in this book (Chapter 8).

Table 3.1 The levels of coaching

		Authors				
		Marc Khan Coaching on the Axis 2014	*Peter Hawkins Leadership Team Coaching 2017*	*Paul Lawrence & Allen Moore Coaching in Three Dimensions 2018*	*Goldsmith and Silvester Stakeholder Centered Coaching 2018*	*Hawkins and Ryde Integra-tive Psycho-therapy 2019*
Levels	Level I	Individual centric / Dyadic	Team facilitation	Traditional Coaching	Client centered	Objective
	Level II	Relational	Team coaching	Dialogic Coaching		Inter-subjective
	Level III	Systemic	Systemic team coaching	Systemic	Stakeholder Centered	Systemic
	Level IV		Eco-systemic team coaching			Ecological

An integrated model of systemic coaching

Building on the work of these various writers and our own development of this field over many years, we now define *Systemic Coaching* as:

> *Individual systemic coaching is a collaborative and dialogical inquiry between two people (coach and coachee), exploring how the coachee can learn and develop in relation to the worlds they are embedded within, in a way that creates positive benefit for them and all the nested systems of which they are part.*
>
> *Systemic coaching recognizes that all learning and development is relational, between an organism or living system and the wider living eco-systems it is nested within.*
>
> *Business systemic coaching is systemic coaching that focuses on creating value for the individual client and the teams they are part of, the organizational client they work for, as well as the organization's stakeholders and the wider communities and the ecology that the organization is part of.*

We will now unpack this dense definition and offer what we believe are the underlying principles of systemic coaching.

1   In executive or business coaching there are always at least two clients.
2   Focussing on connections not separate parts.
3   We see systems in relation to other systems.

4   Understanding how all systems are nested within larger systems that are, in turn, also nested within them – we live in the world and the world lives in us.
5   We are part of, and affect, all systems we observe and engage with.
6   We cannot be completely objective, as we bring our own background, culture, values and bias.
7   Systemic coaching is not just about what we focus on, but also about how we focus and from where we focus.
8   Systemic coaching requires systemic perceiving, systemic thinking, systemic being and systemic relating.

1. In executive or business coaching there are always at least two clients

As touched on in Chapter 1, many supervisees talk of their coaching client as being the individual they meet with. They fail to recognize that the organization where the coachee works (and who is normally paying for the coaching) and the relationship between the organization and the individual are both important clients in their own right.

In *Leadership Team Coaching* (Hawkins, 2011a, 2014, 2017a), I, Peter, used the Parsifal myth to illuminate this issue, calling it the Parsifal trap after the legendary Knight of the Round Table who spent his life learning to ask the key question "Whom does the Grail serve?"

Coaches fall into the Parsifal trap when they see coaching as an end in itself and fail to work with their client in asking: "Who and what does our coaching serve?" and "How can we ensure a legacy from this coaching for the individual and the organization (at least)?" If as a coach I am going to create sustainable value, I must be clear about what and who I am serving in my work. As a minimum, I need to ensure that my coaching is in service of the individual client, the teams they are part of, their organization, and the wider system that the organization serves, including the more-then-human ecological world. In addition, as a coach, I must be in service of the relationships that connect and weave between all these parties, for none of these entities can be successful by themselves and their value is intrinsically bound together. I need to be focussed on the unrealized potential in all parties and the connections between them as well as assisting in realizing that potential. However, in serving the individual it is important that I am not just serving their fragmented or egoistic self or acting as an agent of a more senior manager. Instead I am helping the person find their calling, their service and their purpose in doing what is necessary in their organization and in the wider world.

Likewise, in team coaching, becoming a high-performing team is not an end in itself, but merely a means for the team to be better able to "co-create value with and for all their stakeholders" (Hawkins, 2017). In serving the organization we need to ensure that the work with the individual or team is not just an end in itself but is enabling the team to more effectively lead and manage the organization through its next phase of development, so that the organization can fulfil its potential and make a better contribution to the wider world.

Thus the systemic coach needs to create the contract with the coachee and their stakeholders. The coaching needs to be a partnership and a joint enterprise between the coach and the coachee, in service of the individual development of the coachee but also of all the people and systems their work serves and is connected to – the relationship between them and the wider ecosystem as well as the coaching profession.

2. Focussing on connections not parts

Increasingly it is recognized that the most important organizational issues cannot be resolved by trying to fix problems just within one part of the organization, for the organization is an interrelated whole. Eve thinks of this like balloons that have been made into animals: what you do to the balloon in one place influences the shape elsewhere. Also, many of the organizational challenges transcend the boundaries of the organization and involve the wider system of stakeholders, without which the organization has no life or meaning. These stakeholders include customers, suppliers, partner organizations, employees, investors, communities in which the organization operates and the ecological environment.

Gareth Morgan (1986) has written about the change in dominant organizational metaphors, which has moved from seeing organizations as machines to seeing them as living organisms. This shift of dominant metaphor has been further developed by subsequent writers (Senge, 1990, 2008; Senge, Flowers, Scharmer, and Jaworski, 2005; Senge and Kofman, 1993; Cooperrider and Whitney, 1999; Scharmer, 2008, Scharmer and Kaufer, 2013; de Gues, 1997; Hutchins, 2012, 2016; Hawkins, 2017a). This brings with it a shift in focus from parts to connections; from individuals and individual teams to relationships; from events to patterns; and from linear cause and effect thinking to process thinking. Cooperrider and Whitney (1999: 19) argue we should: "view organizations as living spiritual-social systems, mysteries of creation to be nurtured and affirmed, not as mechanistic or scientific operations with problems to be solved."

A system is defined by Capra (1996) as "an integrated whole whose essential properties arise from the relationships between its parts"; and by Peter Senge (1990) as "a perceived whole whose elements 'hang together' because they continually affect each other over time and operate towards a common purpose." A heating system and a bicycle are systems, as their purpose can only be achieved by the whole working interconnectedly together, and not by the sum of their parts. A living system can be a plant, a living animal, a human or a family. It can also be a coral reef, a woodland, or indeed 'Gaia', Lovelock's (1979) term for the whole envelope of interdependent life that surrounds our planet. A system can also be a family or tribe, a coaching relationship, a team, a whole organization, or a business ecosystem.

Survival and success are never unitary but always relational and yet we mostly behave as if the individual, team or organization can succeed by sub-optimizing their part of the wider system.

Peter has defined *systems* as:

> An integrated whole whose essential properties arise from the relationships between its parts.

He then defines systems thinking:

> *Systems thinking* looks at how the whole system is more than the sum of its parts – how it connects and functions within its boundaries over time.

Which he sees as different from *Systemic thinking*:

> *Systemic thinking* – sees systems as always engaging, developing and changing in relation to the nested systemic levels within them and the systemic levels they are nested within. It perceives the dance between systemic levels and the holographic nature of the universe.

3. Always seeing systems in relation to other systems

Systemic coaching recognizes that the concept of an individual separate from their contexts is both an abstraction and unknowable. As a coach we get to know the client as they show up in the context of coaching, or more precisely how they show up in the coaching session with us, as organized by their organization, through the lenses in which we, the coaches, view individuals. These lenses are shaped by our own culture, education and personal conscious and unconscious biases and mind-sets.

From a mixture of their own narratives, compared to the 360-degree feedback and views gathered through multi-stakeholder contracting (see chapter 6), we may form a view of the individual as they show up and are perceived by their colleagues and stakeholders. But this is also inevitably partial and temporal. This means our own views of the individual should be at best tentative, temporary and exploratory – partial understanding awaiting to be changed by further experience and correction. The psychoanalyst Wilfrid Bion encourages us "to impose on [ourselves] a positive discipline of eschewing memory and desire" (Bion, 1970: 31) and so we can engage the other with what the great poet Keats called 'negative capability' (Keats, 1970), the capacity to stay with unknowing and partial knowing so new awareness can emerge between us. Otto Scharmer, an influential innovator in the fields of organizational change and leadership, similarly encourages us to start with an open mind, open heart and open will (Scharmer and Kaufer, 2013: 16).

There is never a text without a context or a coachee without a systemic context; the work of the systemic coach is to listen not only to the coachee but to the systemic contexts they inhabit, both inside and outside work. Then, most importantly, to listen to the relationship between the two, for all learning and development happens in the relational field between the individual and their systemic contexts, both developing and evolving in responsiveness to the other. We also need to keep in mind that we as coaches also are bringing in all our systemic contexts.

The implications of this for coach training is that all coaches need to be trained, not only in coaching, individual psychology and development, and understanding organizations and business, but also in systemic thinking (see Chapter 13). This essentially includes developing one's personal epistemology (i.e. theory of knowledge) from one that focuses on individuals, problems and snapshots in time, to one that sees all issues in their wider context, over time and sees patterns and knows how to create shifts at more fundamental systemic levels.

4. Understanding how all systems are nested within larger systems that are, in turn, also nested within them

We can recognize that any system we look at has systems within it and in turn is part of larger systems. Atoms have protons and electrons and a nucleus within them, and in turn are parts within a larger system of the molecule. Teams are made up of individuals, and in turn are part of a function, which is part of an organization, which is part of a business ecosystem, which is part of a sector, which is part of human activity which is part of the wider ecology. Everything in the Universe, as far as we can know, exists within interconnected nested systems. Let's imagine a set of Russian nesting dolls: each fits inside the other, but systemic understanding tells us that while the smallest exists in the largest, the largest also exists in the smallest (see also Chapter 10, p153). The individual is part of their family, community and organizational cultures, but these cultures also reside within them, how they move, behave, think and in the language they use. Also, we are all part of the wider ecology but the ecology is also within us, in the food we eat, the air we breathe, and the way it shapes our evolution. What we put into the environment therefore we do not get rid of. Take the increasing proliferation of unbiodegradable plastics. As humans we have created this plastic from the earth's resources; then, when no longer wanted, we have abandoned it, and it either enters landfills, affecting the earth in which we grow food, or turns up in the sea and eventually many of us eat fish containing micro-beads of plastics.

Nearly a century ago renowned psychotherapist Carl Jung talked about the collective unconscious: something that unites us all. Ultimately, we are all connected and interrelated because we, humans and non-human living beings, exist within the one eco-system of our planet; we pick this up later in our call for ecological thinking.

If we think about this further, we start to realize the next principle, that of interconnection and interdependency:

> So long as the smaller systems are enclosed within the larger, and so long as all are connected by complex patterns of interdependency, as we know they are, then whatever affects one system will affect the others.
>
> (Berry, 1983: 46).

Yet what we normally look at, think about and talk about, are separate things. Our very language names things as being separate. We tell our children "that is a tree," "that is a leaf," "that is mistletoe growing out of the tree, but is not part of the tree." Part of the way our left hemisphere neo-cortex works in order to analyze the world and solve problems is to break things down into their constituent parts, to create boundaries. To make sense of the world we apply the analytic scissors and create cuts in the seamless web of life (Bateson, 1972), but we then forget that it is our own thinking that has created the cuts and the boundaries, and we think the cuts and boundaries exist 'out-there' in the world.

5. We are part of and affect all systems that we observe and engage

It is important that we recognize that every system we are studying, we are studying from within our own systemic position. In one sense we are part of any system we are studying, and inevitably have some effect on that system. From both the early Hawthorne experiments in factories (Landsberger, 1958) where workers modified their behaviour when they knew they were being observed, and the work of nuclear physicists such as Bohr (1934) and Heisenberg (1958), we have learned that whether we are studying human groups or subatomic particles, we are influencing that which we are researching. Secondly, we bring with us all of our ways of thinking, framing, language and making sense that are part of the systems and cultures that we are nested within. The beliefs and mind-sets of our family, community, culture and species are not only what we are nested within, but they are nested within us, and form the lenses and filters through which we perceive the world.

6. Systemic coaching is not just about what we focus on, but also about how we focus and from where we focus

Systemic coaching is not just about what we focus on. Moving the focus from an individual to a team, to an organization etc. is important but not by itself systemic. Paying attention to multiple levels of systems is what we would describe as systems coaching. For coaching to be truly systemic, we need not only to

Table 3.2 Levels of System and Levels of Systemic Focussing

Level of focus	Level of focussing			
	Attempted objective observation	Dialogical and relational engagement	Attending to the 'here and now' relational system	On the limits of our culture and consciousness
Individual				
Individual relational patterns				
Immediate stakeholder context				
Wider systemic levels				

broaden out what we are focussing on and become aware of the dynamic relationship between multiple levels of systems, but also shift how we focus and where we focus from. We would like to offer an important distinction between using the term 'systems' to refer to what we are looking at; and using the term systemic to refer to where we are looking from and how we are engaging with the world.

Much coaching has emerged from the fields of counselling and psychotherapy. We cannot observe, study, or engage with another individual through a quasi-empirical scientific approach. As with counselling and psychotherapy, in coaching (and other human interactions) we only know the other in and through the context in which we meet them, in and through the relationship we co-create with them and in and through our subjective ways of making sense of the encounter.

7. Systemic coaching requires systemic perceiving, systemic thinking, systemic being and systemic relating

So often the word systemic is associated with systemic thinking and is seen as a cognitive process where we think about systems, but we would argue that we should also engage with *systemic perceiving, systemic being* and *systemic relating*.

Systemic perceiving begins with recognizing that we are part of every system we see and hear, and that we only perceive the world inter-subjectively, (Hawkins and Ryde, 2020; Stolorow and Atwood, 1992; Atwood and Stolorow, 1984) in other words, through our own subjective lenses and from our particular place in the system.

Systemic perceiving changes how we listen, where we focus, and how we feel and sense. When we listen systemically to another, we do not listen as one separate individual entity listening to what the other is talking about, but rather we listen through the other to how the world is showing up through them. By the world we include how their team dynamic and organization culture are being enacted through them and how their social, ethnic and national cultures are speaking through them. We listen to the holographic field, where the dynamic dance in one level of the system may be a small replication of the dynamic echoing through other levels of system. We need to listen empathically to the other but without seeing the world through their eyes; to engage with wide-angled empathy (Hawkins, 2019) where we have empathic compassion not just for the individual client but for every person and every system within their story. This helps us avoid locating the problem or the conflict in a person or part of the system outside of the coaching room, which can quickly lead to 'blaming them' or to the 'drama triangle'(Karpman, 1986) in which the client is the victim, 'the other' is the persecutor and the coach is a collusive rescuer.

As a systemic coach we would always view the problem or conflict as being in a relationship, connection or partnership, and as being co-created by multiple parties. We would endeavour to listen without judgement of either the client or any other party within their story. We would listen with our whole body, not just our ears, allowing us to hear the tonality, tempo and timbre of the voice and the breathing pattern of the other, the harmonics that carry so much more than the simple melody. We would also look 'with soft eyes' not overly focussed on data and content but looking for the pattern that lies behind the separate points. Our colleague Nick Smith uses the metaphor of the 'magic eye' pictures that were popular in the 1980s, where you needed to defocus your gaze to see the 3D picture hidden behind what appeared to be many coloured dots.

Systemic being changes our intention and how we show up. In Hawkins, 2018, there is a list of 13 'Systemic Beatitudes', or attitudes of being, that are pointers to how to show up systemically. It entails an intention to be present not just to the other individual or team, but to all that we can sense in their wider ecosystem. To be in service of not just what the individual wants, but what their world requires of them and from their coaching.

Systemic relating is always triadic rather than dyadic, which means it is not just a dialogue between two individuals facing each other but a trialogue, where the two individuals are shoulder to shoulder collaboratively inquiring into the joint purpose of their work together, what the future and the coachee's stakeholders require, and the emergent potential that is waiting, within the individual and their wider contexts, to come alive. This is why, mirroring this physically, we both like to work side by side with people looking ahead to what is needed, rather than sitting opposite them

A seven-eyed model of systemic coaching

The seven-eyed model of coaching supervision (Hawkins, 1985; Hawkins and Smith, 2006, 2013; Hawkins and Shohet, 1989, 2000, 2006, 2012) has been written about widely. Many have seen this model as a collection of seven places the supervision can focus on and seven sets of tools and methods. In doing so they have failed to recognize that it is fundamentally systemic. This model, although developed as a way of understanding supervision and training supervisors, can also be applied directly to understanding coaching. For – like supervision – coaching is a relational system that attends to the coachee's relational systems, and both systems always operate within a larger systemic context. In the coaching version of the seven-eyed model, systemic coaching can focus on a number of interconnecting areas and we will now outline these separately, while recognizing that they are all systemically interconnected (see figure 3.1).

Mode 1. Focuses on the coachee's work situation, exploring and understanding together the challenges their work is presenting, their team and how it operates, their organization and its processes and challenges.

Mode 2. Looks at the choices, conscious and unconscious, that the coachee makes in their response to the Mode 1 challenges and widens the options of how they might respond.

Mode 3. Focuses on the coachee's relationships to various others at work and how these are being co-created.

Mode 4. In Mode 4 the focus is more on the internal world of the coachee, including the reactions and re-stimulation the coachee experiences in relation

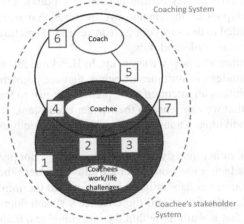

7.	The wider contexts
6.	The Coach's self reflections
5.	The coaching relationship and parallel process
4.	The coachee
3.	The coachee's relationships with their stakeholders
2.	The coachee's actions, behaviours and interventions
1.	The coachee's work/life challenges

Figure 3.1 **The seven-eyed model of coaching**

to the various situations they are faced with. This might lead to exploration of some deeper patterns of behaviour and emotional patterns and belief systems that underpin these (see four levels of engagement in Chapter 7).

These first four modes are looking at the coachee and their world. However, the coaching is also happening in a relational system co-created between the coachee, the coach and the work – thus a system that the coach is part of.

Modes 5 and 6. In Mode 6 the coach needs to focus beyond the data they are hearing and seeing and become aware of the coaching relationship and attend to how the stories that the coachee brings are impacting on themselves. Often the most difficult issues the coachee needs to communicate cannot be articulated, as they are what Bollas (1987) describes as "the unthought known" – something we sense but do not have language for. The supervisor needs to use themselves as an instrument that resonates with what is non-verbally expressed – and this impact can be noticed and commented upon. What we cannot articulate we may be doomed to replicate.

Only when the coach is able to comment on their own perceptions and subliminal experiences as part of the coaching system is it appropriate to also reflect on the coaching relationship as it emerges live in the process (Mode 5). By utilizing Modes 5 and 6 the coach can explore what needs to shift in themselves to shift the coaching relationship to enable the coachee, in turn, to shift their relationships and engagements with their various systemic contexts at work. Although our understanding needs to start 'outside-in' and 'future-back', creating change needs to start in the 'here and now' in the live coaching relationship and thus coaching Modes 5 and 6 are critical. We have to remember that the only parts of the wider system that can change in the coaching are the ones present in the room – the coachee, the coach and the coaching relationship. However, if part of a system changes the whole is impacted.

Mode 7. The seven-eyed model emphasizes that everything that the coachee is attending to in their coaching is nested within wider systemic contexts which is what Mode 7 attends to (see figure 3.2). In 7.1 the coach encourages the coachee to see the wider contexts of the issues they have brought. In 7.2, the coachee is encouraged to understand that the choices they make when trying to respond to the various situations they struggle with also arise from within the wider systemic conflicts, team dynamics, organizational culture etc. In 7.3 the coach may help the coachee explore how the difficult relationships they bring are not just interpersonal conflicts driven by personality differences but driven by the systemic dynamic of each of them carrying different organizational and systemic needs that have not yet been acknowledged and connected. In 7.4 the focus is on the wider contexts of the individual beyond the situations they are bringing. This includes how the situation is coloured by what is happening in their life beyond work, in their family, social and community world, as well as how it is coloured by their past experiences and their sense of purpose and ambitions for the future.

This coaching relational system is also embedded in a wider systemic context (Modes 7.5 and 7.6). This includes how the coaching has been set up, framed and contracted (see Chapters 5 and 6). It also includes the organization the coach

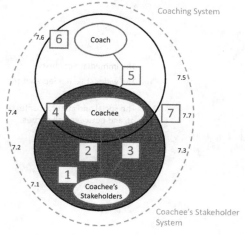

7.7	The wider contexts
7.6	Coach's stakeholders
7.5	The context and stakeholder's of the coaching relationship
7.4	The coachee's work and life context
7.3	The context and stakeholders of the coaching relationship
7.2	The training and background that shapes the coachee's actions and interventions
7.1	The coachee's organizational stakeholder's contexts

Figure 3.2 **The seven perspectives of Mode 7**

works for and the professional bodies they are part of, who have their own expectations of what happens.

These are the immediate and different contextual areas in the first circle of outer nested systemic levels (7a). Beyond this are the social contexts both parties belong to. Further out (7b) are the systemic cultural contexts of both parties in the coaching and the intercultural dynamics that are co-created in the coaching dialogue (Ryde, 2009, 2019). This next further level out (7c) is one interconnected world of human population and what is happening globally, as we explored in the previous chapter. These levels are all contained within the ecological world that includes the human and 'more than human world' – the world of coevolution (7d) (see figure 3.3).

These wider systemic levels that we are all nested within do not just exist out there, but flow through all the levels within them. The organizational culture is not something external to us, but becomes part of us, our ways of being and perceiving. Peter once defined organizational culture as "What you stop noticing when you have worked somewhere for three months," because it has become part of you. Likewise, the ecological system is not apart from us, we are a part of it, and a very small but dangerously impactful part.

Conclusion

To address these critical challenges to the coaching profession we have been developing ways of fundamentally shifting the paradigm and practice of coaching in ways that:

1   Deliver value not just to the individual, but all those wDho are affected by the work of the individual coachee;

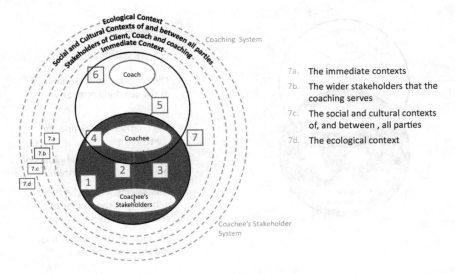

Figure 3.3 The Wider Dimensions of the Seven Eyed Model

2   Introduce the needs and voice of the multiple stakeholders both into the contracting for, and in the process of coaching;

3   Raise the level of challenge in the coaching room, while still staying true to the role of the coach and enabling the explorations of the issues the coachee brings;

4   Ensuring that the focus of the coaching is both 'future-back' and 'outside-in' and the coaching counterbalances, rather than replicates, the dynamic of the urgent current issues that drown out the important future challenges.

In our definitions we have tried to capture the essence of systemic coaching of individuals in a systemic context and in later chapters we will go into far more detailed exploration of each of the elements, showing practically how this approach changes fundamentally:

- How organizations can manage coaching in a systemic way (Chapter 4).
- How multi-stakeholder contracting happens (Chapter 5).
- The process of a systemic coaching session and ongoing relationship (Chapter 6).
- The different tools and methods that a systemic coach uses (Chapter 7).
- How individual systemic coaching connects with systemic group coaching and systemic team coaching and systemic OD (Chapter 9).
- How systemic coaching requires that the coach continues to undertake systemic supervision for their work (Chapter 10).
- The way we need to think about ethics beyond an individualistic frame to understanding complex systemic ethics (Chapter 11).
- The way we need to evaluate and asses coaching (Chapter 12).
- The way we need to rethink how we train and develop coaches (Chapter 13).

Chapter 4

Developing systemic coaching from the organization's perspective

Introduction

Having described the core elements of systemic coaching in the previous chapter, we will now turn to what organizations can do to ensure that coaching delivers value beyond the individual to the organization and all its stakeholders. This will include how to create a coaching strategy and infrastructure for all coaching activities, whether delivered by external or internal coaches or by line managers or human resources, and how to create a coaching culture whereby a coaching approach is built into the very fabric of how the organization operates and partners with its stakeholders.

As we move through this chapter, we encourage you to consider your thoughts – whether as an organizational representative or a coach – regarding these questions, and perhaps you might add your own ideas about

- What needs to be in a coaching strategy and what makes it effective?
- What are the mutual roles of the organization and the coach in a coaching relationship?
- How might we create a coaching culture or support its creation?
- How can we deliver value that goes beyond the coaching relationship to benefit the organization and its many stakeholders?

Coaching strategy

To create a robust and sustainable coaching strategy and culture requires building a strong foundation. In Hawkins (2012) Peter suggested that there were three key pillars that support coaching at work (see Figure 4.1) and that if any of these are missing, there is a danger that coaching can become marginalized, or be swept away in the next round of organizational cuts, restructuring or new initiatives.

1. Coaching strategy

The first pillar underlines that a coaching strategy has to be firmly grounded in the organization's purpose and mission, its strategy, its development plans and its people development policies such as talent retention and recruitment; otherwise

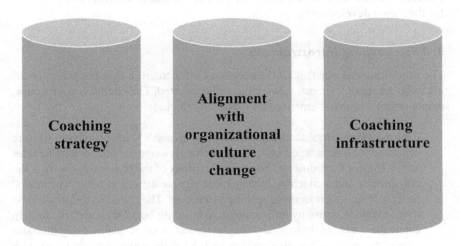

Figure 4.1 The three pillars of coaching culture

it may be lost among the many documents that get left in bottom drawers. It is essential that the strategy is developed collaboratively across the organization, involving stakeholders and then regularly updated as context and practice change. The strategy also needs to engage people and be communicated and discussed with staff so it is a 'living' strategy.

2. Aligning the coaching culture with the wider organizational culture change

The second pillar aligns the creation of a coaching culture to the wider changes in the organizational culture. To thrive, organizations have to stay ahead of the world in which they operate, both in terms of strategy and culture, the latter being a particular challenge. Many have heard Peter Drucker's phrase "Culture eats strategy for breakfast" and, some add, for lunch and dinner, too! We know from the roads littered with failed change initiatives that organizational cultures are pervasive and inherently conservative and can slow down or even prevent all forms of strategic change unless the cultures are also carefully developed. Creating a coaching culture is a means to an end, and a key part of creating a more general culture of continual learning and development to enhance the capabilities and capacities of all staff and the whole organization. This increased capability and capacity is in service of individual, team and organization performance while in turn, high performance is in service of creating greater shared value for the organization and all its key stakeholders. Other examples of a coaching culture could be demonstrated in how meetings are run, the type of conversations that are held and the level of responsibility people are taking at all levels, including for their own development.

3. The coaching infrastructure

The third pillar ensures that all the necessary infrastructure is in place for coaching to be successful, robust, sustainable and integrated. This includes governance, management and involvement of all parties. We include

1   A strong sponsorship/steering group. This group needs to have members who are central to the organization indicating coaching's longevity and ideally includes senior leaders from different parts and functions of the business, as well as the HR director and a coaching manager and representatives of other 'customers' for coaching – such as those seeking promotion. They need to be people who have influence, visibility and budgets. As a strong board they are able to help create the coaching strategy, allocate the resources, drive quality evaluation and review processes while also making high level decisions, ensuring a fit with the organization's changing strategy and development. The 2016 Ridler Report, drawing on information from more than one hundred survey respondents, along with interviews and focus groups, examined key factors in setting up coaching successfully and states that "Coaching needs a high-level sponsor" (2016: 16).

2   A management group. This will drive, co-ordinate and integrate coaching processes and activities. The size of the organization and the stage of coaching's development within it will determine the exact composition, but at a minimum there would be a part-time coaching champion supported by a wider group, even if a small one, so that responsibility is shared and there is resilience in the system should the person leave.

3   A community of practice. This third pillar should always involve the coaches, in order to ensure that they can be partners in creating a coaching culture committed to the organization's success. This is essential for the establishment of a community of practice. They will be brought together regularly, virtually or face-to-face, both for their own continual learning and development and to ensure they are briefed on the organization's strategy and development, as partners. They need to be committed to the development of the coaching culture within their organization as well as to their individual coachees and their own learning, and this way of thinking may not automatically be adopted (St John-Brookes, 2014). The three pillars are rarely (all) put in place prior to an organization engaging with establishing coaching activities. In Hawkins (2012) Peter shows how many of the organizations he studied only addressed the need for such foundations once they realized they had a lot of coaching activity, without any effective integration or evaluation of what their coaching investment delivered.

Creating a coaching culture

Having carried out research on creating a coaching culture (Hawkins, 2012) and reviewed much of the literature in this field (Clutterbuck, Megginson and

Bajer, 2016; Hawkins, 2012; Clutterbuck and Megginson, 2005; Hardingham et al, 2004; Caplan, 2003; and many others), Peter integrated these elements and arrived at a new aspirational definition of a coaching culture (Hawkins, 2012: 21) that we have developed further in the light of ongoing developments in systemic coaching:

> A coaching culture exists in an organization when all the staff and other stakeholders experience a coaching approach as a key aspect of how engagement takes place. This will be true at all levels and in all functions and the result will be increased individual, team and organizational learning, enhanced performance, high levels of engagement and a sense of shared value for all stakeholders.

Developmental stages in creating a coaching culture

As we consider engaging stakeholders, one of our organizational challenges relates to determining where organizations are developmentally in their use of coaching. Peterson (2010) describes four typical stages in the use of external coaches:

1   Ad hoc coaching that is driven by individuals within the organization seeking coaching and then potentially extolling its benefits;
2   Managed coaching driven by a sponsor or champion;
3   Proactive coaching driven by business need;
4   Strategic coaching driven by an organizational talent strategy.

The first stage is often driven by the enthusiasm of a few senior executives who have found coaching personally beneficial. Not only do they recommend it to others, they also tend to bring in coaches through recommendation and without monitoring either quality or expense. Maxine Dolan discovered Tesco spending over a £1,000,000 annually on coaching when she took over responsibility, with no monitoring of either its appropriateness or effectiveness (Hawkins, 2012).

The succeeding stages move from the appointment of a key individual, to the provision of a more centralized plan for coaching and expenditure, to the third stage of alignment with business outcomes that includes consideration of who would most benefit from coaching and finally, to alignment with business strategy, change and cultural considerations.

We can see a similar pattern in the growth of internal coaching:

1   Unconnected ad hoc internal coaching driven by individual staff members who have undertaken coaching training independently of the organization.
2   Connected ad hoc internal coaching by individual staff members who trained independently but are brought together in some way by the organization.
3   Managed coaching, driven by a champion or sponsor involving some selection of coaches for training in coaching skills.

4   Proactive coaching driven by a business need – including bringing coaches together, collating emerging cultural themes.
5   Systemic coaching where coaching is directly linked to changing business strategy. There will be a formal process for the selection of coaches and clients, and an evaluation process, collation of themes and a desire to cover areas like multi-stakeholder contracting in training (see Chapter 12) and there will be ongoing continuing professional and personal development and supervision in place.

We are not suggesting that we should necessarily aim for the highest stages – as this depends on the organization and its context. We agree with Knights and Poppleton when they suggest that:

> One size clearly does not fit all in relation to organising coaching services. What's important is having a clear understanding of the organizational context for coaching, then establishing the enabling processes that are congruent with that understanding and intent.
>
> (Knights and Poppleton, 2008: 10)

The choice of who sponsors/leads coaching activities remains a key issue. That person's "power" within the organization, their access to resources and the ear of the top team will determine how coaching is positioned and develops.

We interviewed a number of leaders about how they had developed a coaching culture, one of whom was Donalda MacKinnon, the director of BBC Scotland, who is also a trained BBC internal coach. She took over as director in late 2016, with responsibility for over 1000 staff working in English and Gaelic and a budget of £114m. In addition, following some widely publicized cases that highlighted unequal earnings for some high-profile female employees, Donalda was asked to sponsor a project looking at career progression for women and improved workplace culture in the BBC. The report *Making the BBC a Great Workplace for Women* (BBC, 2018), had 30-plus recommendations that were endorsed by the BBC Board and she now oversees their implementation. The recommendations included mentoring to be made available to women and men at all grades, and for coaching to be offered to new parents back from maternity, adoption or shared parental leave and to people returning to work from extended leave or career breaks after caring for family members. Thirty-one percent of women had left after their last maternity leave. Donalda's interview demonstrates how coaching skills can be integrated into action to achieve lasting systemic culture change.

> Taking over as Director I wanted to achieve cultural change as quickly as possible, and with the launch of a new channel in 2019, and a new BBC Charter in place, I undertook the biggest restructure for one or two decades. I set up a number of workstreams including People and Culture. The desire

to reflect and look at culture influenced our appointments process, to recruit people who wanted to be on that journey. Training as a coach, the theory and practice, equipped and influenced me, as it underpinned the importance of listening conversations, while not necessarily being in "coaching mode." This was particularly appropriate in developing a new television channel at the same time as taking a multi-platform, multi-disciplinary approach and in encouraging teams to work collegiately and inclusively.

Putting coaching training into practice, allowed deep listening, being present for individuals and teams and through this we have witnessed renewed energy and productivity.

A year into the role Tony Hall (the Director-General, the top BBC leader) asked me to sponsor a workstream related to career progression for women, gender balance and workplace culture. Drawing on my coaching approach, I brought together a range of individuals and ensured we consulted widely across the BBC, including holding day-long events to find out what people really felt, to give people a voice and let them be part of the solution and have ownership of the recommendations. To find solutions we asked what would make a difference: in groups, in teams and among individuals, the principle being that, together, we would come up with workable solutions to the challenges that prevent career progression and good culture. In addition to management consultants who bring their own expertise, I believe it is essential that we ourselves engage in the process of self-examination and exploration to arrive at solutions which have a greater likelihood of achieving lasting change for the better.

The seven steps

In 2012 Peter developed a model that suggested seven steps are necessary to establish a full coaching culture, building on earlier work (Hawkins and Smith, 2006). They are not always done in this order but this is the most frequently used sequence:

Step 1 Developing an effective panel of external coaches

Step 2 Developing the internal coaching and mentoring capacity

Step 3 The organization's leaders actively support coaching endeavours and align these to the organizational culture change

Step 4 Coaching moves beyond individual formal sessions to team coaching and organizational learning

Step 5 Coaching becomes embedded in the HR and performance management processes of the organization

Step 6 Coaching becomes the predominant style for managing throughout the organization

Step 7 Coaching becomes how an organization does business with all its stakeholders

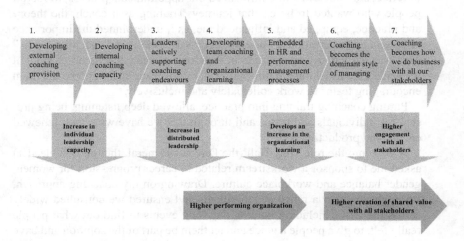

Figure 4.2 Developing a coaching culture – outcomes

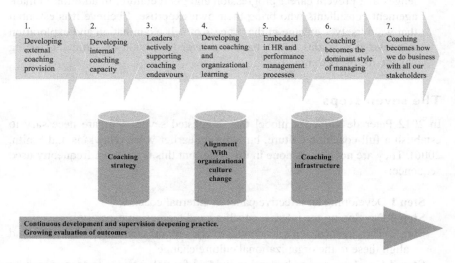

Figure 4.3 Coaching strategy: steps to creating a coaching culture

Even with these steps in place, there are other elements that can determine the depth of the foundations of coaching within an organization and its becoming a full coaching culture. The initial input costs of developing a coaching service, of providing elements like learning and supervision (if internal provision), may mean that the outputs, the business benefits, may take time to be visible and acknowledged. Peter has used Figure 4.2 to explore with senior executives that output benefits in business outcomes only start to emerge when you have supported the coaching efforts with some of the later steps in the coaching culture journey. He will also discuss the key role of evaluation.

Coach selection

If an organization decides to create a structured coaching process, the following nine stages can be useful to ensure the best organizational return.

1. Diagnosing and defining the need

This starts with a coaching strategy as outlined previously and goes beyond simply introducing coaching to examine why it is needed and the outcomes it will contribute to. We would ask questions like:

- What is the developmental journey needed to help the organization's leaders and managers to make this shift?
- How will coaching play a part in this wider development journey?
- What are the particular outcomes, we want coaching to deliver on this journey?

2. Creating a coaching policy and guideline

The answers to these questions will inform the organization's coaching policy, built on the foundation of the coaching strategy, which will provide more detail of how coaching will be provided to contribute to the organization moving forward. These responses can be developed into information freely available to all leaders and managers in the company. It will cover:

- WHY: The purpose of external coaching in the organization and how it links to the current business, leadership and change strategies in the organization.
- WHAT: The organization's definition of coaching.
- WHO: Both who is eligible for external coaching as well as whom the organization employs as external coaches.
- WHEN: The circumstances in which coaching is most useful, e.g. at transitions in role, linked to attending leadership programmes, preparing for future role etc.
- HOW: The processes of applying or being selected for coaching, of being matched with a coach and of contracting, reviewing and evaluating the coaching.
- WHAT IS EXPECTED: The business, performance and personal outcomes that the organization expects and that the individual can expect from coaching.

- WHERE: The person to go to for further information or for pursuing coaching options, e.g. performance or development review with the line manager, HR, coaching manager etc.

A good example of a coaching policy and guidelines is the one developed by Thomson Reuters Executive Coaching services (see Hawkins, 2012: 49) and the BBC who provide an online brochure with an overview of coaching that covers the following areas (see box) before interested leaders can then link to a site to assess their eligibility. All coaching engagements for leadership and transition coaching in the BBC require the manager's involvement and a three-way meeting at the start and end. There is also an agreed evaluation by the coachee and manager at the end.

BBC Guide to coaching and the skills (2019) involved

- What is leadership coaching in the BBC?
- What does a BBC leadership development coach do?
- What might a BBC leadership development coach be helpful for?
- What skills can you build with leadership development coaching?
- What coaching programmes does the BBC offer?
  Executive
  First 100 days transition coaching
  Leadership and development programmes
- What makes a successful coaching relationship?
- Development goals
- Ending a coaching relationship
- Confidentiality
- Are you eligible for leadership coaching (which leads to another site)?

3. Defining requirements and setting coach criteria

We next consider which coaches will be appropriate for the organizational outcomes required. This will include, among other things, their background and experience, training and accreditation/credential and their cultural fit. We also acknowledge that there needs to be a range of coaches available to provide sufficient challenge across the leadership community.

There are a variety of criteria for coaches available, including those from the professional coaching bodies such as the Association for Professional Executive Coaching and Supervision (APECS), Association for Coaching (AC), Coaches and Mentors of South Africa (COMENSA), European Mentoring and Coaching Council (EMCC) and International Coaching Federation (ICF). Some books on coaching also contain information on coaching competences, capabilities and capacities (see Hawkins and Smith, 2013; Passmore, 2016 and Chapter 13 of this book). These can be adapted by the particular organization to fit its own coaching requirements.

Peter has described three fundamental and integrated capabilities from an executive coach that he visualizes as a three-legged stool made up of coaching craft, psychological understanding including adult development, and business and organizational understanding. He sees good coaching supervision as essential for the stool to be effective, connecting the three legs. Peter believes this connecting seat has to be provided by a coach supervisor who is experienced in all areas the three legs represent (Hawkins and Smith, 2013; Hawkins, 2012; Hawkins and Schwenk, 2011). To join the legs coaches will also need good systemic understanding, so that they can notice and attend to the interconnections between the individual, team, departmental, organizational and wider stakeholder and system dynamics.

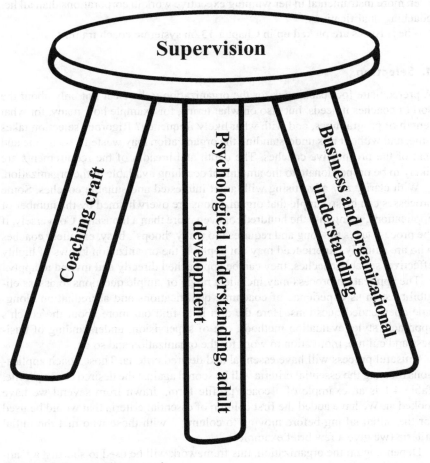

Figure 4.4 The coaching stool

The first leg comprises skills in the craft of coaching and establishing and maintaining effective coaching relationships. Every coach should have completed professional coaching training and be actively participating in continuous personal and professional development, including supervision.

The second leg is psychological understanding essential for a coach to be alert to psychological conditions that may require referral for more specialized help. This understanding will include the area of adult learning and development, personality types and learning preferences.

The third leg provides an understanding of organizational behaviour and the world of business. This requirement is likely to be met by the coach having previously worked as an executive themselves. The coach may also have completed a business or organizational qualification such as an MBA, but of itself this may not be sufficient. Eve has noted that her MBA and experience as a senior leader has been more instrumental in her winning executive work in corporations than all her coaching qualifications.

These issues are picked up in Chapter 13 on systemic coach training.

4. Selection

A prerequisite for coaching is for the organization to be clear not only about the sort of coaches it needs, but also on what terms, for example how many, for what length of programmes, and with what likely frequency? Rigorous selection takes time, and without this understanding the organization may waste its own time and that of the prospective coaches. The depth and breadth of the requirements are likely to be proportionate to the amount of coaching available in the organization.

With clarity any advertising will target interested and suitable coaches. Some processes can be so simple that organizations are overwhelmed by the number of applications, going into the hundreds or even more than a thousand. Conversely, if the process takes too long and requires too many 'hoops', busy, excellent coaches who are suitably experienced may not apply. If the organization knows of highly effective, suitable coaches, they can be approached directly and invited to apply.

The application process may include a range of simple questions to assess eligibility such as experience of coaching, qualifications and accreditation alongside open-ended questions. Here the aim is to find out more about the coach's approach, style, evaluation methods, use of supervision, understanding of business and culture, motivation to work for the organization and so on.

A useful process will have essential and desired criteria. Those coach applications meeting the essential criteria will be scored against the desired coach profile. Table 4.1 is an example of a coach profile form, drawn from several we have looked at. We have added the first column of essential criteria that would be used for the initial sifting before moving to column 2 with those who met the initial criteria (we give a few brief examples).

Depending on the organization, this framework will be used to shortlist a manageable number of applications for more in-depth assessment; however, some

Table 4.1 Coach selection criteria profile

Area	1. Essential requirement	2. Desired requirement	3. Applicant's score	4. Weighting of element	5. Weighted score (2 × 3)
Previous coaching experience	e.g. 3 years minimum	Specific experience of working in executive coaching for 5 years			
Coach training and recent CPPD	Evidence of regular ongoing continuing personal and professional development				
Relevant business/sector experience	Not essential				
Business qualifications	Not essential				
Membership of a professional body	Full membership of APECS, AC, EMCC, ICF etc. acceptable				
Accreditation by a professional body*	Not essential	At least at professional level from APECS, AC, EMCC or ICF or country equivalent.			
Professional indemnity insurance	Yes – to minimum level of £5m				
Psychological training or experience	Yes				
Professional supervision	Yes – name of supervisor required and evidence of a year minimum and currently in supervision	Examples of how supervision has been used to make a difference provided			
Model of coaching	No one model essential				
Ability to handle ethical dilemmas	Completion of a dilemma in form				
Qualities and personal attributes necessary to match to the internal values	Not essential				

Source: *In the 2016 Ridler report 68 percent of reporting organizations required accreditation

organizations with very large numbers of coaches to appoint may do a paper exercise only. Whatever is decided we reinforce the idea of proportionality to the work offered and the need to ensure that leading coaches, who may go through a number of these processes, may be put off if they are too long and demanding.

There are a variety of assessment options depending on the time and resources available:

- A short presentation by the coach on their approach to coaching, the models and processes they use and how they believe they could add value to the organization;
- One or more in-depth interviews, ideally to include the HR/coaching manager and senior executives who are potential users of coaching;
- A live observed coaching session with a volunteer from the organization; for this, organizations may use a video camera and have observers watch in an adjoining room;
- A written reflection by the coach on both the interview and their coaching session;
- Written or verbal answers to how the coach would approach a number of prepared possible coaching situations;
- An interview with the coach's supervisor to get a verbal reference as well as the written one.

Peter helped an international bank review their selection process and asked them what questions helped them separate the coaches they accepted (33% of those interviewed) from ones they turned down (67%). They mentioned two open questions:

- Please describe an ethical dilemma you have faced in your coaching, and how you dealt with it.
- Please tell us about a time that you have used supervision to improve the coaching you were doing with a client.

They reported that those accepted were able to give meaningful answers to both questions. The other factor that distinguished successful coaches was the congruence between how the coach described their coaching approach and what they actually did in the coaching demonstration, showing an alignment between their espoused theory and their theory in use (Argyris and Schön, 1978).

Some organizations have also chosen to outsource the selection of their external coaches and/or the managing of the external coach panel. This is sometimes combined with the same provider ensuring that all coaches continue to meet the requisite criteria and are given supervision geared to the needs of the particular client organization. This has been commissioned by large global organizations who find it difficult to recruit, quality assess and keep aligned a global panel of coaches. Case study G from Nick Smith is one example of this (p 256–260). When this is the process used it is important to ensure that coaching is equally as embedded in the organization as if it was wholly managed in-house.

There is an increasing focus on the selection of coaches. The 6th Ridler Report (Mann, 2016: 17) concludes that "selecting the right quality of coach and ensuring organizational fit is a precondition for success." One participant, Samantha King, Global Head of Executive Development from Standard Chartered, reflects that:

> we have often been surprised to find numerous accredited coaches . . . who stick to one approach or even a more formulaic set of questions or who may lack contracting confidentiality or rapport-building skills. The risk with coaching is that it is, by its very nature, mostly unobserved, and many coachees generally don't know what "good" looks like. We look for the rare coaches who offer a range of flexible tools, approaches and deep skills to draw form, who are hugely invested in their own personal development, with varied experience developed over time with a diverse range of leaders.
>
> (quoted in Mann, 2016: 60)

One of the biggest shifts over time in coach selection, highlighted by the Ridler reports, is the requirement for individual accreditation by a coaching professional body. This shifts from 54 percent in 2013 to 68 percent in 2015 (Mann, 2016: 59).

When Eve started coaching full-time in 2007 she was surprised at the wide variety of approaches organizations adopted.

> There were the organizations who had heard about me from someone and asked how much I charged, then, if the fee was acceptable, when could I start? In such cases, even the most rudimentary questions were not always asked: qualifications, supervision arrangements, professional body membership and professional insurance (which is not available in all countries). In contrast there were national registers' processes that were time-intensive and demanding, for example with the NHS (the National Health Service) that required a three-stage, three-month process: written application, requiring accreditation, interview, and assessment centre. The written application was substantial, with 15 questions, of which the 15th required two lengthy case studies. Sample questions included:
>
> How do you describe your approach to coaching? Please include any underpinnings you draw on and a typical process for your coaching
>
> How do you evaluate the effectiveness of your coaching practice?
>
> Please share an example of an issue you have taken to supervision over the last 12 months. Describe what you learnt in supervision and the impact your learning had on your coaching practice and/or a specific coaching assignment.

When it comes to internal coaching, the first question is who the organization wants to select as coaches and the reasons for that choice. This varies, from human resources and learning and development specialists to leaders, or it can be a mix. What commitment will you require from the coaches, and their line managers? When Eve applied to train as a BBC internal coach, her line manager had to approve the application that included an outline of the minimum time requirement that the manager and potential coach had to agree to. On top of this there is the training that will be put in place and the ongoing CPD and supervision.

5. Coach on-boarding, briefing and alignment

Once the selection is completed, to ensure that organizations get best value from their coaching many following good practice will provide an induction, either through a briefing event or through virtual webinars. Ideally, they will involve a senior executive who can provide context for the coaching, by the organizational mission (purpose, strategy, core values and vision) and will explain how the coaches can best add value to both the organizational and individual clients they will be working with. Other elements the briefings could cover include

- How the coaching process will work – coach matching, initial meetings, three-way contracting, review, evaluation, reports etc.
- What feedback and psychometric instruments the organization uses, their availability and process for using them (360-degree feedback, Myer-Briggs, Firo-B, Hogan, Insights Discovery, Belbin etc.).
- What evaluation criteria and feedback processes are used for assessing both the coaching and the coach.
- How the collective organizational learning from the coaching will be harvested and how the coaches will be involved with this.
- General contractual arrangements, such as confidentiality, handling conflicts of interest, ethical boundaries, cancellations, complaint processes etc.
- Invoicing and payment methods.
- How the coaches will be kept updated on changes in the organization and in the coaching policy and operations.

The aim is not only to provide information, but also to begin the process of building a committed community of coaches, coach managers and senior executives who share the joint endeavour of taking forward the organization, its strategy, culture and leadership. As part of this, ongoing organizational briefings and updates will be arranged, and the coaching lead or sponsor will consider who will do this and when, to ensure that there is continued interconnectedness and clear communication between the different parts of the system. This ensures that coaches have a full understanding of the context within which the coach, your coachee and the wider stakeholders are operating without being 'sucked into' the organization's or the individual's agenda.

6. Matching coaches and coachees and aligning coaching to the organizational needs

There are a number of approaches organizations can use to match individual clients to appropriate coaches.

Open book self selection

In an open book process the organization publishes a directory of the pool of coaches available with a short biography for each coach, including their relevant background, experience, approach, location and contact details. Prospective coachees contact their choice directly to arrange an exploratory (chemistry) meeting and inform the central organizers (also see Chapter 6, p. 78).

Open book joint selection

As self selection, but here the prospective coachee contacts the central coaching manager and discusses their preferences and the manager arranges one or two exploratory meetings.

Central matching of needs to appropriate coaches

In this instance the coaching register is kept centrally alongside a list of which coaches have current availability and recent feedback. These stages are then followed:

- The individual's specific development needs and learning preferences are identified by their line manager, or their HR Partner/Adviser.
- From this information the coaching manager identifies two or three suitable coaches using their knowledge of the pool.
- The individual is given information about one or two suitable coaches.
- They either make an immediate selection or have introductory meetings with both.
- The individual (and possibly coach) notifies the coaching manager of their choice.
- The coaching manager informs the selected coach formally and ensures necessary contractual arrangements.
- The individual has the first contracting meeting with the selected coach and probably their line manager.

7. Harvesting the learning

In Hawkins (2012: 19, 99) Peter poses the following question to CEOs and HR directors who employ a lot of external coaches: "How many coaching conversations do you think happen every month in your organization?"

Very few had a clear idea, but most estimated that it was in the thousands, particularly if you include coaching conversations by line managers and not just formal external and internal coaching.

Then follows a simple but challenging question: "How does your organization learn from these thousands of coaching conversations?"

They are usually puzzled but curious about how coaching can lead to organizational learning and demonstrable organizational benefit.

In large organizations there may be many coaching relationships occurring in parallel. Three- and four-way contracting and evaluation processes (see Chapters 5 and 12) will help the learning to move beyond the confines of the coaching room, but this learning can be restricted to the few people who have been involved in the contracting and 360-degree feedback processes. Due to confidentiality there will be a great deal of organizational learning that remains unrealized. Peter (Hawkins, 2012) developed a methodology for preserving the appropriate confidentiality of the one-to-one coaching relationship, while simultaneously helping the organization learn from the many coaching relationships it was sponsoring and from the collective insights of the external and internal coaching pools. He termed this approach "Harvesting the Learning" and it has four stages (Hawkins, 2012: 100):

1   Regularly bringing together the community of internal and external coaches to hear the challenges the organization is experiencing, providing a forum for questions about its strategy and its plan for the development of its business, its organization, culture, leaders and people.

2   Then working with all the coaches in supervision trios (coach, supervisor and observer) on key coaching relationships with managed confidentiality. The observer is given a pro-forma to capture some of the emerging themes; for example:

   i   Clarity and alignment concerning the direction of the organization and what this requires from leaders and managers.
   ii   The organizational culture, including patterns of behaviour, mind sets, emotions, and motivational roots.
   iii   Connections and disconnections across the organization.
   iv   Connections and disconnections with stakeholders.
   v   How coaching is perceived.
         Each person has 30 minutes in each role, and with both coach and supervisor receiving feedback, providing additional developmental learning.

3   Each trio looks for patterns emerging across the themes collected and these patterns will be entered onto post-its and posted on different themed flip chart boards. The group will then split up into small groups by each themed board and organize the emerging clusters and themes, identifying the patterns that connect them, before feeding these back into the whole group. They are asked to identify the key patterns that will enable or block the organization in meeting its strategic and developmental objectives.

4   These enabling and blocking patterns are then brought together and a dialogue is facilitated between senior executives and the coaches on these emerging key themes. This can either be at the same event or at a later meeting between the senior leadership team and a representative group of internal and external coaches. Having explored the emerging themes, the dialogue can focus on

how coaching can contribute more effectively to the next stages of the organization's development.

This process requires facilitation from a consultant that is not only an experienced coach and skilled coaching supervisor, but also one who understands organizational strategy, culture change, systemic dynamics and organizational development. Most importantly, this facilitator needs to translate between the strategic and business language of senior executives and the more process language of the coaches.

This full process for harvesting the learning may sound rather daunting for coaching communities in the early stages of their development, but simpler forms of the process can be adopted as part of the annual review of the coaching community. This process has been used successfully with organizations in several different sectors. In the case study written by Nick Smith (case study G in Appendix 1), he shows how by having a global panel of coaches that have been selected and on-boarded by the same coach supervisors who will continue to supervise their coaching for the global company, the coach supervisor can themselves carry out this process of harvesting the learning.

8. Group and team and team of teams coaching

There is evidence – as seen in the 6th Ridler Report (Mann, 2016) – that team coaching is on the increase. While it was 9 percent of the volume of coaching taking place in organizations (2016: 34) 76 percent of organizations expected to increase their use of it in the next two years. As part of developing the coaching strategy and reviewing the impact of the coaching provided, those responsible need to look at what time and investment should be spent on providing individual coaching, and what investment should go into group coaching, team coaching, systemic team coaching and team of teams coaching. All these approaches have the potential to maximize the impact of the coaching for the organization and its stakeholders, and to provide the link between individual learning and development, team learning, organizational learning and the organization growing its capacity to create more value for all its stakeholders. We explore this in more depth in Chapter 9.

As we have outlined in this chapter, in our view coaching in organizations does not start by suggesting to an individual or team that they might benefit from coaching. Coaching begins by the organization looking at its strategy and considering what will be required in the future from all its stakeholders for it to be successful going forward. Only then can the organization look at what this will require to be different from its current culture (both as described and as experienced by those within the organization), its collective leadership and its management and employees. This can lead to the creation of an organizational development plan that plans how to develop not just leaders and managers, but the functions, teams and connections right across the business – as well as its external stakeholder relationships.

This developmental plan may well include addressing the following questions:

- Where can we achieve the best impact from our coaching endeavours?
- Where can individual coaching be most effective? And where can group coaching or team coaching or inter-team or team of teams coaching be most effective?
- What part of this coaching can be best delivered through e-coaching, peer coaching, internal coaching or external coaching?
- How do these various forms of coaching need to be monitored, supervised (see Chapter 10), ethically ensured (see Chapter 11) and evaluated (see Chapter 12)?
- What challenges might surface and how might we respond to them? What and who might help us do this?

As we have observed, an organization's coaching strategy needs to be built on both its learning and development strategy and its organizational development strategy, which will ensure delivery based on the future needs of all the business' stakeholders (see Hawkins, 2012).

Without this flow and linkage, it is very hard for those tasked with managing coaching in an organization to achieve effective targeting of resources or to achieve the potential benefits from all the coaching activity. It will also be difficult for the organization to fully implement its approaches to stakeholder contracting, involvement and benefit, since the people giving input will unavoidably speak from their personal view point as to what is needed regarding coaching of an individual or team, rather than have the foundation and clarity to voice what the organization, the future and the wider stakeholders will need from the individual members or teams and from their coaching.

To help tease out some of these issues, we might start with some simple questions such as:

Who are you here to serve? List your critical stakeholders and what they need from this (named intervention).

Thinking of the investors complete the following sentences by stepping into their shoes:

- As an investor what we appreciate from the (named group, team or individual etc.) is. . .
- As an investor what we need different from them is. . .

Now step into the shoes of the customers – internal and/or external customers and complete:

- As the customers of the organization what we appreciate is. . . .
- As the customers what we need different from them is. . . .

Next, step into the shoes of other stakeholders: employees, team members and so on. Then we can ask: what does this tell us our next steps need to be?

Conclusion

In this chapter we have shown how organizations can play their part in ensuring that the coaching they provide delivers value beyond the individuals lucky enough to receive it directly. To do so we have shown ways of:

a)   Developing a coaching strategy, aligned with and in support of their business strategy.
b)   Building the right infrastructure to develop, align, support and evaluate all the many coaching activities within the organization.
c)   Developing from providing a lot of coaching to developing a coaching culture, where coaching approaches are built into the ways the company, manages, leads and appraises its people and engages with its stakeholders.
d)   Selecting, on-boarding and regularly briefing external and internal coaches.
e)   Finding methods for harvesting the organizational learning from the many individual coaching assignments and feeding this back to both senior leaders and those responsible for organizational, team and individual development across the business.
f)   Thinking about the investment in individual coaching, group coaching, team coaching, systemic team coaching and team of teams coaching that we explore further in Chapter 9.

In the next two chapters we will explore what all coaches can do to increase the value that is created from their coaching. Firstly, in Chapter 5, through greater and more effective stakeholder involvement in both contracting, and secondly, in Chapter 6, by how the coach uses a systemic coaching process that focuses not only on the needs of the coachee but also on the needs of all those who the coachee's work serves.

Chapter 5

Multi-stakeholder contracting

Introduction

In this chapter and the following two, we explore ways of working as an individual coach that maximizes the potential value the coaching creates, not just for your coachees but also the many stakeholders their coaching serves. These chapters are based on the shift to a systemic paradigm, where we no longer just think about coaching an individual but also about coaching with and through an individual to create benefit for all the people, systems and organizations that the individual engages with. Working this way reminds us of a Sufi teaching story, which goes like this:

> You think that because you understand "one" that you must therefore understand "two" because one and one make two. But you forget that you must also understand "and".
>
> (Quoted in Meadows, 2008: 12)

If you have ever been coached or are currently, can you think of all the people, organizations and systems (including the ecosystem of the more than human world) that could or would have benefited from the coaching? Try and list as many as possible. Now ask how the needs of all these were brought into the coaching and how you and the coach attended to them. In this chapter we will explore first how to change whom we view as the client, and then explore contracting in ways that mean we are basing the coaching, that is the work the coach and the coachee do together, on the needs of the individual and the many systems they are nested within.

Over the next few pages we will:

- Examine what research tells us about effective contracting.
- Explore the conditions for success.
- Consider what can happen when we either fail to contract at all or do so ineffectively, with short case illustrations in part drawn from an amalgam of issues brought to us in supervision.
- Consider the phases of contracting.

- Provide frameworks that can be used successfully by practitioners and commissioners.
- Provide some practice tools including for situations, when no representative of the organization is directly involved.

From one client to two clients to partnership in service of the many

This relates to a question posed in Chapter 3 that relates to the coaching and supervision spaces: "Who is the client?" What was your initial response? Framing the question in this way could suggest a binary response, either the coachee or the organization. One can find advocates of either. St John-Brooks' research (2014) with internal coaches quotes one respondent who thought that employers' interest was so fraught with difficulty it was not worth considering, while another thought the primary responsibility should be to the organization. In Eriksson's research the executive coach group's more personal and holistic individual 'life as a whole' approach contrasted with the purchasers' "more result-oriented focus with a task/result oriented focus tied to company development" (2011: 4–5). Scoular (2011) argues strongly that the organization is the client, while Huffington (2006) and Kahn (2014), among others, see both as important. Bresser and Wilson (2006: 11) say that the "effective coach needs to balance these competing priorities."

We suggest that we need to go further to avoid juggling between the individual and organizational client or finding a midpoint compromise between two sets of needs. Systemic coaching seeks to discover the work that needs to be done in the coaching that will develop the partnership between the individual client and the organizational client, in ways that further the co-creation of value with and for all stakeholders.

The history and development of contracting in coaching

From our experience, contracting and re-contracting lies at the heart of our work as systemic coaches and supervisors. This may be explicit or implicit but underpins the interrelationship, the 'mutuality' (as described by Martin Luther King when he said "all life is interrelated, and in a real sense we are all caught in an inescapable network of mutuality, tied in a single garment of destiny" (King, 1964)), between the coach, client and the context (including the stakeholders) and the work that needs to be done, as demonstrated in our 3Cs model (figure 5.1):

In a study of ethics in coaching, Pomerantz and Eiting (2007: 96) highlighted some of the challenges from their research, such as:

- Multiple clients in a company.
- Clients who do not have the capability to be successful.

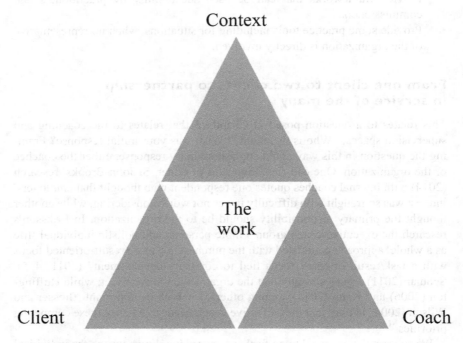

Figure 5.1 The 3Cs model

- Client's bosses who want more information shared with them.
- Clients who want to leave the company.
- Dual relationships.

They note that contracting is central to ethical considerations and offer six ideas for dialogue between the coach and the person hiring the coach "to raise client and organizational awareness about ethical coaching practices" (Pomerantz and Eiting, 2007: 97). This includes contracting for expectations, working in partnership with HR, setting clear boundaries and "defin[ing] and set[ting] up a firewall around confidentiality and anonymity with the client, with the sponsor or HR representative and with anyone else to whom you are accountable within the client company or organization" (2007: 97). They also refer to agreeing how feedback will be done, how support will be provided once the coaching is over, and discuss situations when a different form of support might be needed, such as therapy.

There are many elements to contracting, and here we will examine a few, drawing on some of the relevant literature. Lee reminds us that contracting begins from the moment we as coaches, mentors or supervisors are first asked about our interest in an assignment, not just within the formal setting of a contracting meeting. In Table 5.1 he differentiates five types:

Table 5.1 Lee's types of contracting

1	Pre-contracting, the decisions that precede the formal contracting efforts
2	Change contracts, describing the ways the client (individual coachee) hopes to develop as an executive with the support of the coach and sponsoring organization
3	Process contracts, which contain the methods and responsibilities of the coach, the client, and others that combine to make coaching happen
4	Business contracts, specifying the commercial and legal arrangements between the coach and the sponsor
5	Psychological contracts, the tacit but potentially powerful expectations among the parties

Source: Adapted from Lee (2016: 40–41)

In Table 5.2 Hawkins and Smith (2013: 175) describe six areas the contracting process covers.

Table 5.2 Hawkins and Smith's processes in contracting

1	Practicalities – such as the timing and frequency of sessions, payments, and agreements on cancellations or postponements
2	Boundaries – for example between coaching and other helping professions such as therapy, and around what is confidential
3	Working alliance– how the coach and coachee will build trust, mutual expectations, learning style; this also covers the relationship with the organizational client(s)
4	The session format– this covers the session detail including any approaches that might be used
5	The organizational context– this covers the expectations of stakeholders and includes examining any coaching policy; the ongoing role of the sponsor(s) in supporting the coachee; how evaluation will be done; mutual responsibilities
6	The professional context– such as observing a professional body's codes of ethics and complaints procedures

Other authors have provided guidance for contracting beyond the individual. Kilburg defined executive coaching as one that necessitated organizational benefit:

> executive coaching is defined as a helping relationship . . . to assist the client to achieve a mutually identified set of goals to improve this or her professional performance and personal satisfaction and consequently to improve the effectiveness of the client's organization within a formally defined coaching agreement.
>
> (2000: 65–67)

While he offers a coaching services agreement (2000: 235–236) he is not explicit about the organization being involved in contracting and the option is offered for the sponsor/supervisor to sign it 'if appropriate'. Both Rostron (2013: 264–266) and Kahn (2014: 69, 85) provide useful contracting questions, with Bluckert noting ten key questions related to contracting (2006: 13) (Table 5.3):

Table 5.3 Bluckert ten contracting questions

1	Is it a two- or three-party contract?
2	What are the desired outcomes of coaching?
3	What will be expected of each party (coach, client and sponsor)?
4	What is the confidentiality agreement?
5	What are the reporting arrangements?
6	What will be the scope and method of assessment?
7	How will the coaching intervention be structured?
8	Where will the coaching take place, how often, and what levels and availability of support, if being offered?
9	How will the coaching process be reviewed and evaluated?
10	What are the business arrangements – fees, cancellation terms and invoicing procedures?

Bluckert further suggests that if the contract is two-way, "You will want to satisfy yourself that not having a third-party organizational sponsor is appropriate" (2006: 13).

Rostron's overview when setting up the contract includes initial questions such as: "What are the needs of the individual executive client versus those of the organization?" She also focuses on clarifying outcomes and their evaluation, checking the coachee's readiness for coaching, and considering feedback and monitoring mechanisms (2013: 264–265). One professional body, the EMCC (2011), has provided a Commercial Coaching Agreement for its members, prepared with legal advice from an international law firm. Bird and Gornall highlight the need for a checklist of things to consider and agree with corporate clients and sponsors at the point the coaching relationship is established (2016). Turner and Hawkins' research (2016) offers detailed guidance for handling such meetings (see the following sections).

What does research tell us about what is effective?

Current research by David Clutterbuck and Eve with 100 supervisors and 149 coaches globally, suggests that supervisors believe half of the issues brought to them by executive coaches (51%) were related in some way to the original contracting with their clients (Turner and Clutterbuck, 2019). Interestingly, executive and business coaches believe this figure to be lower – with just over a third of issues relating to contracting (34%). This disparity may indicate that contracting could be given more emphasis, for example in coach training to improve practice and confidence in this area and highlight that contracting could be done more comprehensively and effectively. In the same research three themes emerge as most important in contracting with a client or supervisee. However, within this, fewer coaches believe the relationship is one of the most important areas (Table 5.4).

One of the most comprehensive studies on multi-stakeholder contracting was undertaken by us in 2014, with 651 surveys completed: 569 coaches, 52 organizational representatives and 30 individual clients (Turner and Hawkins, 2016). The vast majority of coaches (87.8%) who took part in the survey had experience of multi-stakeholder contracting, a figure that rose to 96.0 percent for those working as a coach for ten years or more. There was little variation in this across the world. The overall result is similar in organizations where again the majority (81.3%) of those responding said that a line manager, HR, L&D or a coaching manager had been involved in such meetings. Most of the coaches and organizations that involve other parties in the contracting considered it good practice, although half of the coachees, albeit in a small sample, did not have strong views (see Table 5.5). This client response suggests there is more to do to ensure that all parties to the stakeholder contracting understand why it is being done, and what will make it effective.

Table 5.4 Top three good practice themes in contracting

Top three good practice themes in contracting	Coaches (when contracting with a client, n=142)	Supervisors (when contracting with a supervisee, n=99)
1	Shared understanding of the coaching assignment between the coach and coachee (57.7%)	Shared understanding of supervision (67.7%)
2	Clarity of contracting (55.6%)	Supervisor-supervisee relationship (63.6%)
3	Relationship between coach and coachee (42.3%)	Clarity of contracting (54.5%)

Table 5.5 Views on multi-stakeholder contracting in organizations

Stakeholder contracting is...	Coaches (506)	Clients (25)	Organizations (32)
good practice	81.8% (414)	44% (11)	78.1% (25)
poor practice	1.4% (7)	0%	3.13% (1)
unnecessary	0.2% (1)	4% (1)	3.13% (1)
do not have strong views	16.6% (84)	52% (13)	15.6% (5)

Four-fifths of organizational responses indicated that the client, coach and HR/L&D were most likely to attend an initial three-way meeting, with the line manager being involved for two-thirds of respondents. For coaches this was similar. But other voices were brought into the room, for example through 360 feedback. On the question of who should be involved, context was seen as crucial, as shown in this quote from one of the research participants: "really depends on the specific context of the coaching engagement. No black or white. Key thing is transparency to the coachee at all times!" (Turner and Hawkins, 2016: 57).

Before we enter into a contracting meeting as coaches, we will need to consider what we believe our role is, and the research highlighted three main roles:

1   To ensure that each person is aware of the role they will play in the coaching relationship e.g. individual client, organizational representatives and coach (85.6%, 399).
2   To make sure there is an agreed understanding about what coaching is (81.8%, 381).
3   To be the facilitator of the dialogue (72.8%, 339).

There was consistency about the four circumstances when all the parties to the multi-stakeholder contracting – coach, organization and client – believe it is appropriate:

1   when it serves the client's development: as part of a leadership/management programme, to develop skills for their current role, to support someone preparing to apply for promotion, or to help them develop skills without which they may lose their job or be demoted.
2   When the organization is paying.
3   When the coachee agrees.
4   When the coaching goals lend themselves to evaluation and review.

The research alerts us to some of the main challenges coaches experience in multi-stakeholder contracting (Turner and Hawkins, 2016: 59):

1   That coaching is being used by the organization to deal with something a line manager has avoided;
2   Boundary management between the three parties to the coaching (coach, client and organizational representative);
3   Maintaining confidentiality; this included the organization sometimes seeking progress without the individual coachee's knowledge or agreement for example in 'off-line' meetings or phone calls;
4   Setting outcomes that are agreed between the individual client and the line manager.

Emerging best practice

At the end of our research survey coaches were able to offer their suggestions for what made multi-stakeholder contracting successful. Their responses picked up many of the themes identified earlier. In Table 5.6 we list the ten top themes that emerged (Turner and Hawkins, 2016: 60–61):

Table 5.6 Top ten themes for successful multi-stakeholder contracting

Top theme	Coaches
1 Clarity	Be clear on expectations (of stakeholder, client, and yourself), boundaries, confidentiality, and what coaching is and isn't.
2 Honesty and transparency	Ensure honesty and transparency in communication. Do not fear to challenge the line manager and/or ask the important questions. Coach the line manager so he/she is able to provide meaningful feedback.
3 Leading and planning	Take the lead in contracting. Plan ahead; provide a clear, concise contract.
4 Setting outcomes and measures	Establish clear desired outcomes and measures of success.
5 Impartiality	Be impartial. Listen. Be curious.
6 Engaging and encouraging	Engage with the client and stakeholder as partners. Encourage the individual client to lead the interim meetings. This supports the client in strengthening their interactions with their manager and HR.
7 Flexibility	Be flexible – respond to individual circumstances and stick with professional management practice and responsibilities.
8 Being brave	Be brave and firm. Do not fear to walk away if stakeholder expectations are unrealizable.
9 Understanding the problem	Aim to understand what really lies at the root of the problem.
10 Rapport and a safe space	Put effort into building a positive rapport and creating a safe space.

The need for clarity and transparency is underlined in these recommendations. Drawing on this guidance and our own experience we emphasize these areas as key to being effective in contracting (Turner and Hawkins, 2019: 18–19):

1   Clarifying the aims for the coaching – ensuring alignment between the coachee and the organization and transparency between the stakeholders.
2   A shared understanding of any organizational guidance that would influence contracting, such as procedures for handling bullying, harassment, or breaches of workplace confidentiality.
3   A shared understanding of the ongoing role of the sponsor in the coaching, such as ensuring any additional support is put in place both during the programme and afterwards.

4   A shared understanding of what will make the coaching successful with any measures such as 360 feedback, interviews etc.; evaluation: how, when and by whom this will be evaluated and how information is shared.
5   A shared understanding of what could happen if the coaching:

    a)   Is judged as successful – such as promotion, a new role, involvement in a project, a pay rise, increased responsibility.
    b)   Is considered unsuccessful – such as remaining in the same role, missing out on a financial bonus, being demoted, or even losing their job.

6   A shared understanding of confidentiality and being explicit about the circumstances in which it could be breached, taking into account: the law; health, safety and wellbeing; having supervision; organizational requirements.
7   Copies of, or links to, the professional body code(s) of ethics to which we subscribe and the details of how a coachee or organization can make a complaint to our professional body, should they feel it to be necessary.
8   Using our intuition. If we feel something unspoken is going on, it may be alerting us to something endemic in the system. We need to

    a)   Notice it;
    b)   Catch it;
    c)   Use it as data (of what may be going on in the client, the organization, other elements of the system);
    d)   Act on it (Hawkins, 2019: 71).

The importance of successful contracting, here around a shared outcome, can be seen in this short example from a colleague, coach Joanna, who was working in the technology sector in Europe with a growing, global company. The two directors who had started the business and were jointly responsible for its success had grown apart to the point where they wouldn't even sit next to each other in meetings. They had open disagreements and the tension between them was leading to staff taking sides. Their dispute was a threat to the ongoing success of the business and its stakeholders: staff, board, and customers. But it was not being addressed systemically and was like an unacknowledged 'elephant in the room'. Joanna was brought in to work with the management team.

Joanna recalls that when she tried to contract, it soon emerged that there was no agreement on what the outcomes needed were for the work she'd been brought in to do. Meeting both separately, it was clear that the two founders had their own take on what had caused the dispute, what it involved, and what needed to be done. They were going 'round in circles'. Joanna therefore chose to have a joint meeting with the founders and set up a ground rule of each listening to the other without interrupting. This took some time and drilled down to both the causes of the dispute, and a shared outcome that they could then contract on. Joanna found it uncomfortable going back and forth between them (as did the founders), but believes it was worth the feeling of discomfort and challenge to get to a shared understanding of what the issue was that needed to be dealt with. Without this work it would have been impossible to get to the right solution. She notes that it can be an easy course as a coach to avoid challenge, but it isn't necessarily a good thing for the stakeholders!

Some challenges from lack of contracting

There are many reasons that insufficient attention is paid to contracting. We have heard of several instances through our work as supervisors and experienced them ourselves in our role as coaches (also see Chapter 11 on ethics)! Here are just a few examples of what may happen in individual and multi-stakeholder contracting:

- We imagine that many of us have had an eager client wanting to share their story and is very keen to 'just get on with it'. So, we speed through or omit the contracting, and, for example, don't have a chance to establish how their individual needs both connect with those discussed in the multi-stakeholder contracting or how they might be an addition to what came out in those meetings.
- The sponsor is so busy that we don't clarify fully either the outcomes or what they will see, hear or experience that is different, if it is successful. This leads to a lack of clarity for both coach and coachee. It also challenges how the coaching programme is evaluated.
- We experience the organizational representatives or coachee as so helpful, that we don't like to stress our cancellation terms assuming it will be ok not to; we assume they wouldn't think of cancelling sessions!
- Perhaps we recall the very senior leader who we are absolutely delighted to have secured through a 'chemistry' meeting (well, actually, if we're honest, we really thought of it as a beauty parade where we won first prize). Talking about what coaching is and isn't and clarifying situations when we might need to refer them for another type of helpful intervention, such as therapy, doesn't seem quite the thing to do. After all, that client requiring further support won't be them, will it?
- We are doing our first sessions for an organization we have been trying to win work from for some time and are having an initial meeting with them. Dwelling on confidentiality, when they are saying "yes, yes, we know, we have that sorted with our other external coaches," can make us feel awkward and we skip over elements of it.
- We fail to mention note-taking and discuss how it is used and why, and then may:
  - o sit there wondering why the coachee isn't writing anything down or
  - o notice them watching us taking notes and it seems to be putting them off or
  - o get taken aback when a client (individual or organizational) asks for a copy of our notes
- We have been asked to work with members of the same executive team and been assured that is okay with the team –then discover that none of them knows that we are working with anyone else and then it turns out that there is a truly challenging interrelationship between some people and we find team members complaining about each other.

Contracting process

For us contracting begins from the initial meeting, or even before when you first articulate what you offer as a coach. From the first engagement we are modelling how to have coaching conversations and that includes the agreements we are developing between us as coaches, mentors and supervisors, and the organizational sponsor(s) or gatekeepers.

Underpinning this work is our emphasis on these contracting elements to ANCHOR us:

Agree the outcomes
Normalize collaboration
Communicate and connect
Honour stakeholders
Openness
Review and recontract

Contracting is about creating clear, co-owned contracting partnerships to achieve effective and meaningful outcomes. Little attention has been paid to the phases of contracting, and this begins from the moment contact is made (also see Chapter 6 where we have fully described the early stages of Inquiry, Dialogue, Discovery and Design that are essential foundations in the early stages of contracting IDDD).

Table 5.7 Phases of contracting in a coaching programme – overview

The phases of contracting	Description
1 Pre-contracting – initial contact and decision	The initial contact(s) when the organization and coach (or the contract lead if an associate arrangement) discuss the assignment and an initial decision is made whether to proceed.

2 Pre-contracting – briefings and collaborative inquiry with stakeholders including the coachee (client). All IDDD cycle elements are relevant	Collaborative inquiry between the coach and other stakeholders underpinned by the IDDD cycle, including
	  i) expectations from the coaching – what is needed
	  ii) assessment of the clarity of outcomes as understood by each party
	  iii) practical arrangements such as how many sessions, cost, timing
	  iv) agreement on the use of psychometrics including 360
	  v) agreement on any live observation of the coachee in situ
	  vi) further assessment on whether to proceed.

The phases of contracting	Description
3 Reflection – discussion with supervisor (optional) and personal reflection – this can happen in any phase	The assignment may or may not be straightforward. We may experience complete openness and transparency and feel confident to enter into the contract fully. But if we have any concerns, something doesn't 'feel right', and we want to explore 'what is and isn't in the room', then this is the opportunity to reflect, including with our supervisor. This may lead to further briefings (phase 2)
4 Multi-stakeholder contracting. Again, all elements of IDDD are relevant (also see Chapter 6)	This is the meeting, face-to-face or virtually, with the coachee and the organizational sponsor(s) representing the stakeholders to create a collaborative agreement, emphasizing the development of trust, relationship building and listening. Topics will draw from the points noted above in Table 5.6: i) what coaching is and isn't ii) mutual responsibilities iii) use of tools such as 360, seeing the coachee in situ iv) what success will 'look' like, desired outcomes v) confidentiality vi) re-contracting/meeting again and feedback vii) how success will be "measured," and evaluation by whom and when and consequences of achievement and non-achievement viii) answering questions on all sides
5 Individual contracting. Again, drawing on the IDDD cycle and potentially adding further elements	We do further contracting dialogically, with the individual client building on phase 4, but adding elements that may be private between us and our client. This may include discussing: i) How will we know that our work is being effective ii) How will we be open and transparent with each other? iii) How can we challenge ourselves in service of what is needed from our work? iv) How will we keep our stakeholders in mind and how will we bring any feedback into the room and use it? v) How will we use note-taking? vi) What is the role of silence, questions, tools, models; what is the coach's role regarding giving advice?

(Continued)

Table 5.7 (Continued)

The phases of contracting	Description
6 Multi-stakeholder re-contracting with the sponsor(s) and individual	*Stakeholders:* In phase 4 we will have discussed when we might meet again to consider progress and recontract formally as necessary – perhaps midway through the coaching and at the end. We will also have discussed meetings between the individual client and the sponsor(s) within the work setting and how discussions will be fed back to us as coach. *Individual:* Re-contracting is informal during each session and relates to all aspects of our partnership – our outcomes, how we work together, evaluation, degree of challenge, responsibility and so on.
7 Reflection – discussion with supervisor (optional) and personal reflection	As indicated at phase 3 this can, in fact, happen at any point in the contracting. It is our self-reminder to reflect on our work.
8 Post-contracting	Evaluation is completed based on the agreements made during earlier phases. We also consider the legacy from coaching and how it will be maintained.

Systemic questions for contracting

While Table 5.8 is not an exhaustive list of questions, it gives an indication of what we might use in the different phases of contracting.

Table 5.8 Phases of contracting in a coaching programme including questions

Phases of contracting	Systemic questions – some examples
1 Pre-contracting – initial contact and decision	What is the purpose of the coaching? What are the perspectives of the different stakeholders on the work that needs doing? How aligned are the different stakeholders, including the potential coachee, with the purpose and the outcomes?
2 Pre-contracting – briefings and collaborative inquiry with stakeholders including the coachee (client). All IDDD cycle elements are relevant	What is the work we need to do together? How can we explore further the work that needs doing? Who does your work serve?

Phases of contracting	Systemic questions – some examples
	What do those people value about what you do and what do they need you to develop going forward?
	What are your future stakeholders asking you to step up to?
	What would you regret in two years' time not having explored in coaching now?
	Given those responses, what is the work we need to be doing together?
	How can we explore further the work that needs doing?
	How should we work together to be most effective in achieving what we have discovered?
3 Discussion with coach/ supervisor (optional) and personal reflection – this can happen as part of any phase	Who is our coaching/supervision in service of?
	Which stakeholders have a stake in our work here today?
	How can we bring their perspectives into the room?
	What is the work we need to do to serve the needs of all the stakeholders?
	What has been said and what is unsaid?
4 Multi-stakeholder contracting. Again, all elements of IDDD are relevant	Who are the stakeholders to the coaching?
	What is the perspective of the stakeholders to the coaching?
	What would 'effective outcome(s)' mean for these stakeholders?
	How will we judge whether the coaching is effective?
	How will we ensure we all have the same understanding of the work that needs doing?
5 Individual contracting. Again, drawing on the IDDD cycle and potentially adding further elements	As above and
	What other factors are relevant?
	In what ways would it benefit you and your stakeholders to maintain the status quo?
	What are the consequences of maintaining the status quo? What are the benefits of achieving change?
6 Multi-stakeholder re-contracting with the sponsor(s) and individual	What changes are being made and how have those benefitted the individual and the stakeholders?
	What is the work that needs doing now?
	What/who else should we be considering?
7 Discussion with coach/ supervisor (optional) and personal reflection	As 3

(Continued)

Table 5.8 (Continued)

Phases of contracting	Systemic questions – some examples
8 Post-contracting	What is the legacy of the coaching? How will the learning be maintained? How has this made a difference to the individual and to the stakeholders? What has been the learning for all parties? How will this learning feed back into the organization?

Engaging managers and leaders in contracting

Drawing on the literature and adding suggestions from our own experience, we suggest a range of questions relevant to each phase of the developing relationship. We will pick this up in Chapter 6.

Managers' and leaders' engagement in the coaching process can be variable, and this applies to the commitment to contracting. Where leaders and managers are reluctant there can be many reasons. They include

- Anxiety and lack of confidence for example in giving feedback. From her research Brown believes that "vulnerability is at the heart of the feedback process. This is true whether we give, receive, or solicit feedback" (Brown, 2013: 201). She provides examples of how to do so from a strengths' perspective.
- Time pressures.
- Geographical dislocation – when multinational or multi-regional companies are involved, and line managers rarely see those team members who are to have coaching.
- A lack of interest in managing performance or providing feedback.
- A fractured relationship.
- Disconnection.
- Or simply poor leadership practice with little exposure, themselves, to positive role modelling. How often have we felt that the boss of our clients would benefit from coaching?

In keeping with our aforementioned ANCHOR model, one way to support and engage leaders and managers is to provide them with an overview of the purpose of three- and four-way meetings. The overview of the purpose of multi-stakeholder contracting we recommend includes these elements:

1   To provide context and to get a sense of the organizational culture and norms.

2   To make sure that all parties understand what is meant by coaching and the responsibility that each person has for the success of the programme. This includes, for example:

   a)   Allowing time for the sessions to be held;
   b)   Regular feedback being given by the line manager/other sponsor to the coachee;
   c)   Ensuring the coaching is being undertaken voluntarily.

3   To link the coaching programme into the business', as well as the individual's, desired outcomes, agreeing what will be addressed in the coaching programme while ensuring there is space for other areas that might emerge during the coaching.

4   To ensure there is openness and transparency around the outcomes, and that these are known to the coachee prior to the three- or four-way meeting.

5   To discuss what will happen following the coaching. This includes the result of outcomes either being met, such as promotion, increased responsibility or retention in role, or of not being met, such as failing to gain promotion, being put under performance measures, changing role or leaving the organization.

6   To discuss how coaching will be evaluated and how success factors will be judged.

   a)   What will the coachee/line manager/Head of HR/direct reports/other stakeholders see, hear and feel that tells them progress is being made? Some may be SMART (specific, measurable, achievable, realistic and timely) but that will not always be appropriate.
   b)   At what stages will evaluation be done, by whom, how will it be done and fed back?

7   To discuss how many sessions are likely to be held and at what spacing and length.

8   To agree how often and in what way feedback on the coaching programme will be provided back to the organization. This could be:

   a)   Through a verbal report(s)/discussion(s) by the coachee to the line manager/Head of HR;
   b)   Through a report(s) written by the coach/coachee and explicitly approved by the coachee;
   c)   Face-to-face, through another three- or four-way session, perhaps mid-way and at the end of the programme, with the coachee taking the lead.

9   To make sure that each side feels they have got what they need out of the coaching programme by the end at evaluation: i.e. discussing the creation of a win-win situation.

10 To manage the expectations of all parties in particular:

    a) To be clear what coaching can and can't achieve;

    b) To discuss the importance of continuing the work and trying out actions between coaching sessions;

    c) To discuss what other support might be needed and who will undertake to provide this;

    d) To discuss who to go to should further support needs be identified.

11 To address the issue of confidentiality and what will be shared with the manager such as process issues (how many sessions held) and what will remain confidential between the coach and coachee, namely the content of the sessions. To consider any exceptional circumstances in which this could be lifted, such as the safety of the client or others or in proscribed breaches of the law or of specific company/institution policies.

12 To answer any questions on all sides.

Conclusion

In this chapter we have explored how we can think about and better practice multi-stakeholder contracting, so that the coaching work is carried out in partnership between the coach and coachee and focussed on the needs of the individual and all the many systems they are nested within, and all the many stakeholders that their work and life serves. In the next chapter we will explore the process of systemic coaching, both through the stages of the coaching relationship and within each particular session.

Chapter 6

The systemic coaching process

Introduction

In this chapter we explore the stages of the coaching relationship between the coach and both the organizational and individual partners in the systemic coaching work.

We then go on to look at the stages within a systemic coaching session. There are many models of coaching process, most famous of which is the GROW model developed by Graham Alexander and then made famous by John Whitmore. In systemic coaching where we are partnering with the coachee to deliver value for them, their organization and all the many stakeholders, we use a systemic version of the CLEAR model that Peter developed in the 1980s – and the four levels of engagement.

Before we start you might like to capture the processes you use. Do you find them helpful when working systemically? How do you ensure that the process you use draws in different partners to the coaching? What do you share about how you work with your clients and stakeholders?

Pre-engagement

Before we begin the coaching process, we need to be alert to the many systemic needs and influences on the coaching process. John Whittington reminds us how diverse these can be:

> When you look at your clients, try to see the people behind them: their peers, direct reports, boss and former bosses, their educational and family systems, the possible loyalties and entanglements. Look with great respect for all that they are and come from, all that you know and all that you will never know. Remember that you are only a momentary guest to their immeasurable system of connectedness.
>
> (Whittington, 2016: 82)

When a client organization or individual calls us directly, or a coaching organization through which we work as an associate, we are in "Inquiry" mode. Implicit in our Inquiry is that we are collaborating with both our organizational and individual clients from the start and this underlines all the processes outlined throughout the chapter.

'Chemistry' meetings

Chemistry between a coach and a coachee exists on many levels and starts from the first moment on first meeting, perhaps on the phone when they first inquire about us and continues into the coaching sessions. It is also a two-way, or more, process. Traditionally we think of it as being about an initial meeting between the coach and the coachee to decide 'fit', but in truth the first contact may have come in advance of that, say through HR or L&D or a direct call from the potential coachee. The coachee (and coaching sponsor or lead) will have a reaction to us as coach, and we will, in turn, have a reaction to them.

From some of the descriptions we hear in supervision it seems that some coaches see chemistry meetings as a competition with the prize being the coaching work (also see Chapter 5). The challenge then can be to want to win the work at all cost, and so 'sell' ourselves rather than ensuring that a chemistry session is a good model for what the coaching will be like.

Let's assume we have got around that and are in a genuine place of curiosity. Bluckert (2006: 12) notes that "A positive liking and an immediate empathy for the client will always feel better and we will look forward to the work, but is that best?" He goes on to observe, "on occasions, the most unlikely and least promising of starts can turn into some of our best and most satisfying assignments." This happened to Eve, recently when: "I unusually, felt a lack of empathy towards the client while also experiencing a degree of hostility from the client. She understood the potential benefit from coaching, but spoke about how she resented 'needing' it." Through coaching questions, level 5 pure listening (see Chapter 7), and definitely not feeling the need to win the work, a mutual respect was established and within a couple of coaching sessions a rapport had developed, and they were getting extraordinarily positive feedback on their improved relating. There is learning in reflecting on what it is about a client that makes us feel uncomfortable or even why we label a client as "difficult" (see Chapter 10, Halos and Horns model pp. 162–164). Of course, there may be such a strong clash of values or reaction – perhaps driven by something about them that resonates with someone in our past – that we choose not to work with them.

The challenge works both ways. Bluckert says

The issue of chemistry is a complex one. For some prospective clients the overriding consideration is whether they feel comfortable or not with you. Others may recognize that some degree of discomfort might not be a bad thing – it may suggest a more productive working relationship.

(2006: 12)

We have to accept the client's decision in this, regardless of whether we feel we'd be good for them – in the end for the coaching to deliver value, they do need to go into the relationship with some positivity and trust.

Starting the relationships

There is much evidence in both the fields of psychotherapy and coaching that the most critical ingredient that leads to healing and growth is the relationship (de Haan and Kasozi, 2014, de Haan, 2008). The American existential psychotherapist Irvin Yalom (2008: 204) puts it succinctly when he says: "therapy should not be theory-driven but relationship-driven" and "it is not primarily the theory or ideas, but the relationship that heals." We would echo this by saying it is not the coaching skill or tools of the coach that bring about change but the relationship that provides the container in which life can transform the client.

In systemic coaching, as with any form of coaching, collaboration is the foundation of the working partnership and the heart of an effective contracting relationship. Before we begin a contracting conversation, we will consider this collaborative cycle (IDDD) in the phases of contracting that is central to systemic work. It covers:

1 Inquiry – considering all the voices we may bring into the coaching 'room' and doing this in a way that is outside-in, and future-back; this could include 360-degree feedback but engages widely in stakeholder perspectives and impacts on wider systems. Questions we might include are:

    a) Who does your work serve?
    b) What do those people value about what you do and what do they need you to develop going forward?
    c) What are your future stakeholders asking you to step up to?
    d) What would you regret in two years' time not having explored in coaching now?

2 Dialogue – Here we talk about what is needed as a result of our inquiry; we are sense making.
3 Discovery – What does the Inquiry and Dialogue tells us we need to do? Here we are considering potential 'destinations'.
4 Design – Now we co-design how we need to work together in service of our Inquiry, Dialogue and Discovery. We decide on the journey we need to make because of our collaborative inquiry.

There are parallels to appreciative inquiry and its five Ds model, the stages of Defining the topic, Discovering and appreciating what is currently happening, Dreaming – imagining what might be, Designing – determining what should be and Destiny – creating what will be (Watkins and Mohr, 2001: 25). This will be

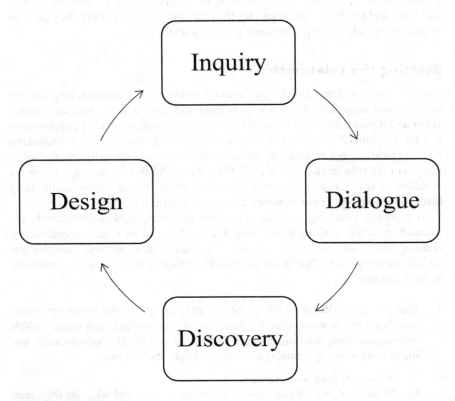

Figure 6.1 IDDD model

done in stages, both in multi-stakeholder contracting conversations and in individual conversation with our coachee (see Figure 6.1).

When first meeting a new client, our approach would start in a way similar to many other coaching approaches. We ask the client to tell us about themselves and be interested in how their narrative unfolds, how it is framed and shaped, and last but not least how they relate to us in their telling. We also ask them what they most care about in their lives and work, to discover more about their sense of purpose, their values and deepest intentions. Bronnie Ware, who spent years working with people at the end of their lives, wrote about her learning and its link to purpose. She lists the top five regrets of the dying as "I wish I'd had the courage to live a life true to myself, not the life others expected of me," "I wish I didn't work so hard," "I wish I'd had the courage to express my feelings," "I wish I had stayed in touch with my friends," and "I wish I had let myself be happier" (Ware, 2011).

What we do somewhat differently to some other coaching approaches is explore their work and how this aligns or not to their sense of purpose, values and intentions. Crucially, we ask them, who does their work serve? (see the Parsifal question in Chapter 1). In this work together, we are discovering the map of their stakeholders, both within their organization, beyond the organization's boundaries and in their personal and family life.

Often, in this process, the differing and conflicting needs of their stakeholder world will emerge. For example: "My boss wants me to ramp up performance, but my team are telling me we are already making too many demands and that they are at breaking point." "My family tell me they never see me, yet I cannot get all my work done without working ridiculous hours." "Our investors are wanting greater dividends, but our customers are saying we are already charging too much."

As coaches or supervisors we need to ensure that we retain our sense of perspective. It is important for the systemic coach not just to focus on individual stakeholder relationships, but to partner the coachee on understanding the web of differing and often competing needs – the complex ecosystem in which they live and work.

This collaborative inquiry process opens up a rich picture in which we can move to a greater 'outside-in' and 'future-back' perspective. We can ask:

- What do these various stakeholders currently value about the work you do?
- What do they need to be different from you?
- How might their needs change in the future?
- Who are the stakeholders we might be ignoring or not noticing that we will ignore at our peril?

Then, and only then can we move to asking:

- In the light of this exploration, what is the work that your world needs us to be doing in our coaching together?
- This is the work you cannot do by yourself and I cannot do for you, but your lifeworld requires us to work on together.

Thus, from the beginning we are co-discovering the work that is required, and not focussing on either the coachee's agenda or the coach's agenda. Instead we consider what life is requiring the coaching to explore and the coachee to develop, keeping in focus the wider needs of all parts of the wider ecosystem.

Contracting with client and stakeholders

If coaching is to deliver value for more than the individual coachee, then the exploration of where the coaching needs to focus and how the work needs to happen needs to go beyond the contracting discussions between the coach and the coachee.

In the preceding chapter we explored the process of multi-stakeholder contracting in the coaching and shared the research we carried out across many coaches and organizations about this issue (Turner and Hawkins, 2016). From this research we discovered that the two classical ways coaches undertook multi-stakeholder input into the contracting process were:

1   To carry out a 360-degree feedback process that collects feedback on the coachee from multiple agreed respondents. Often this was collected by the coach with an agreement to anonymity.
2   To arrange a three- or four-way contracting meeting between the coach, coachee and their line manager, and/or human resources connection, where the manager or organizational representative would be asked what skills or competencies the organization needed the coachee to develop. Sometimes this will draw on appraisal feedback from colleagues.

Both of these approaches are well intentioned but have their own problematics and limitations. The importance of multi-stakeholder contracting and how to manage the difficulties it involves are fully covered in Chapter 5.

Multiple ways of engaging stakeholder feedback

Many coaches use 360-degree feedback, drawing on views from various parts of an organization (peers, direct reports, shareholders, the board, customers etc.). Kegan and Lahey take this further by including family and friends in the feedback. They describe this as "720-degree feedback" (2009: 65). They noted that "including key people in your private life as well as your public life – dramatically increased people's attachment to improving on their . . . goals" (2009: 65). This is something we also encourage as family and friends can provide further insights and help cement commitment to goals.

In relation to the wider team, 360-feedback can be carried out in a variety of ways. The simplest (options 1 and 2) involving emailing a few questions to all direct reports, peers, stakeholders, the line manager and others who know your client well – such as family. The responses are emailed back to the coach and collated into one document. Options 3–5 involve more work on the part of the coach/organization and are more expensive. Option 3 involves a bespoke questionnaire devised internally involving the coachee, coach and organization. Option 4 involves paying to use a questionnaire from an external provider and option 5 is the costliest, involving the coach in doing bespoke interviews. Option 6 and 7 both involve the coachee proactively seeking out structured and direct feedback from key people.

Option I

1   What do I do well, and how does that help you and your stakeholders?
2   What do I not do so well, and what impact does that have on you and your stakeholders?

3   What would you like me do more of and why?
4   What would you like me to do less of and why?

Option 2

1   An alternative version of this is to use what Zenger, Folkman and Edinger (2011) describe as "informal" questions, again getting the responses emailed back to the coach:
2   What skills do you think are strengths for me?
3   Is there anything I do that might be considered a fatal flaw – that could derail my career or lead me to fail in my current job if not addressed?
4   What ability of mine would have the most significant impact on the productivity or effectiveness of the organization?
5   What abilities of mine have the most significant impact on you?

Option 3 (stakeholder value contribution)

Here the individual receives feedback less on their personality and more on how their work creates value for the other internal and external stakeholders. The stakeholders are asked – "How do I currently create value for you and your organization or part of the system?" "How could I create more value for you and your organization or part of the system?" This can be a two-way dialogue with the individual sharing – "This is how I get value from you and your part of the system," and "This is how I could get more value from you and your part of the system." This can lead to a joint agreement of co-creating greater value in their partnership. This form of feedback is more focussed on value creation, than on the inputs concerning behaviour (see Chapter 12 on Evaluation).

Option 4

The coach, client and organization in partnership set up a bespoke online questionnaire that also allows space for some qualitative responses. One might base this on the competencies/specifications for the client's role or on feedback from appraisals. For example, questions might come under several headings such as:

1   Builds good relationships.
2   Communication.
3   Dealing with conflict and challenging situations.
4   Dealing with strategic aspects of the business and contributing beyond their area.
5   Is a positive role model, internally providing calmness and respect under pressure and challenge, and externally with wider stakeholders and in the community.

A key for responses is provided for respondents, for example a five-point scale with: (Almost) Always; Often; Sometimes; Occasionally; (Almost) Never.

The questionnaire ends with opportunities to offer open responses, as the qualitative information is particularly helpful. The standard three tend to be:

6   What could x do more of?
7   What could x do less of?
8   What would you encourage x to continue doing?

Option 5

We now turn to off-the-shelf questionnaires. There are literally hundreds, if not thousands, available, costing from a few dollars to many hundreds. In Chapter 9 you will learn of a bespoke one for team coaching. Some of those questionnaires that are highly validated and based on several years of research require people to have training to give the feedback. Other 360-degree feedback providers allow people to purchase them and provide the feedback without specific training. The key is appropriateness for the context in which the 360-degree information is being gathered.

Option 6

Another option offered here is to develop a bespoke 360 interview protocol, drawing on questions agreed in partnership with the client and organization and then conducted by the coach, preferably face-to-face but otherwise by video or phone one-to-one. This would, at a minimum, include three peers, three direct reports, the line manager and representatives of other parts of the business including HR and stakeholders such as customers and shareholders. The coach would then collate the report and provide it to the coachee. This is the most expensive option because of the time taken to both conduct the interviews and collate the report. It also allows the most systemic approach.

Option 7

This option entails agreeing the questions to be used and the stakeholders to be approached, following which the coachee interviews each of the stakeholders, and records the data, which they then explore with the coach. This removes the coach from being the 'go-between' and can open up important new conversations in key relationships, as well as developing the coachee's ability to be a proactive requester of useful feedback (an important leadership skill in itself).

Option 8

It is also possible and useful to involve the coachee's team in ascertaining some of the coaching focus, alongside the three- or four-way contracting. This is another way to engage the wider organization (we describe ways of doing this in Chapter 9 on team coaching).

With all these options it is crucial to contract the following aspects at the start: who will compile the 360, who will see it, will it be shared with the line manager and if so, by whom, and so on? It is also important to agree how it will be used, both by the coachee and potentially the organization.

Another consideration is whether the respondents offering feedback do so anonymously. Kahn argues contributors should be named, since "anonymity introduces a limiting and potentially destructive element into the feedback process, that ultimately can prevent the process from potentiating the positive change it seeks to achieve" (Kahn, 2014: 72). His belief is that "for feedback to be truly meaningful, it needs to be located in a context . . . systems thinking exposes how we are essentially relational beings and that what we know, and indeed who we are, is located in the context of our relationships" (Kahn, 2014: 73). As feedback is relational it is less valuable when taken out of its context. As Kahn says, if a client tries to work out who said what, this may be a defensive reaction, but it may also be an attempt to understand the feedback better by remembering the context (or 're-membering' i.e. reconnecting to the context). It is also the case that already existing tensions may be exacerbated by comments made anonymously, increasing the receiver's anxiety within a sub-optimally performing team. A counter argument is that anonymity may facilitate more honest feedback or ensure people feel safe to offer it. If this is the case, it would suggest the organization should explore what needs to change in its culture to facilitate more direct feedback.

The organization, coachee and coach will have agreed at the outset how the 360 results fit into the overall contracting. Will the results be left for the coach and coachee to refer to as appropriate, or will the organizational sponsor or HR use the results to specify or add to more formal outcomes?

How to explore 360-degree feedback

Before reporting back any feedback, we have repeatedly discovered that the biggest trap is failing to first ensure that the recipient is a curious inquirer, and that you have established a partnership of joint discovery. This applies whether you are sharing data from an employee engagement survey, team 360 or individual 360/720 inquiry. Without this preparation, we unintentionally recreate echoes of receiving an 'end-of-term' school report, or other form of external judgement, which naturally elicits a defensive and even dismissive response. Just think of times you have witnessed a senior team receive employee feedback – what was their response? – how many times did they respond with

- I do not think we asked the right questions.
- Was this a representative sample?
- At least my function's figures are not as bad as some.
- We sent this out at the wrong time.
- I am sure all companies get low scores when going through rapid change.

We are sure you could add to this list.

To set the right context and avoid data being seen as judgement rather than useful information that gives us a wider perspective, before sharing any feedback we ask the recipients (coachee or team or organization):

- What do you hope to find in the feedback?
- What do you fear you might find in the feedback?
- What are the most important questions you would like the feedback to help you answer?

We find this helps the coachee(s) be curious and see the data as a useful resource in answering their own inquiry questions.

The process of coaching sessions

When we coach, one of the approaches we are informed by is the CLEAR coaching process model that Peter first developed in the early 1980s (Hawkins, 2011a). This has parallels to, as well as differences from, the GROW model. (Downey, 2003; Alexander and Renshaw, 2005; Whitmore, 2017). It has five stages:

Contract, listen, explore, action and review

When coaching systemically each of the CLEAR stages has a different and more extensive focus:

Contract: Traditionally we would begin individual coaching sessions by asking the client what they would like to explore or think about in today's session. This question sets a relationship where the individual coachee is the client and customer, and the coach is the supplier – there to enable the thinking of the coachee. With a systemic coaching approach, we are dialogically thinking together with a broader focus; we would more commonly ask: "What is the work we need to do together in this coaching meeting?" We might also begin the session by asking the coachee what will make this session of value to them, the people they lead and work with, the organizations they work for and the wider stakeholder systems they serve.

Then, as they engage in bringing material from their work, we will **Listen** with systemic ears (Hawkins, 2018), listening to the reality of the client, the people they work with and lead, the organization they work for and the relationship between the organization and the individual and the organization and its complex web of stakeholders. Clients' stories are often 'sticky' so that the coach may get caught within the story and conceptual frame of their client. Coach training, in being client-centred and primarily empathic to one's client, can mean that we start to see their world through their eyes and vicariously share their emotional reactions to situations and other people. This can take the coaching relationship into the enactment of the drama triangle (Karpman, 1968) where the coachee becomes the victim, portrays the organization or others as the persecutor and the coach becomes the rescuer. This drama triangle can increase powerlessness and, over time, the roles can turn, the persecutor feeling persecuted by the rescuer etc. (Hawkins and Shohet, 2012: 190–192; Hawkins, 2014: 392). It is important that the coach can practice "wide-angled empathy" (Hawkins, 2019), not just for the client, but for everybody and every system within the client's story. The coach has to listen from multiple perspectives, not only to what is shared but what is not said and possibly ignored and also listen to how the relationship is emerging between themselves and their client.

In the **Explore** stage the work is to think about the issue from multiple perspectives. Traditionally we may have asked the coachee: "How else could you make sense of this?" "What else might you do?" "Who do you know who would handle this well and what would they do?" These are all questions to expand the coachee's options and creativity in responding to the situation they are exploring. In systemic coaching we would also invite them to see the situation from other places in the system. We might, for instance, encourage them to sit on different chairs to represent different places or roles in the system or imagine those people sitting in the chairs and how they would respond – their boss, their team, their customer, investor etc. We would also encourage them to embody these different perspectives and tap into their embodied knowing or even ask them to role play or constellate the key aspects of the system they are inquiring into (such as, their team, their organization or the wider stakeholders. Or we might suggest they make a picture sculpt (see pp132–3).

In helping the client explore their own development, we might adopt Peter's favourite strategy question (Hawkins, 2005), which is:

"What is it that you can uniquely do, that the world of tomorrow needs?"

This question can be valuable not only for the individual coachee, but can be asked at all different levels of the system to benefit the individual, team, division, business unit, organization, stakeholder community, business sector, nation etc.

In the **Action** stage in traditional coaching the coachee would be asked to create an action plan – having explored the situation and generated new options and possibilities. This may be built on by asking specific questions such as the what, when, with whom and how of each action, in order to make the plan very specific. However, with the work that has been done by Peter and Nick Smith (Hawkins and Smith, 2010, 2014, 2018), we discovered that one of the most repeated patterns in coach supervision would be coaches being frustrated that they had coaching sessions where the coachee had an 'aha' moment of insight and turned this into a very clear action plan, but then came back a month later, having not followed through on their plan. At this point in supervision the coach would often blame the client and use phrases like: "they were clearly not committed" or "they lacked the courage", rather than look at how the coaching needed to be different to ensure greater follow through. Our own exploration of this led to adopting the phrase: "If the change does not start in the coaching room, it is not going to happen outside the room." We also began to realize that whereas insight and good intention often happen in the neo-cortex and with words – change is always embodied.

Systemic coaching focuses on helping the coachee to embody the transformational change in their self that is needed to enable a shift in their relationship with other individuals and groups. If this is done sufficiently the coachee is more likely to have the desired impact on the wider system with which they engage. This stage often involves a "fast-forward rehearsal" (Hawkins and Smith, 2006: 224, 2010: 232). One of us coached a very tall team leader, who explored his difficulty in challenging his team. He had been very tall from a very young age and had learned to hide his size, by sitting in a way where he was almost folded in on himself. In 'rehearsing' how he wanted to be in meetings, he suddenly discovered a way of sitting that felt both more open as well as authoritative, without being dominating. He rehearsed how to challenge from this new position and afterwards reported finding new energy and said: "for the first time I can allow myself to be powerful and seen."

In the final **Review** stage, it is important to reflect back on the agreed contract and the value we have jointly created for all parts of the system, as well as the experiments that the coach has committed to trying out. We will review these at the beginning of the next coaching session. In the original CLEAR coaching model, at this stage we would ask the client: "what has been useful in this coaching session and what could be more helpful next time?" Without realizing it we were putting ourselves as coaches back into the supplier mode and putting the coach back into the role of customer, who we were asking feedback from on 'our' performance. In many talks Peter has commented on how: "for many years, I thought I was asking for feedback from my client, but I wasn't – I was asking for reassurance. The client would duly oblige and often tell me, how useful it all was, and that they wanted more of the same."

The Systemic Coaching approach uses a very different question:

- "If your stakeholders x and y (often we would name the appropriate ones relevant to what we had been exploring) were in the room listening to our coaching session, what would they have valued about the work we have been doing together, and what would their challenge to us have been?"
- "What is the future work that life is asking us to go on to address?"

Reviewing and evaluating the coaching together

It is important that reviewing and evaluating is not left to the end of a coaching relationship, for by then it cannot be used to inform, improve and integrate (the three "i"s of reviewing) the coaching relationship and process. Previously we have shown how reviewing should be an integral part of every coaching session.

In Chapter 5 on contracting we showed how multi-stakeholder contracting can include multi-stakeholder reviewing and evaluating at the midpoint of the coaching programme. We both ensure we do 'mini reviews' throughout our coaching sessions, as well as the reviews at the end of each, the beginning of the next and at the end of the relationship.

At the end of the programme once again multi-stakeholder involvement is very valuable, and can ensure:

1   The coachee is supported in integrating their new ways of thinking and being into their work and work contexts. This will support a lasting legacy from the coaching.
2   The individual coachee can explore how they might increase the ripple effect of their learning and development to maximize the learning and development of all those in their circle of influence.
3   That processes that have worked well and those that have been difficult or could have been improved are appreciated by the coach to inform and develop their growing capability and capacity.
4   In the same way, sponsors and managers of the coaching processes in the organization can harvest the learning for renewing and redesigning the ways it commissions and organizes coaching to deliver optimal benefit for the individual coachees, their teams, customers and organization (see Chapter 4 on harvesting the learning).
5   There may be useful organizational learning that needs to be shared to create wider benefit.

Four levels of engagement

So far, we have explored the linear and surface dimensions of the coaching process, both at the organizational level, the coaching relationship level and the process of each session. Now we need to explore the depth dimension. Peter has developed over many years, with his colleague Nick Smith, a model of four levels of engagement. (Hawkins and Smith, 2010, 2014, 2018). We start here and continue this topic in Chapter 7.

Level 1: data and narrative

At the first level, data, we are listening to the narrative of the coachee, their story about the situations they wish to explore and the problems they want to manage better. At this level we need to realize that this is the world as seen through their eyes, their patterns and their lenses and practice "wide-angled empathy" (Hawkins, 2019: 74) for everybody and every system in their story. We listen not just to the story but also how they tell and frame the story, and how they engage us as listener. We begin to ask questions to discover how much the situation concerns a one-off problem, and how much it might

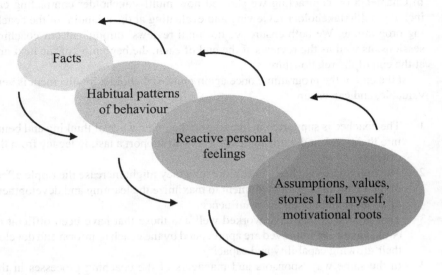

Facts

Habitual patterns
of behaviour

Reactive personal
feelings

Assumptions, values,
stories I tell myself,
motivational roots

Figure 6.2 **Four levels of engagement**

be a symptom of a deeper, and longer running, pattern for the coachee. We
might ask:

> "Has a similar situation happened for you before, what did you then?"
> "How often to you find yourself in such eventualities?"
> "What do you think you did that might have triggered this reaction?"

These questions can help us move to the second level of engagement, exploring
the patterns of behaviour.

Level 2: patterns of behaviour

Our identity and personality are constructed out of many patterns of being in the
world that we have developed and often engrooved throughout our life. These are
not just patterns of repeated behaviours, but are also brain patterns of neuronal
synaptic connectivity that become the dominant architecture of our brains. These
patterns of adaption and ways of coping with the world have mostly been laid
down early in our lives, as ways of coping with frightening experiences, overwhelming emotion, or situations we have found challenging to deal with. They
were once helpful and necessary patterns. The difficulty is that they can still operate long beyond their usefulness and become a restriction on fully and receptively
responding to new current situations. Instead, they step in and we automatically
react from our well-practiced pattern. In coaching, the coach and the coachee

can gradually notice such patterns with compassion and without judgement. We attempt to create some distance to witness our reactive behaviours and hence establish more choice about how we respond when these patterns are activated. Neuroscience research has shown that the more we can widen our own internal windows of tolerance (within the brain), the more we widen our external windows of tolerance (within our lives) and can respond rather than react more often to potentially triggering situations. We will explore what this requires from the coach in the next chapter.

Level 3: emotional patterns and triggers

As we get caught into reactive patterns of behaviour as explained previously, these patterns are often triggered by past feelings and emotions, and in turn trigger emotion in the present where they do not belong. In psychotherapy we might help the client go back to the earliest emotional triggers of their patterns, but in coaching we usually stay more present focussed, asking the coachee to notice the feelings that come up for them in relating the relevant story, or to recall the feelings they had at the time. For some coachees who operate with left-hemisphere dominance and are quite split off from their bodily sensations and feelings, this can at first be difficult. In the next chapter we will offer some tools for overcoming this, through body awareness exercises and visualization. When coachees have a stronger awareness of their feelings, they become more able to monitor and witness them, and then they are less likely to be 'run by them'. There are many senior executives, who were very successful up to the point they ruined their reputation by one or more events where they were hijacked by their emotional eruptions.

Level 4: mindset, assumptions, beliefs – the stories we live within

Beneath the behavioural patterns and the emotional patterning lie what Stolorow and Atwood (1992) call "the organizing principles" of our mind. We are normally unconscious of these, as they are the lenses through which we view the world, the frames through which we think, the ways we create meaning. Although normally these are hidden to us, they can be uncovered in coaching and as a coach we could ask:

"What is the story you tell yourself when these events occur?"
"How would you describe yourself when you are in these situations?"
"How do you know that is true?"

The coach can catch the patterns of framing that the coachee uses and gently at first and then more robustly, interrupt these with reframes (see next chapter). At this level of engagement, we need to walk carefully, as we are dealing with the belief systems a person has used as a foundation for constructing their identity; sometimes simple assumptions exercises may gently help unlock these (Ryde et al, 2019: 45). However, this is also the most transformational level of engagement and leads to the longest lasting change. At Level 4 we are helping the coachee unlearn and relearn their assumptions, limiting mind-sets, and outdated narratives, helping them free themselves, expand their capacity to be aware and, by accepting aspects of themselves, becoming more able to have empathy and compassion for a greater number of others.

Case study/interview

Mark Kahn is the Group HR Director for Investec, a provider of financial products and services, who is also author of *Coaching on the Axis* (Kahn, 2014).

> **Question:** How satisfied are you with the coaching on a scale of 1–10, that has been carried out by the internal and external coaches in your organization?
>
> **Marc Kahn:** The majority of coaches are trained in a counselling-based approach. In Investec we are coaching an individual in an organization. So, I would respond: coaching generally – 2–3 out of 10, in Investec – 5.
>
> There can be an unconscious conspiracy between the coach and client to create the closed dyad, partly because it is easier work – multi-client work is unsettling, complex, disturbing, risky and ethically challenging – client also wants to feel in control of the narrative and the relationship.
>
> To get from 5 to 8 we need a macro paradigm change – from Newtonian–Quantum physics, from monotheism to polytheism – from linear thinking to complexity thinking – understand how we are a collective in complex ways – thinking in parts is short-termist and at worst counter-productive.
>
> We are early in this paradigm shift – this is necessary to shift coaching and needs to be applied to how we train, supervise and take leadership in the coaching profession.
>
> Currently most coaching focuses on improved competencies, behaviours, attitudes, with no link to how this creates value for the organization. There needs to be more research on value creation and outcomes. This research could combine both rigorous qualitative and quantitative methods.

Conclusion

In this chapter we have explored many dimensions of the coaching process:

> The systemic organizational process that begins with setting up the organization's coaching policies and architecture, and the selection of the external or internal coaches. It continues through the stages of implementation, review and evaluation and renewal and redesign.
>
> The coach-coachee relational process, from deciding whether they will work together at the first meeting, as well as what work needs to be addressed.

This is constantly reviewed and upgraded in the light of multi-stakeholder engagement, developing a strong working alliance and relational container, right through to final review and evaluation.

The process of each coaching session – following the CLEAR model, which ensures that the sessions deliver, not just insight and awareness, but embodied learning and new implementable actions.

The process of enabling in-depth change by moving down the four levels of engagement, so that coaching is moving from: solving immediate problems, to shifting deeper patterns of behaviour, to addressing the emotional patterns that trigger the difficult behaviours, and finally, how these are rooted in fundamental assumptions, belief systems and internal and internalized narratives.

We now have maps of the various dimensions of the systemic coaching journey. In the next chapter we will look at some of the tools and methods we will need to take with us on this journey and use at various points along the way.

Chapter 7

Systemic coaching methods, approaches and tools

Introduction

In the last chapters we have been exploring the dimensions of the coaching journey: the organizational journey, the journey of the coaching relationship, the process of each coaching session, both horizontally through time and vertically in terms of levels of engagement. By now you may be saying, "this all sounds very complicated, so what do you actually do?" or "Enough of maps! I want to go out and see the territory. What would I see if I was a fly on the wall in one of your coaching sessions?"

Well, firstly it is possible for you to go and see Peter carry out a one-off systemic coaching session on video, and twice stop and receive feedback and reflect out loud before continuing the session. This can be accessed from www.wbecs.com/wbecs2018/presenter/peter-hawkins/?tab=full_smmt_5603.

Meanwhile in this chapter we will show some of the activities, processes, tools and methods a coach deploys in coaching sessions and relationships. As in the earlier chapters it would deepen the learning if you as the reader also moved your thinking to the world of practice and difficult challenges. We invite you to think of a recent situation, when you were trying to help someone who had a stuck situation and your intent was to try and help them see the situation more systemically. You may find it helpful to write a short vignette of this situation, including the approach you used and what more was needed. This will help you enter this chapter curious to find the methods and tools that will be most helpful for you and your clients.

Building the relational container

To do good work a coach needs to build, with the coachee, a strong enough relational container, which generates the necessary psychological safety and trust for both parties to be vulnerable and not knowing. The coachee is then more likely to be open to exposing their vulnerabilities and the unintegrated parts of themselves. Part of building such a container is carried out through clear contracting and boundary setting, as we explored in the previous two chapters. However, the inner work is about creating the necessary level of relational resonance to allow empathy, trust and an inner sense of being attuned to and received by the other.

Relational resonance is created by the coach being fully present, undistracted, open and curious, non-judgemental and listening to the coachee, not just with their ears, or even their cognitive understanding, but listening with their emotions and whole body.

When we watch coaches in training work in threes with each other, you can see when and if relational resonance develops. Gradually both parties relax, their breathing patterns become more synchronized, there is often an unforced mirroring of their body movements and gestures, the music of their voices come into harmony. After this, a softness and open wondering inquiry starts to emerge.

Normalizing

Many of our coaching clients will sooner or later say to us, "You must think I am weird or crazy," or "I am sure you have never met anyone like me before." As we open up those maybe unrecognized parts of ourselves, we may find them mirrored back to us and accepted. We are then more able to become vulnerable and less worried about how we may be seen.

One of the important roles of the coach is to normalize these feelings, to reassure coachees that they are not mad, or indeed unusual. It is important to let them know you have met many others with the same patterns or feelings and when appropriate acknowledge that you have experienced something similar.

Another common theme concerns "the imposter phenomenon", where externally successful people – research showed this was particularly the case with female leaders – can feel a yawning gap between how they perform and are seen externally and how they feel internally (Clance and Imes, 1978). Clance and Imes describe how "The fear that 'my stupidity will be discovered' is constantly present" (1978: 4). So, such leaders become fearful that: "If only people really knew what I am like inside, they would stop trusting me, respecting me or following me." One type of this pattern particularly found in women, is the sense, that if they display confidence, they will be disliked for it:

> The phenomenon may be further maintained in response to the negative consequences that are likely to befall the woman in our society who displays confidence in her ability. Margaret Mead (1949) has noted that the successful or independent woman 'is viewed as a hostile and destructive force within society'.
>
> (Clance and Imes, 1978: 5)

In more extreme cases some of our clients talk about their fear that they might be publicly exposed as a fraud. Again, the job of the coach is to normalize this experience; to tell the coachee they are not alone, and many successful people have the same fears, particularly those so busy building external success, they have not given much time to do the work of going inside and integrating parts of themselves that have been left behind.

Moving into dialogical inquiry: coaching beyond questions

One of the underlying assumptions of some coach trainings and coaching books is that all interventions are questions. This approach is built on the assumption that the client already has the answers and the coach uses questions to help dig these out.

In dialogical coaching we believe that answers and new awareness are to be found through the collaborative inquiry of the coach and coachee exploring together, combined with the agenda or curriculum that life is providing for the coachee. This three-way triangle of coach, coachee and context or life's curriculum (see the 3Cs model, Chapter 5) provides the dynamic interaction in which new learning can be created. The coach is not only listening to the coachee but also alongside the coachee, both listening to the challenges and lessons that life is providing, recognizing that often the wider systems have greater knowledge than we do.

The work of coaching is for the two partners to walk together to the edge of their joint unknowing and, through exploration, discover new thinking and new meaning that neither knew before they entered the room. Often the answers are not in the coachee or the coach but lie in an exploration that involves the wider field of the systemic levels that the coachee's life is embedded within. This requires the coach to spend the minimum amount of time asking questions that the coachee already can answer, to move to inviting the coachee to talk about and share the background to the issue they have brought and to interventions that deepen and extend the exploration.

This means the coach needs to listen at many different levels.

Level One is to be fully present and attentive, completely open and focussed on the coachee and what might emerge.

Level Two is to be able to let the coachee know you have understood what they are telling you about, through accurate listening – playing back to the coachee what you have understood, in ways that are open and tentative, and encourage the coachee to expand on what they have said so far and at times correct what you have understood.

Level Three – empathic listening – listening not just cognitively but with our whole being, emotions and body and the coachee senses we get what it feels like to be them. However, if we just stay emotionally empathic and resonating with the client, we will begin to see the world through their eyes and feelings, so it is important to move on to the next level.

Level Four – wide-angled empathic listening, where we adopt an attitude of empathy for every person and organizational system in the coachee's story. We imaginatively place ourselves in the shoes of all the others and how they might feel and perceive the situation. This helps us not to locate the problem or conflict in others who are not present in the room, but to see the situation from multiple perspectives, locating the conflict in the connections rather than the parts. This is listening not just to the person, but through the person, to hear how the wider systemic levels – of the team, organization, culture, and social belief systems – are speaking through them. The coach can then listen to what is said and what is left outside the narrative and outside the room.

Level Five – pure listening, is listening from a position of unattachment, open heart, open mind, open will (Scharmer and Kaufer, 2013), open to whatever emerges, and not feeling any pressure to solve the problem, or to offer our thoughts or make the situation better.

Dialogue is not just created by the depth of listening of the coach. It also requires an inter-subjective (Stolorow and Atwood, 1992; Hawkins and Ryde, 2019) and dialogical way of being (Bohm and Nichol, 1998). This requires us to not try and see the coachee as an objective other we can investigate, but recognize we can only know them relationally, in how they show up in relationship to us, perceived through our own individual way of being.

Bringing in the different worlds – 'outside-in' and 'future-back'

One of the distinguishing features of systemic coaching is that it not only invites the coachee to focus on the needs of their stakeholders and the wider systems they are part of, but directly and indirectly brings those 'outside-in' perspectives into the room. This can be done through involving multi-stakeholders directly in the contracting and review as we explored in Chapters 5 and 6.

It can also be done by psychodramatically inviting the coachee to step into the shoes, adopt the perspective of and speak as one of their stakeholders. This can be done, not just by adopting the position of a significant individual, but also a wider system, for example stepping in to the shoes of one's team, or another function.

Another distinct feature is the focus on 'future-back' thinking and exploration, rather than only reflecting on past situations. This has already been indicated in some of the questions we introduced in earlier chapters. Questions like: "What do you need to focus on to be ready for what you will need to face in the future?" "What do your future stakeholders need you to be developing now?" "What might you regret in two years' time, not having explored in this coaching?" Coaching, like leadership, needs to be working with all three time horizons: (1) the immediate business as usual; (2) innovating for tomorrow; and (3) future foresight requiring radical change (see Chapter 1 and Sharpe, 2013).

Working with the relationship live in the room

One of the most transformative aspects of coaching is the relationship between the coach and the coachee. A great deal of research on psychotherapy and coaching has shown that the most critical factor in any therapeutic or coaching process is the relationship (see de Haan et al, 2016, 2008; Hawkins and Ryde, 2019: Chapter 7). When we presented the seven eyes of systemic coaching in Chapter 3, we showed the importance of Modes 5 and 6 where we focus on the 'here and now' relationship between coach and coachee live in the room.

The relationship, however, must not just be a safe, trusting and supportive context in which the coachee feels safe enough to be vulnerable and explore aspects of themselves as well as the external situations they are facing. It also needs to be a place where the coachee's fundamental patterns of relating can become available for reflection and experimentation. Rather than just focus on exploring the relationships outside the room that the coachee is bringing to explore, at least once or twice in every session, it is useful to bring the focus back to the current experience and dynamic.

For instance, if a coachee says "Everyone lets me down" and this becomes a constant refrain and pattern, the coach might ask: "In what ways have I let you down, or you fear I might do so?" Or if a coachee talks regularly about their difficulty in standing up to people, the coach might ask: "How might you need to stand up to me in this relationship?" "Perhaps you could experiment with how you might do that, right now."

This movement from the external, to the internal present, moves from talking about situations, to witnessing them as they are happening live in the room, to finding and trying out news way of changing the pattern.

Four levels of engagement

In Chapter 6 we introduced the model of 'Four Levels of Engagement' (Hawkins and Smith, 2013). At the core of creating transformational change with the coachee is the coach's ability and capacity to explore the deeper levels of story and assumptions that keep the current way of seeing and acting in the world in place and will undermine any attempts to create a shortcut to sustainable change.

We will now explore the tools and approaches that show how to broaden out each level of engagement and how to move from one level of engagement to the next.

Level one: from surface data to deeper narrative

The coachee offers us the surface structure of their story, which can be thought of as a jigsaw puzzle with many of the pieces missing. Often as coaches we can get lost when we ask about the pieces of the jigsaw that have been laid out rather than listening to the gaps and inviting the coachee to explore the empty spaces.

Bandler and Grinder (1979), in their very early work, showed how we can listen for the deletions, distortions and generalizations in the language of the surface structure story and then invite the client to create the missing pieces of the jigsaw to discover the deep structure that underpins their story.

Generalizations

Generalization is the process by which elements, or pieces of a person's model, become detached from their original experience and come to represent the entire category of which the experience is one example. Thus, a person may express their feelings and feel hurt and generalize that into a rule such as "Don't express feelings." Transactional analysis would describe this as developing an inner script.

Examples of generalizations

1   Lack of specification in subject – "People don't like me."
2   Lack of specification in object – "It's too late."
3   Lack of specification in verb – "By rushing ahead we will regret it later."

Often the best form of intervention with generalizations is for the coach to provide a linking word or phrase which becomes a 'nudge' into further exploration. Here are some examples in relation to the above examples of generalizations

1   "People don't like me."

Such as . . . ?
"John and Carol in my team."
And I know that by . . . ?
"Because they never look at me in meetings."

Here we have helped the person go from a general statement about the whole team to two particular team members. Then to a belief system that people who do not look at me must dislike me. This then becomes a distortion that can be unpacked (see ahead).

2   "It's too late."

To . . . because now . . . ?

3   "By rushing ahead we will regret it later."

. . . rushing ahead of . . . we will regret not having . . . ?

Deletions

Deletion is a process by which we selectively pay attention to certain dimensions of our experience and exclude others.

Examples of deletions

1   Comparatives/superlatives.

e.g. "Carmen is so much better than I am."

2   "Have to."

e.g. "I have to keep going."

3   "Necessary."

e.g. "It is necessary that we need to keep up a united front".

4   "Must."

e.g. "I must be prepared, with no weaknesses in my preparation."

Again, linking phrases and one-word interventions can help move the client from limiting beliefs to open exploration.

1   "Carmen is so much better than I am."

At . . . because she . . .?

2   "I have to keep going."

In order to . . . so that . . . ?

3   "We need to keep up a united front."

When we . . . in order to . . . ?

4   "I must be prepared, with no weaknesses in my preparation."

Otherwise . . . ?

Reframing distortions and assumptions

A third form of "Linguistic Unclarity" according to Bandler and Grinder (1979) is where an individual uses language to imply a truth, which is either an assumption, a distortion or logically invalid.

Examples of distortions and assumptions

1   **Process into event – nominalization** e.g. "The CEO's impossible demands are driving me mad".
2   **Implied cause/effect** e.g. "He makes me angry when he doesn't respond." "This change process is a nightmare."
3   **Mind reading** e.g. "The members of my team don't like me."
4   **Confusion of map with territory** e.g. "All I.T. staff are emotionally illiterate."

5 **Presupposition** e.g. "I'm afraid that this change process will turn out to be as big a disaster as the last one."

6 **A generalized rule** e.g. "You can't do that in our organization."

These are referred to variously in the cognitive behavioural field such as cognitive thinking traps and ANTS (automatic negative thoughts).

When there are nominalizations, with implied cause and effect, the client needs help to turn the event back into a process and then challenge it. This can best be done by gently reframing their statement

1 "The CEO's impossible demands are driving me mad."

> *You get "mad" when you receive requests from the CEO that you feel to be impossible.*

When there is an implied cause and effect, often the person is putting themselves in the passive or even victim role. Here the reframing needs to locate them back in the world of choice.

2 "He makes me angry when he doesn't respond."

> *When you don't get a response from him, you get angry.*

When there is an assumption that can sound like it is built on mind-reading or on confusing the map and the territory, the coach can challenge the belief.

3 "The members my team don't like me."

> *How do you know that is true?*

4 "All IT staff are emotionally illiterate."

> *What have you experienced, seen and heard that led you to that conclusion?*

Where there is an implied presupposition, the coach can help the client unwrap the assumption about the past experience that is colouring how they are responding to the current experience.

5 "I'm afraid that this change process will turn out to be as big a disaster as the last one."

> *The last change process failed because . . .*
> *The key learnings from that experience were . . .*

6 "You can't do that in our organization."

> *Yet* (this is Peter's favourite short reframe that stops the past controlling the future!)

The aim is not to challenge all generalizations, deletions and distortions, for to do so would soon grind down conversation to a mechanistic analysis and might well lead to insanity! However, the more you can be aware of where the gaps in the jigsaw are, and the more skilled you can be in recognizing the processes, the more options you have in facilitating another person to reconnect more fully with their experience and thus increase their options and choices.

Moving from the deeper narrative to discover the pattern of the behaviour

Often traditional coaches will explore the presenting issues one at a time and help the coachee resolve each one but fail to go deeper to discover the coachee's pattern of behaviour that is co-creating these issues. The issues are often the symptoms of a well-ingrained pattern of being and acting and will continue to appear until the pattern is addressed. In life we often try to solve the problem that is 'out there', by changing our job, where we live or our life-partner. But as we often point out, what we fail to learn in one role, one place or one relationship, life will generously provide the same lesson in the next role, place or relationship.

Each of us has clients who have brought an issue about one or other of the members of their team that was not performing, wanting to explore whether they should go through a disciplinary process, terminate their role or support them with more coaching help. Peter recalls that in one situation the first problematic team member his client discussed was sent off on a secondment to another part of the organization. But at the next session there was another problematic team member he needed to deal with. Peter asked him to describe an example of a good team member that had worked for him and he paused and looked worried and said, "I am not sure I have ever had one – but they would be someone who just got on and did high quality work." Peter added "which is. . . ."– "Well, work I don't have to correct or change and would bring positive feedback from other parts of the organization."

It soon emerged that he had never articulated to himself or his team what good work looked like or his expectations of them, a pattern that ensured that he was constantly disappointed and frustrated when his team members had failed to recognize or deliver on his unspoken expectations.

We will now explore three other powerful ways to help your client move from exploring specific situations to discovering their patterns of behaviour.

> **Shadowing** – an approach where the coach spends time observing the client as they carry out their work – noticing the pattern they display as they show up in different work settings. An example of this is shown in the case by Julie Zhang (see Appendix 1, case study A, p235), where she shadows her client and also sits in on his team meeting, providing real-time feedback. She writes: "With shadow coaching, I was no longer only relying on what Lee brought into the coaching dialogue. I could be in the situations real-time with him, replaying the process, provoking him to think both 'inside-out'

and 'outside-in'". We have also shadowed clients when they have made important presentations at conferences, led 'town hall meetings' with their employees, chaired a Board meeting and when they have been engaging live with their key stakeholders.

Pattern based feedback – the coach when shadowing, carrying out fast-forward rehearsals, or reviewing a 360-degree feedback exercise with the coachee, can focus on giving immediate pattern-based feedback. Feedback is always most helpful when it is as close to the event as possible. It is also very helpful when it enables the coachee not to feel criticized, but to see a repeated pattern of behaving and how it is linked to different contexts. When coaching a middle manager and spending three hours shadowing him, the coach shared the reflection that they noticed the coachee became physically changed and was different when they went in to see their boss, from when they were chatting with peers in the corridor, and how they had been when they had gone to the office of one of their direct reports. This led to a very useful exploration of their 'deference' in different situations (Hawkins and Smith, 2006).

Videoing – It can be useful before important meetings as mentioned earlier to coach the leader through a 'fast-forward rehearsal' (Hawkins and Smith, 2013, 2018), where they can try out new ways of engaging. This process can be further deepened by making a video recording of the client and then doing a structured review while watching it back. Kagan (1980) developed an approach called IPR – interpersonal process recall, in which he discovered that if you watch a video of yourself within 36 or 48 hours of it being filmed, you have the same bodily responses and emotional reactions as you had at the time, but with a greater capacity to reflect on them. He provides a series of useful questions that can be used in this video review process. These include questions like: "What are the patterns you notice in your behaviours and ways of engaging? What were the most helpful ways of engaging you notice you did and what were the least effective?" The coach can also freeze the frame at a point where the coachee was clearly triggered into a reaction and ask the person what they were feeling at that point/and what they are feeling now watching. This leads into the next section of noticing the reactive feelings that drive the behaviours.

The Thinking Environment® – Eve draws from her training with Nancy Kline (Kline, 1999, 2015)."The Thinking Environment®" was originally developed in response to the question: "If action is only as good as the thinking behind it, how do we create the conditions for the highest quality thinking?" (Adshead, Hathaway, Aspey and Turner, 2019: 147). This led to the "Ten Components of a Thinking Environment" to support the client's own thinking but noticing this works best in the presence of another person, the coach or thinking partner. Contracting is crucial and while questions are offered at the request of the coachee, using what Kline has recently described as "Eleven 'Innate' Breakthrough Questions" (Kline, 2019), Eve has found it powerful for clients to identify their own systemic patterns.

Interventions for moving from patterns of behaviour to embodied emotions

Echoing

Many traditional coaches wait until the client has finished their sentence and then paraphrase what they have heard. In our experience this often has the effect of showing understanding but reducing the emotional charge inherent in the original telling. Peter encourages coaches he trains and supervises to move from serial listening to parallel active listening, where they can echo words or phrases in the coachee's narrative that have a particular emotional charge, evidenced by how they are said, with a change of volume, tempo, timbre or pitch. The coach might amplify this emotional charge in their echoing it back, so the coachee can hear the harmonics of their story as well as the melody.

Here are some lines from the opening of a recent coaching session showing the words echoed by one of us as the coach:

> "There are so many demands **bearing down** on me."
> "I feel **run-ragged**."
> "I am constantly **chasing round** to ensure everything has been done."
> "But I can't **bear** to have our work not done **properly**.

In the metaphors are the small shoots of the coachee's feelings, most of which were under the ground of self-control and steely determination. The echoing and slight amplification helped the client not only feel emotionally received but helped her hear how much she felt driven and 'done to', by the demands and responsibility. Only when she was in touch with the embodied feelings, and had them recognized, was she able to move on to explore her assumptions and belief systems that were keeping this pattern in place. (We explore this further ahead.)

Non-verbal interventions

When teaching coaches how to enable clients to contact and express more feelings, many would believe that this is done by asking the client, "How are you feeling?" This intervention can take the client away from what they are feeling in order to think about their feelings and find a way of articulating them to the coach. To deepen contact and expression of feeling is often best enabled by non-verbal interventions. To give an example: when a client is half-expressing their grief, a long out-breath through the mouth by the coach can not only show empathy but give permission to the client to go deeper and express their feelings more.

A coach having matched the non-verbal posture, gestures, voice tonality, tempo and rhythm of the client to establish rapport might also change their non-verbal signals to mismatch for change. In the example mentioned previously, when Peter had a client who had listed all the many demands that were bearing down on her, and she felt she had to shoulder, once he had empathized and non-verbally matched her, he suddenly changed tempo and volume and said: "SO . . . once we have taken these demands off your shoulders, where do you want to put each of them?" The power of the intervention was less in the question than the non-verbal mismatching.

Moving from feelings to assumptions and mindsets

Returning to the client we explored earlier when we were looking at patterns of behaviour, the one who always felt let down by his team members, once he recognized that he never shared his expectations and defined what 'good work would look like' to his team members, he set about committing to changing this pattern. For a few weeks it led to some improvement, but as coach, I (Peter) sensed a level of continuing frustration. He told me how some of their team "were still not getting it." "Why can't they see what I need without me having to explain to them all the time?" As he looked past me, he clenched his fists and hissed loudly through his teeth and tightened jaw. I could sense a deeply ingrained emotional pattern was re-emerging, and gently asked them: "Do you feel that I see what you need in this coaching?" thus bringing it into the here and now relationship, to re-establish relational contact. "Oh, you are different!" he said with the same tone of exasperation, "You are paid to listen to me." I noticed I felt somewhat dismissed and wondered to myself if this was how others felt.

I asked him when in his life he had felt others had noticed his needs, without him having to explain them first, in a genuine tone of loving concern.

There was a long pause. He slowed down and I felt a tearfulness in both of us, even before he said: "Probably not since I went off to boarding school." I took a pause to let that sink in for us both, and then asked – "How old were you?" Gradually he told me of how at age seven, his mother had become seriously ill and how he was sent off to boarding school. How he only discovered about his mother's death by being called in to see their housemaster in "a cold prison-like classroom" and was not allowed to go to the funeral, as it was considered this would be too upsetting for him.

Gradually we discovered how in reaction to this traumatizing event, he had developed a longing to have his feelings and needs recognized, but also a fear of this happening, and how he had never developed the language and relational skills of asking for what he needed. His needs felt unseen and unseeable.

I asked him what his internal caring parent would say to that seven-year-old inside him. Gradually he developed a capacity to reparent his hurt inner child, to see and hear it, to notice when it was clamouring to be noticed and responded to, and to stop blaming others for not mind-reading his thoughts.

Shining light on the hidden areas

In coaching it is important not just to focus on the urgent issues that are top of the mind for the coachee, but to invite in important deeper areas that the client may otherwise ignore or be reluctant to bring to coaching. One way of inviting these areas into the coaching is to offer one of the following sentences for completion.

1 **Sentence completion**:

    a) What I would least like to bring to you for coaching is . . .
    b) What I would least like my staff to say to me is . . .
    c) What we can't talk about here is . . .
    d) What I half know now but will come as a surprise or shock to me in one year's time . . .
    e) What I might regret in a year's time not talking about today . . .
    f) If I was not frightened of hurting your feelings, I would tell you . . .

2 **Overcoming change inertia and resistance – Kegan and Lahey's four-column exercise**

When running masterclasses in leadership team coaching, I (Peter) often ask participants what percentage of actions that they agree at 'team development events' subsequently get enacted. The figures shared are very disappointing, ranging from 0 to 30 percent! This is also very human, for as the old proverb says, 'the road to hell is paved with good intentions'. One approach to exploring resistance to change is built on Kegan and Lahey's (2009) 'Immunity to Change' methods of helping individuals and teams to understand the competing demands, assumptions and beliefs (often subconscious) that will undermine the conscious agreements made.

Our adaptation of their approach for systemic coaching is as follows.

Step 1: Ask the coachee to list all the intentions they have for change and tick those that they are successfully implementing and put a cross against the ones that they are struggling to make happen; then to create four columns;

Step 2: In column one list the ones they are struggling to implement;

Step 3: Work out what they are doing or not doing instead for each of these unfulfilled agreements, and enter these in Column 2;

Step 4: Identify the competing commitments that are driving these alternate actions and behaviours and put these in Column 3;

Step 5: Explore the collective assumptions, beliefs or fears that underlie these competing commitments – e.g.: 'I assume if I did x, then y would happen';

Step 6: Explore how to overcome these limiting beliefs, or at least experiment with discovering whether they still hold true. This can be done by using some of the following belief inquiry questions:

- In what way does that belief serve you?
- In what way has that belief served you?
- Is that belief happening right now?
- How is it happening?
- Where do you feel it?

These latter questions help the coachee inquire into how the belief is embodied and has emotional ties that keep it anchored and continuing in their behaviour.

Another approach is offering the coachee sentences to complete such as:

a)   I believe this in order to . . .
b)   I first learned this when . . .
c)   The payoff for holding onto that belief is . . .
d)   If I stopped believing that . . .

Completing the four levels of engagement and moving to action

As can be seen in the last section, working with the four levels of engagement is not a linear journey down through the levels. When we have discovered the emotions and beliefs that are keeping the patterns of behaviour in place, it is necessary to come up and help the coachee explore and develop new behaviours and experiment and rehearse these live in the coaching room.

There are three main ways of encouraging these active embodied experimentations:

1   **Using the coaching relationship.** This is done through discovering ways of changing the pattern of relationship that has happened between the coach and coachee (see preceding section and also Mode 5 in the coaching model – Chapter 3). When one coachee said they found it almost impossible to give others direct feedback that might sound critical, one of us asked them to experiment with giving us direct feedback on how they experienced us in the coaching – what they appreciated and what they thought we could do better as a coach. At first the second part was vague and mumbled, but by the third experiment it was strong, clear and embodied.

2   **Fast-forward rehearsals.** This is an approach developed by Hawkins and Smith (2013, 2018) where the coachee is invited to take a future situation where they want to apply the new way of behaving and relating and to rehearse it several times live in the coaching session. The coach, rather than fully entering the role play, stays alongside the coachee, giving them direct feedback on how they come across and prompting possible opening phrases, or shifts in their embodiment, or tonality, volume, eye contact etc. for the next iteration of the role play. Eve recalls a client where she was facilitating a fast-forward rehearsal and it wasn't going very well. She got out one of her toys, magnetic monkeys (which represented a range of things including where responsibility sits and whether something has been successfully 'handed over') and used it as a prop. The monkey went backwards and forwards between them as the rehearsal went on, until the coachee finally noticed they had 'got it'. It was creative and fun and led to an embodied 'Eureka' moment. The client reported that was the most transformational moment they had ever experienced in their many years of work as a senior leader!

3   **Visualization**. For some more introverted and sensitive coachees, another approach is to ask them to close their eyes and visualize a future scene where they will be behaving differently and to notice and report out loud what they see themselves embodying, doing and saying differently. They then are asked to notice how this is received and responded to and notice how they then respond to that reaction. Again, multiple iterations can be used with feedback and processing in between each.

In neuro-linguistic programming (Bandler and Grinder, 1979) this would be termed 'anchoring' the new state. Another way the coach can further increase the bridge from what is discovered to embodied new action back at work, is through inviting the coachee to send them an email on how the 'difficult' meeting or presentation went, as soon as it happens. We have discovered that this increases the way the coachee holds your support (in absentia) at the event.

Opening to the positive, purposive and potential

So far in this chapter we have spent a lot of time exploring how we unlearn old habits and deconstruct some of our stuck patterns of behaviour, emotional reactivity and outdated beliefs that no longer serve us. We believe that this is an essential stage of the coaching and human development process. However, we are also both strong believers that, in coaching, helping the client develop and build on their positive strengths, discover their fuller purpose and open up more of their potential, is just as important.

There is increasing evidence that organizations that are 'purpose led' rather than focussed on short-term targets and profits are far more successful in many ways. Such companies:

* **Attract and retain the best employees** – People are 1.4 times more engaged, 1.7 times more satisfied and three times more likely to stay in a company with a strong purpose (The Energy Project, *What is the quality of life at work*, 2013).
* **Build loyalty and trust with customers** – 89 percent of clients/customers believe a purpose-driven company will deliver the highest quality products and services (Edelman, *The Good Purpose* study, 2013).
* **Increased return for shareholders** – Purpose-led companies outperformed the average performance of the S&P 500 by ten times between 1996–2011 (Raj Sisodia, *Firms of Endearment*, 2007).
* **Create shared value for all their stakeholders** –including investors, customers, suppliers and partners, employees, communities where they operate and the wider ecology – which in turn builds loyalty, trust and lasting partnerships.
* **Build a sustainable enterprise**

- **Have greater protection against reputation damage including against viral social media negativity**

Individuals also live healthier, happier and more fulfilled lives when they have a sense of purpose.

The desire to be connected to something beyond ourselves was reflected in a survey of 735 managers by the Roffey Park Institute in the UK, that found 70 percent were looking for a greater sense of meaning in their working lives (Holbeche and Springett, 2004, also see Chapter 8).

In this aspect of the coaching we draw on three key strands – positive psychology, transpersonal psychology and universal spiritual approaches.

Positive psychology

Positive psychology began as a new domain of psychology in 1998 when Martin Seligman chose it as the theme for his term as president of the American Psychological Association. Other key developers of this field of psychology were Mihaly Csikszentmihalyi (1999), Christopher Peterson (2013) and Barbara Fredrickson and Losada (2005). Appreciative Inquiry had already been developed by Cooperrider and Srivastva (1987), who pioneered the use of an appreciative approach to bring about collaborative and strengths-based change.

Martin Seligman and Csikszentmihalyi (2000) define positive psychology as: "the scientific study of positive human functioning and flourishing on multiple levels that include the biological, personal, relational, institutional, cultural, and global dimensions of life." They focus, not on mental illness but on 'eudaimonia', the Greek word for 'the good life', and on the factors that contribute most to a well-lived and fulfilling life.

Seligman (2011) defined flourishing or positive individual health and wellbeing using the acronym PERMA, which stood for: Positive Emotions, Engagement, Relationships, Meaning and purpose, and Accomplishments.

- **Positive emotions** are not just happiness and joy but also excitement, satisfaction, pride and awe, amongst others. These emotions are frequently seen as connected to positive outcomes, such as longer life and healthier social relationships.
- **Engagement** refers to involvement in activities that draw and build upon one's interests. Mihaly Csikszentmihalyi explains true engagement as flow, a state of deep effortless involvement, feelings of intensity that lead to a sense of ecstasy and clarity. The task being undertaken needs to call upon higher skill and be somewhat difficult and challenging, yet still possible. Engagement involves passion for and concentration on the task at hand and is assessed subjectively and most completely when the person engaged is completely absorbed, losing self-consciousness.

- **Relationships** are essential in fuelling positive emotions, whether they are work related, familial, romantic or platonic. Humans receive, share, and spread positivity to others through relationships. They are important not only in bad times, but good times as well. In fact, relationships can be strengthened by reacting to one another positively. It is typical that most positive things take place in the presence of other people.
- **Meaning** is also known as purpose and prompts the question 'Why?'. Discovering and figuring out a clear 'why' puts everything into context from work to relationships to other parts of life. Finding meaning is learning that there is something greater than one's self. Despite potential challenges, working with meaning drives people to continue striving for a desirable goal.
- **Accomplishments** are the pursuit of success and mastery, and sometimes can help us develop a sense of self-esteem and worthwhileness even when accomplishments do not result in immediate positive emotions, meaning, or relationships. Examples of this include a young musician or gymnast practicing for hundreds of hours, or an athlete or sportsperson spending much of each day exercising their skill, or an artist developing their craft.

Peter's colleague and friend Malcolm Parlett (2015) writes about psychological health coming as a result of developing "whole intelligence." He explores in depth five different aspects, which he first called "capacities" and more recently "explorations," of whole intelligence, while recognizing that, to be whole, they are indivisible and co-arise together. The five are:

- **Interrelating:** Role modelling and building a climate of deep respectfulness, acceptance of differences, building of trust, countering shaming, stereotyping, fears of 'otherness' and of un-constructive conflict.
- **Responding to the situation:** Awareness of the field, recognizing different constructions of shared 'reality', encouraging ownership, staying in the present, noticing what is being avoided, building resilience, exploring figure/ground, 'response-ability', finding their leadership.
- **Embodying:** Slowing down and 'getting out of one's head', encouraging sensory engagement, working with the felt sense, expanding awareness to the non-verbal, the non-human; the aesthetic qualities of the situation, recognition of fluctuating energy, acceptance of 'feeling data'.
- **Experimenting:** Encouraging playfulness, artful discovery, living with uncertainty, humour; discerning when the experiment is to enhance stability, coherence, and lack of change; acknowledging that 'familiarity boundary-stretching is inherently shame/embarrassment inducing'.
- **Self-Recognizing:** Sharing of self-experience, slowing down and allowing time for integration, modelling non-judgmental approaches to others and their fantasies, choices, narratives; investigating values, habits, growing edges, life themes, self-organization.

Coaching can help the coachee focus on these areas of flourishing and develop their 'whole-intelligence'.

Transpersonal psychology

Transpersonal psychology "has been called the Fourth force in psychology, complementing the first three forces of Behaviourism, Classical Psychoanalysis and Humanistic Psychology" (Centre for Transpersonal Psychology, 2019, online). It is a hugely diverse and rich field whose roots belong to many great thinkers of the 20th century, drawing on Eastern and Western philosophies and is spiritual rather than necessarily religious (including Bucke, 1901; James, 1902; Grof, 1975; Jung, 1966; Maslow, 1962; Assagioli, 1993; Ferrucci, 1995; Wilber, 1993). Its influence in coaching has been considerable. Whitmore and Einzig (2016: 163) note how Assagioli's emphasis on the super-conscious,

> on our future and the development of our potential, on accessing more of our intuition and inspiration, and our higher feelings (eg altruism, care, service) is every bit as important as examining our past or feelings and events we may have repressed.

They offer ten key questions to guide transpersonal exploration such as "What brings you joy?" and "What do you see when you step back and view the whole?" (2016: 170–171). Firman and Vargiu talk of two types of meaning, the "meaning of our own individual existence, and the meaning of the world we live in – ultimately of life itself" (Firman and Vargiu, 1977: 60). We will explore this link with life itself in the next chapter on eco-systemic coaching.

Spiritual approaches

Systemic coaching by its very nature embraces a wider universal spiritual (with a small 's') way of seeing and being in the world. For each of us, meaning and purpose will mean something different as it is about our personal interpretation of our world and our journey through life. When Jaworski describes his inner journey to "unity consciousness" and the "interrelatedness of the universe" (1998: 56), in doing so he is reflecting the spiritual perspective of an underlying belief in connectedness. This is what many spiritual traditions would describe as 'the oneness of being' or 'non-dual consciousness'. This awareness brings an understanding that each of us is nested within many systemic levels – our family, history, community, country, culture, species, the-more-than-human world, the Gaia ecosystem of our earth, the universe; also our team, function, organization, business ecosystem, the earth etc. Not only are we nested within each of these systemic levels, but they are all nested within us. It is not just an individual who turns up for coaching, but their organization and its culture, their team and family, and the ecology. In working with one individual the whole of life is present, both in them, in us and in our inter-subjective relational meeting.

Conclusion

Having looked at the 'why', 'what' and 'how' of individual systemic coaching, in this chapter we have explored coaching methods we have found helpful for systemic coaching that works both at depth and breadth. The depth work is in moving from exploring problems to discovering the coachee's habitual patterns of behaviour and the emotional patterns, assumptions and beliefs that keep these habits repeating. The breadth of the work is in listening at depth not just to the individual coachee, but to the many nested systems they exist within, and which also live within them. These nested systems in work include their team, function, organization, the stakeholder world of the organization, the communities where it operates. The nested systems of the individual outside work include their family, community, culture and the historical dimensions of all three of these.

Both sets of nested systems are contained within the 'more-than-human' world of the ecology we all live within and are dependent upon. In the next chapter we will explore how the wider systemic levels of our ecological environment are present in every coaching session, either consciously and overtly or unconsciously and hidden.

Chapter 8

Eco-systemic coaching towards developing ecologically conscious coaches

Introduction

In January 2019, Zoe Cohen wrote a blog *Where were all the coaches when the planet warmed by 3 degrees?* an echo of the talk by Peter, *What were the coaches doing while the banks were burning?* from 2009, mentioned in Chapter 1. The ecological crisis is a much, much, greater global challenge than the economic crisis of 2008–2009 or any global event that our species has had to face.

The ability of each of us to make a difference has been illustrated by school-children. In the months after August 2018, when a sole Swedish school student, Greta Thunberg, stood in front of the Swedish parliament with a placard staging the first 'school strike' against climate change, frustrated by global government inaction, the movement spread worldwide, supported by thousands of scientists. In March 2019 an estimated 1.4 million schoolchildren walked out in 128 countries (Carrington, 2019, online). In a newspaper article Greta and other students argued that

> This movement had to happen, we didn't have a choice. The vast majority of climate strikers taking action today aren't allowed to vote. Imagine for a second what that feels like. Despite watching the climate crisis unfold, despite knowing the facts, we aren't allowed to have a say in who makes the decisions about climate change. And then ask yourself this: wouldn't you go on strike, too, if you thought doing so could help protect your own future?
>
> (Thunberg et al, 2019, online, Courtesy of Guardian News & Media Ltd)

Six months later, in September 2019, in a mass day of protest, schoolchildren were joined by adults around the globe as many millions demonstrated, in 160 countries (CNN, 2019), in advance of the UN Climate Action Summit. Protests were held on some of the Pacific Island nations most under threat from the climate crisis and rising sea levels, with protestors demanding urgent action.

We believe that the ecological crisis is far and away the largest challenge facing every individual, organization, country and indeed, the whole human species. Yet when discussion happens about the ecological crisis in coaching conferences, training or supervision, we often hear some worrying responses. To quote just a few:

- "Addressing the ecological challenge is not our job."
- "As coaches we need to be neutral and have no agenda."
- "Our job is to focus on the personal, not the global."
- "We can only focus on what we can change, not what we cannot change."

We would agree that it is very important that the coach refrains from preaching or campaigning, or in any way imposing their values and beliefs upon the client, but we should avoid joint "illusion, delusion and collusion" (Heron, 1996). Josie McLean, a leadership coach in Australia encourages coaches to "be transparent about what you believe in. Not to persuade, but to be honest" (Scotton, 2019).

We contend that the ecological dimension is present in every coaching session, overtly or covertly, consciously or unconsciously. It is present physically, as the ecology is not something out there, but is also inside us and between us – it is in the air we breathe, the food we eat, the chairs we sit upon. It is present implicitly or explicitly in every conversation, not just in the content we discuss but the whole language we use that artificially separates the human and the more-than-human worlds, nature and culture, denying the environmental costs of our activities. Our job as coaches is not to bring the ecology into the coaching relationship, for it is already there. We do have a role to uncover the ecology, surface it, and explore how we are responding and taking responsibility; and as we will see in the following section, we believe that is more often the case than we may believe and consider. Not exploring the ecological has a price not just for the environment and the future, but for our own psychological and physical wellbeing in the present.

An example from a couple of coaching sessions illustrates this better. In the first the client, working in a resource-intensive industry under the media spotlight, was discussing the need for increasing expansion to hit global ROI requirements from shareholders, but was also conscious of its reputation. By inquiring "What other costs might be considered?" and "How does the company want to be seen in relation to its impact?" and "What impacts might be relevant here to your reputation?" the client saw some opportunities and potential connections that were useful both to the organization and to the ecology.

The second example involved a global company that regularly flew executives around the world, business class, for meetings. A coaching question on their espoused values, and their desire to be a "thought leader" led to a decision to reduce the number of face-to-face meetings and introduce more virtual sessions, and to use that as an example of role modelling their values for the organization.

Before we continue in our dialogue with you, we wonder what questions you are holding about the ecology and coaching. We may not address all of them, but we hope the dialogue will continue:

- How far, if at all, do you believe, as coaches, the ecology is part of our coaching?

- What is your thinking about the world you want to leave to those who come after you? What is your clients' thinking?
- How does the ecology come into our decision making about the clients we take on, the ones we choose not to work with, if at all?
- What was your reaction to Zoe's question, quoted at the beginning of this chapter: "Where were all the coaches, when the planet warmed by 3 degrees?"

Five ways of surfacing the ecological dimension in systemic coaching

The ecological dimension is present in every coaching session. Our job as coaches is to bring it to the surface and to open up the space for the ecological dimension to be more fully part of the work. The ecological dimension can appear as a strand of the coachee's life history, or in a variety of current life experiences such as: the coachee describing trips they have made, or their concerns about their living environment or their polluted journey to work; in memories of a particular landscape, or their attachment to a particular pet animal. It increasingly emerges as an anxiety about the future of the Earth through television programmes about melting ice flows or plastic in the oceans, and as concern for family, children's and grandchildren's future.

We have found five main ways that coaches can open up this important area.

1. Inviting the ecological dimension in

We have shown throughout this book different ways of inviting into the coaching process the wider systemic levels of the coachee's lifeworld. The eco-systemic level is a wider systemic level we are all nested within and which is nested within us. It is now the largest and most critical stakeholder of every individual and every organization. One colleague said at a conference: "We have to remember that every organization is a wholly owned subsidiary of the ecological environment, and the environment can shut down any enterprise or species!"

A simple way is to include some questions into the opening chemistry or contracting meeting, such as:

"How does your work contribute positively and negatively to the wider ecology?"

And/or:

"How do you experience your relationship with the wider ecology?"

We have found that both questions produce a wide range of answers, but always provide a sense that the ecological dimension has a place at the coaching table that the coachee can return to and explore further.

2. Through the window

The wider ecology is often most obvious in the coaching situation as seen through the window. Peter has countryside views from his coaching room, and many clients will stop and briefly stare at the view before sitting down. Some will take a deep breath as if drinking in this wider nature. Others will be drawn to the woodland, or a flock of birds, or the animals in the field and comment on them. Some will say, "you must find that view very distracting when you are trying to work at your desk", and Peter will reply: "I find it constantly resourcing and nurturing my work."

Even when coaching many floors up in one of the major banks in Canary Wharf, Peter often pauses with the client at the window, attending to what the coachee's comment on and how their breathing changed.

Many of us will be coaching in rooms in urban landscapes, some with no window or natural light. Some of our supervisees have plants in their coaching room, or pictures, or wallpaper of woodland, countryside or seascapes. Eve has a large painted pebble, a gift from a family member, that anchors her and reminds her of the sea. There are many ways of providing a window to the wider ecology, no matter how enclosed the room.

3. Opening the window

The great psychoanalyst Carl Jung tells a beautiful story about a patient who, despite his efforts, remained psychologically inaccessible and addicted to her rationalism and knowing best. Jung found himself hoping something unexpected and irrational would turn up to burst the intellectual bubble around her. He writes:

> She had an impressive dream the night before, in which someone had given her a golden scarab. . . . While she was still telling me this dream, I heard something behind me gently tapping on the window. I turned around and saw that it was a fairly large flying insect that was knocking against the window-pane . . . I opened the window immediately and caught the insect in the air as it flew in. It was a scarabaeid beetle . . . whose gold-green colour most nearly resembles that of a golden scarab. I handed the beetle to my patient with the words, "Here is your scarab." Jung, C.G

(1969: 109–110)

This experience was enough for the patient's rationalism to be dented and for the treatment to begin, successfully. *In one coaching session Peter also had a dramatic moment when a buzzard banged into the window of the coaching room, chased by a red kite. This shock opened new feelings and awareness for the coachee – both about being chased and hunted in his work but also the thrill of the wild, and how he longed for this.*

There are other ways of opening the window, when access to the wider ecology is less available. One helpful approach when a person is feeling depleted and under-resourced, is guided visualization – inviting the coachee to close their eyes and picture a place in nature where they have felt nurtured and grounded. Some go to a favourite holiday destination, others return to an important river or wood from their childhood. We encourage the coachee to experience their feelings when they are in this setting, to feel the support that comes from the many elements of this special place; the support of the earth, the freshness of the air, the beauty of the setting etc. They can be invited to discover how this and other places they find nurturing can be a fuller resource for them in their work. Holder (2019: 138) suggests three reflective questions, which she uses in creative forms of writing. They work well in conversations, too:

"What about this place brings you alive?"
"Who do you know yourself to be in this place?"
"What does this place know about you?"

From such 'opening of the window' some coachee's have changed their route to work, so they walk via a local park and 'listen to the trees'; others planned restorative weekends walking, climbing, swimming in natural settings; one person took up restoring their garden, another volunteered with the Woodland Trust. This practice is borne out by a study of salivary biomarkers by Hunter, Gillespie and Chen (2019) in research participants who lived in urban settings. It showed that taking at least 20 minutes out of our day to stroll or sit in a place that makes us feel in contact with nature significantly lowers our stress hormone levels.

4. Coaching outdoors

An increasing number of coaches are incorporating coaching outdoors, rather than in a closed room. Clearly this is easier in some locations than in others and it is important to contract carefully for including this option. We recommend that if you want to include this possibility, you mention it as a future option at the first contracting session and are sensitive to the coachee's response. We also believe that it is necessary to establish a strong enough focussed and holding relationship between coach and coachee indoors that can maintain the work in the less bounded situation of working alongside each other outside.

Giles Hutchins, who has written extensively about future-fit organizations and leadership, and how we can to do business the way nature operates (Hutchins, 2012, 2014, 2016), offers the following stories about coaching individuals out of doors:

I have been coaching the Global CEO, the Founder/Owner, and the UK Head of Brand and Operations of an international consumer goods company. The company has been experiencing significant growth, and also growth-pains within its culture and people. I coached each of the three key leaders (individually and together) in nature, and also in urban settings near their offices. The nature-based coaching consists of walking through fields and woodland while applying insights from the natural world regarding living-systems, and 'nature-as-metaphor' for how the organization is going through a period of transformation (death/rebirth). The seasons in nature (winter/spring/summer/autumn) are applied to organizational development and personal leadership development. The inter-relational and ever-changing nature of life is applied to the personal and organizational challenges the organization is facing. Embodiment and experiential exercises, as well as guided meditations and fire-side deep-listening, are undertaken during these nature-based coaching sessions to help integrate the coachee's different ways of knowing – intuitive, rational, emotional and somatic intelligences.

The result is that the coachees always prefer having the coaching sessions in nature rather than near their office, even though it means travelling time for them. The insights coachees experience in nature enables them to gain a far deeper perspective on the underlying systemic issues at play within their personal, organizational and wider societal-ecological systems they live within. I have personally witnessed the coachees having 'ah-ha' moments and psychological threshold-shifts that simply would not have happened as quickly and as safely in an urban setting.

Another of Giles' coachees in nature, Katherine Long, herself a professional coach and supervisor, writes,

When you spend time reflecting on your purpose in the natural environment, the answers come so swiftly. Nature provides abundant living metaphors that speak deeply to our human condition. Whenever I am coaching or being coached in nature, I can trust that profound change will follow. It is a form of coming home and a form of healing.

A colleague, Sarah McKinnon from GP Strategies, works coaching and developing groups of leaders in eco-systemic thinking, perceiving and being, using outdoor forest settings. She tells the following story.

A group of typical leaders arrive for a day or longer, and by the time they leave they are visibly more fully themselves, somehow more coloured in and awake to the whole of themselves.

As we walk through the woods, we use the woodland metaphor to explore, with genuine curiosity, how those intricate systems are always connected, evolving, challenging, collaborating as well as fighting for survival. With little effort this segues into the leader's recognition and reflection into their own nested systems – work, societal and physical wellbeing.

People, who arrive bent upright at the start of the day, are later happily kneeling in mud, feeling an embodied connection with themselves, the group, their many different human communities and the wider ecology.

5. Nature-assisted coaching

A number of coaches have also been extending coaching to partnering with other mammals such as horses (equine-assisted coaching), elephants and dogs. Here the animal becomes a third partner in the work. Because the animals have well-developed limbic resonance, the coaching can help the coachee leave their verbal left hemisphere neo-cortex forms of communicating and relating and discover more about their own embodied forms of communicating, relating, building trust and giving clear signals etc.(see Hall, 2018).

Peter's colleague David Jarrett wrote the following example about coaching using horses:

> Horses' reactions to our energy and intention help us to increase our self-awareness and to learn more about how we respond to challenges. They act as a mirror to give us a better sense of how we 'Show Up' in a given moment in a very inviting and easily accessible way.
>
> Through Equine Assisted Coaching we help people learn to really notice how the receiver of our instructions is feeling, about what we have said or done or the way we came across.
>
> We use the responses of the horse or horses to guide the coach's questioning about whether people are aware of the feelings in their own bodies, for example allowing people to notice their stress or anxiety and how to release them, so as to be a calm supportive leader.
>
> The session releases boundaries, accelerates awareness and stimulates new conversations far more rapidly than 'thinking' alone. Hence we call it an experience with horses.

David also uses his large farm to assist leadership development learning from nature in how to think eco-systemically. He writes

> teams use the 150 acres of natural ecosystem, commercial cider orchard and countryside to debate naturally occurring challenges and dilemmas. These are related back to the delegates' organization to find new systemic approaches to work situations; e.g. How does the tree disease ash dieback require decisions now about culling in a coppiced wildwood to protect future trees? This question generates debate regarding restructuring and redundancies. Coaching in this setting delivers greater benefits by taking the issues into a naturally connected ecosystem, just like any business.
>
> Delegates take the complex ecosystem organisations (the business), appreciate the elements (teams) and hidden interactions (culture and personalities) within it as well as the relationships across the boundaries with stakeholders. They explore new approaches and behaviours which enable them to work in partnership with the ecosystem and better partner with the complex nested systems of their organization.

Exploring physical ecosystems and debating their challenges enables delegates to gain novel insights, transfer these to their context and robustly embed new approaches and behaviours within the business.

Giles Hutchins describes how:

> The key to coaching in nature is holding a psychologically-safe space for the coachee while walking in nature or siting around the campfire. Due to the nature of my work – ecosystemic leadership coaching – I proactively ensure we dialogically 'work-with-nature' (you might say 'commune-with-nature') by drawing upon different resources, such as living-systems-thinking, complexity theory, complex adaptive systems, biomimicry, nature-as-metaphor, presencing, connecting to the living-systems-field (aka, Source), threshold-crossings and liminal spaces, deep ecology, ecopsychology, organization-as-living-system and systemic sustainability.
>
> Safely held coaching sessions in nature enable a deeper richer opening-up and heart-felt sharing to occur. I believe it is the most powerful way for us to gain true relational perspective on ourselves, our habituations, constrictions and blind spots. I also believe it to be a powerful way for us to glimpse beyond the illusion of separateness, to gain perspective on the anthropocentric mechanistic lens we all-too-often view ourselves, each other and the world through. Hence, we tackle our systemic issues at root.
>
> Through nature-based coaching, the coachee has a direct embodied experience of opening-up to the inter-relational nature of the more-than-human world we are part of. It is only from this perspective (what adult developmental psychologist Clare Graves (1974) labels 'Tier 2 consciousness' and business specialist Frederick Laloux (2014) labels 'Teal') that we are able to ensure a perspective that widens beyond the narrowed-down perspective that created our problems in the first place.
>
> In nature coachees feel more able to enter the vulnerable liminal psychological space where deep healing and transformation truly happens. This level of psychological deep-space cannot be cultivated so quickly and safely when indoors. Here are some of the words/phases coachees feedback to me after sessions in nature: rejuvenating, transformative, full of synchronicities, deep surrender, letting-go while opening-up, deeply connecting, existential, worldview-shifting, recharging, revealing, invigorating, re-wiring.

One of our colleagues, Catherine Gorham, a coach and supervisor, underlines the need for careful contracting for coaches and supervisors when working with nature:

> pay attention to the 3 Cs of – Contracting, Containing and Connecting – which all require some adjustment from indoor practice with particular attention to concerns in the moment around privacy, emotional upset or overwhelm.

Developing our ecological consciousness as coaches

We believe that becoming ecologically conscious is a continuous journey that needs constant attention and support from our friends, coaches, supervisors and peers. It requires both developing our eco-literacy and our eco-awareness. We need to learn not only about the wider ecology and the ecological crisis that is affecting us all, but engage in deep emotional self-reflection. Through doing this we may encounter a wide range of emotions, including our own denial, disavowal, fear, grief, guilt and shame in relation to what human beings have done to the earth we share with so many other sentient beings – and how the earth's suffering will increasingly affect all of us.

What is ecology and an ecological perspective or epistemology?

The word 'ecology' comes from the Greek word oikos, meaning household, signifying the household of the whole planet. Capra and Luisi (2016: 341–342) define ecology as "the scientific study of the relationships between members of the Earth Household – plants, animals and microorganisms – and their natural environment, living and non-living."

Ecology is not the study of plants, animals and microorganisms per se but the study of their multi-directional relationships to each other and their ecosystem. If the dominant metaphor of the scientific enlightenment was the machine, the dominant metaphor of ecology is the network.

One of its first originators was the English zoologist Charles Elton, who wrote *Animal Ecology* in 1927, where he described the networks of food chains and food cycles, which provide the interdependency of many differing species. He also introduced the concept of the ecological niche – which he described as the role an animal plays in a community in terms of what it eats and is eaten by. Since then this term has taken on greater and more complex meanings.

It is ecology that has provided us with the notion of nested systems we briefly addressed in Chapter 3, where we discussed personal niches, nested within social cultural niches, nested within local regional and cultural niches, which in turn are nested within biomes. Biomes are the major climatic ecosystems affecting the various biological ecosystems within them. Ecologists describe eight such biomes on our planet: tropical, temperate, conifer forests, tropical savanna, temperate grassland, chaparral (shrubland), tundra and desert (Capra and Luisi, 2016: 344). These biomes are nested within the biosphere of all terrestrial living organisms which Gaia theorists (Lovelock, 1979; Lovelock and Margulis, 1974) see as closely interacting with the lithosphere (the Earth's rocks); the hydrosphere (the Earth's oceans) and the atmosphere (the Earth's air) to form Gaia – the ecosystem of ecosystems in, on and around this planet. They see Gaia as a complex, evolving, living organismic system.

Ecology is a fast-growing inter-disciplinary field of inquiry, and like many potent concepts and new paradigms it has many children, not all of whom get on well together or even speak to each other. For our purposes in understanding the role of ecology in coaching, we need to understand just a few of these: sustainable ecology, eco-literacy and deep ecology.

Sustainable ecology emerges from the recognition that for the first time in Earth's history one species, Homo sapiens, is putting at risk the survival of all life on our planet. In this new epoch, called the Anthropocene, we are witnessing the sixth mass extinction of species (Leakey and Lewin, 1996) caused by massive human population expansion, deforestation, agriculture, atmospheric pollution, plundering of Earth's biotic resources, human-caused climate change and other interconnected processes. "Vertebrate populations have fallen by an average of 60 percent since the 1970s" (Laybourn, Langton and Baxter, 2019) and the rate of deforestation has continued to grow. Sustainable ecology recognizes that you cannot separate out human sustainable development from creating sustainable ecosystems, and many argue that we have for the first time created one interdependent global niche (Senge, 2014) and now need to discover how to enable an interdependent sustainable planet.

Deep ecology was the term coined by Arne Naess (1987, p.40) to distinguish it from 'shallow ecology', which was a study of our ecosystems as if they were separate from ourselves, displaying a human-centric concern focussed on how nature can be best sustained for the benefit of Homo sapiens.

> Deep ecology does not separate humans – or anything else – from the natural environment. It does see the world, not as a collection of isolated objects, but as a network of phenomena that are fundamentally interconnected and interdependent. Deep Ecology recognizes the intrinsic value of all living beings and views humans as just one particular strand in the web of life.
>
> (Capra and Luisi, 2016: 12)

Deep ecology argues that the only way homo sapiens can reverse the trajectory from being the destroyers of sustainable ecology to becoming positive contributors to ecological health is by embracing a fundamental shift in consciousness – from seeing nature as outside ourselves, and the environment as something that surrounds us – to realizing that nature and the environment are also part of us, and that we are an indivisible part of the wider ecosystem.

Wells and McLean (2020, in press) note, "For the last 300 years, the western world has been governed by a paradigm that was shaped by . . . The Enlightenment" closely linked to Sir Isaac Newton. They observe that as a deeply religious man his "worldview was deeply dominated by the Bible" which suggests that "when mankind was placed on Earth, he was set above all other creatures and his role was to dominate all things on Earth". This separation of 'man' from the animal kingdom and from other living creatures contained in the Holy scriptures of the Old and New testaments continues to pervade all modern western life. As Naess (1987) writes:

> Care flows naturally, if the "self" is widened and deepened so that the protection of free nature is felt and conceived as protection of ourselves . . . just as

we need no morals to make us breathe. . . . If your 'self' in the wide sense embraces another being, you need no moral exhortation to show care.

Eco-literacy is not just knowing more about the ecologies we are nested within and the relationship between humans and their environment – it is also about a metanoia – a fundamental change in the perspective from where we are looking. We believe that human beings naturally mature from being physically merged, to being ego-centric, to being socio-centric, to being self-authoring, to being more globally human-centric, to being eco-centric (Wilber, 2006; Hawkins and Ryde, 2020). As coaches we urgently need to help a much greater percentage of the human population to develop along this path in order to reach eco-centric ways of thinking and being. There is an urgent need for the different 'helping' professions to 'come out' and become a more impactful part of the solution, and reduce how they are part of the problem that contributed to us getting here, with an overemphasis on individualism, growth and the dualistic split between the human and the more-than-human world (see Hawkins, 2017c).

Deep ecology argues for an eco-literacy that is not just conceptual, but emotional and embodied, where we overcome the dangerous splits of self and other; my tribe and the enemy; my species and others that I can exploit; humans and lesser-beings; humankind and nature. 'Them' are all 'us', and self-care now needs to embrace the whole world.

The ecological awareness model

This model was developed by Peter Hawkins and Judy Ryde (2020) originally for psychotherapists but we have adapted it for coaches and coachees as a map to help us do the deep emotional self-reflection and change work that is required if we are going to help others develop their ecological consciousness.

Stage 1: overcoming denial

The first barrier to facing the global ecological crisis is our individual and collective wilful blindness (Heffernan, 2011).

Josie McLean (2017: 16) notes that "the human family are in a state of perpetual denial, unable or unwilling to implement the actions that we know are needed." Capra and Luisi talk of the 'illusion of perpetual growth' and believe that the

> obsession of politicians and economists with unlimited economic growth must be seen as one of the root causes, if not the root cause, of our global multifaceted crisis . . . the absurdity of such an enterprise on a finite planet should be obvious to all.
>
> (2016: 366)

"Earth Overshoot Day" – the day when we have used more from nature than our planet can renew in a year – moved from 29th September to 29th July in 20 years

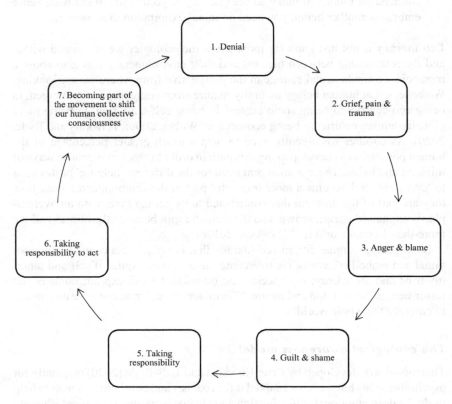

Figure 8.1 The ecological awareness model

(Earth Overshoot Day, 2019). To understand the role of ecology in our work, and therefore in our training, we need to hold our 'varifocal lens' – bifocals and single vision lenses are no longer enough.

Weintrobe (2012) and her co-writers distinguish between three types of denial.

1   **Denialism**. "[I]nvolves campaigns of misinformation about climate change funded by commercial and ideological interests" (2012: 7). It sets out to cast doubt and confusion and undermine belief in the scientific evidence and even in experts per se.
2   **Negation**. They see this as similar to the first stage of Kubler-Ross' stages of grief and mourning, where there is a refusal to believe that a person has died and to accept the loss. It is a psychological process of protection from a shock or trauma we are not yet prepared to face.

3   **Disavowal**. This is where we paradoxically both acknowledge what is happening and at the same time split off from this knowing. "This is seeing it but with one eye only" (Weintrobe, 2012: 7). We both know and don't know simultaneously, and Weintrobe sees this as the most prevalent and dangerous form of denial. "This is because the more reality is systematically avoided through making it insignificant or through distortion, the more anxiety builds up unconsciously and the greater is the need to defend with further disavowal" (Weintrobe, 2012: 7). Charly Cox is a UK coach and founder of *The Climate Change Coaches* (2019), which brings the principles of behaviour change to the problems facing our environment. They use coaching tools to shift people from the powerlessness that generates this 'knowing and not doing' disavowal to a sense of capability and action around climate change.

As we work through our various forms of denial, including our negation and disavowal, and can find our way through some of the contradictions reported in the media (and the denialism spread in some) and repeated by people we know, we can then find ourselves having to face up to feelings of guilt and shame in what we and our species have done to the world. At this stage, it is easy to either fall into the defence of splitting, where we project all the guilt on certain industries, politician or countries, or to take on board and introject more guilt and responsibility than is rightfully ours. The first process leaves us angry from a victim position – 'it's all them', and the second generates feelings of being overwhelmed – 'it is all me': the recognizable survival responses of 'fight' and 'freeze'. Both types of reaction regularly arise in our clients. We will explore these two opposites in Stage 3: Anger and blame and Stage 4: Guilt and shame. To limit these amygdala survival-driven reactions, we all need the space and support to experience our grief and loss, to register the trauma of what is happening and address our fears of what is to come.

Stage 2: addressing the pain, grief and trauma when we become aware of what we have done to our planetary home

Gradually, individuals are waking up to the grief of what we as human beings have done to our planetary home. Film makers, television producers and enlightened authors, journalists and artists are helping by developing well designed 'alarm clocks' to wake us up from our slumber and denial. Programmes like the BBC's "Blue Planet" help us see how over-using plastic and just throwing it away causes great distress to marine life, which has to survive amidst great islands of plastic waste, becoming ensnared in it and digesting it. Such programmes also show how micro-plastics enter the food chain, affecting all forms of fish and amphibians as well as the birds and humans who eat the fish.

We are repeating for emphasis that some scientists describe our current era as the sixth extinction crisis, or as the Anthropocene – the first extinction crisis caused by human beings, rather than the climate and geological causes.

To wake up to the great destruction we as homo sapiens have caused on our planet and to overcome the pervasive denial of the extent of what we have caused involves going through the cycle of shock, anger, grief, guilt, depression, feelings of hopelessness and despair, before we can truly integrate and become congruent with the wider ecosystem of our more-than-human world.

This process is increasingly showing up in the coaching room, sometimes consciously, but more often unconsciously. Some clients will discuss how upset they have been, or are, at witnessing, directly or indirectly, the tearing down of woods, the loss of many bird species, air pollution, the waste floating in the seas. Others have concerns about what their company is doing, and how the supply chain is dependent on non-renewable resources of the earth; others about their carbon footprint growing from their enormous travel miles. Some coachees will have free-floating grief, anxiety about the health of their children or grandchildren or focussed concerns such as their children's asthma being caused by their school close to polluted main roads, or even whether it is right or safe to have children at all.

Concern about our planet's future is prevalent, encompassed by the term "eco-anxiety." Castelloe notes this is "a fairly recent psychological disorder afflicting an increasing number of individuals who worry about the environmental crisis" (Castelloe, 2018, online). Zoe Cohen (2019, personal communication) argues that rather than a diagnosable illness, she believes ecoanxiety

> a right and proper state of waves of experiencing the waves of loss and grieving that are inevitable when we connect with the reality that faces us – and we work through it ourselves and together, and keep working with and through it as we empower ourselves to act.

Stage 3: anger and blame

Some individuals bypass the stage of grief by going back into 'disavowal' as the grief is too hard to bear, and they lack the support from others necessary to express it and be heard. Others go straight from awakening to the reality of the climactic threat and eco-destruction, to anger and fury at those they blame and see as more responsible than themselves for the growing catastrophe. For some this will be local or international politicians, for others the carbon fuel industry and for some the whole capitalist-consumerist culture. Anger can be a healthy response leading to thoughtful activism. Anger can also be an avoidant emotional mechanism, where one's own responsibility is projected on to distant others and we enter the blame game and 'drama triangle' (Karpman, 1968), where we cast ourselves as victims to external persecutors, and consciously or unconsciously wait to be rescued.

Stage 4: dealing with guilt and shame

The work of coaching includes developing our capacity to acknowledge our own destructiveness, and the pursuit of our self-interest which involves collusion with ecological destructive forces. This involves working through our appropriate feelings of shame. Judy Ryde (2009) points out that guilt is something to be established – am I or am I not partly responsible and should I acknowledge my appropriate guilt? Shame is the feeling we have when we start to take responsibility for how we are part of the ecological destructiveness that human beings are enacting on our local and planetary ecosystems. We start to feel shame for the effects of our consumer choices, our travel, our use of carbon-based energy and our collusion in turning a 'blind eye' to what is happening. We as human beings (including coaches and coachees) are equally capable of being destructive and shame is a feeling which usefully alerts us to these actions and encourages us to repair any damage we do. Feelings of shame can become hard to live with, if we do not respond to their call and take reparative action. Turning away from feelings of shame may well lead us back into disavowal, as we saw previously. The aforementioned ecological awareness model shows how guilt and shame fit into the process towards responding appropriately to the ecological crisis. These feelings can deepen our awareness of our own part in damaging the ecology and lead to more thoroughly taking responsibility, which is the next stage in the process.

Stage 5: taking responsibility

Coaching can play a key role in helping us to get beyond our own turning a blind eye to where our consumer products come from and the ecological cost of their raw materials, production and transportation; to move on from trying to rationalize away the carbon footprint of our air travel, or pollution of our car or central heating; and to look squarely in the eye at our own personal responsibility. Only when we can look with open eyes at our part in the collective destructiveness are we able to respond, able to develop our response-ability. Only then can we develop an appropriate course of action that is neither taking too little or too much of a personal share of the collective guilt.

Stage 6: taking responsibility to act – finding a sense of greater purpose in your work

Insight and accepting responsibility are both critical but not sufficient by themselves. "To know and not to act on the knowledge, is to not know" (Latour, 2017: 140), for as Bateson (1972) teaches us real learning begins not by absorbing facts, but by a difference in the choices we make. As coaches we need to avoid the perpetual wringing of hands, the cycles of 'isn't it awful' and 'if only' and ask: 'so what can you do that will make a positive difference?' Most of the steps we can each take are important, but for most of us in the privileged west, not nearly enough. So these actions are a starting point, and we should be careful that they are not the personal equivalent of industries 'greenwashing' their products, to provide a false complacency that leads us back into smugness and disavowal.

This step is also about helping all our coaching clients find a greater sense of purpose in their lives such as asking Peter's favourite strategy question "What can

I uniquely do that the world of tomorrow needs?" We know that people who have a sense of higher purpose in their work, are more committed, successful and more fulfilled and so are the organizations they lead (Edelman, 2013; Renshaw, 2018; Reiman, 2013; Sisodia, Wolfe and Sheth, 2007; Holbeche and Springett, 2004). Holbeche and Springett's research with 735 leaders found 70 percent were looking for a greater sense of meaning in their working lives (2004: 3). Meaning was seen as "connecting with others, having a sense of personal purpose, a heightened understanding of what is really important, of what it is to be human . . . a sense of community" (2004: 4).

Stage 7: becoming part of the movement to shift our collective human consciousness

We cannot just take responsibility for our individual actions. The crisis is such that creating change one person at a time will not be sufficient. We have shown in previous chapters that we are inextricably intertwined and interdependent. In this we are like the Bodhisattvas in the Buddhist tradition, who recognize that individual enlightenment is not an end in itself, but a blessing that necessitates us to return and enable others to also open their awareness, liberate their mindsets and be part of shifting human consciousness. The simple question: "How can you use what you have learnt to help others?" can be really helpful at this stage.

It is also important as coaches that we are not there to judge, moralize, campaign or convert our clients to our ecological stance or beliefs. Firstly, we need to ensure that we are neither in denial, disavowal or into just blaming others for the ecological crisis; that we have moved beyond grief and frozen powerlessness; and that we are constantly looking at the reality of the ecological crisis with our eyes wide open. It is essential that we have worked sufficiently through our own ecological awareness cycle – worked through our own despair, hopelessness, anger, grief, guilt, so we can truly listen and be open to the deep ecological feelings and responses of our clients without becoming reactive, judgemental or minimizing what is present within us and outside us. We need to listen with 'ecological ears' to the ecological field within and around our client, to the emotional responses they have to enable a constant moving around the ecological awareness cycle and enable a fuller life-embracing response at each stage and in each cycle.

Conclusion

In this chapter we have described how we can recognize the ecology present in every coaching session, whether recognized or not. The ecology is not something out there and the ecological crisis is not something in the future; they are both here and now. As the climate crisis becomes even greater and its consequences more present, its impact will be experienced in every organization, something every manager and leader will need to address. We, as coaches, can either stand on the sidelines picking up the pieces, or like those colleagues who we have quoted in this chapter, make it more central to our work. As this chapter has also shown, the ecosystem can actually be our best teacher in thinking, perceiving and being systemic.

Going back to Zoe Cohen's challenge at the start of this chapter: "Where were all the coaches when the planet warmed by 3 degrees?" How would you like to be able to answer that if your future grandchildren asked you that question in 30- or 40-years' time? What would you like to tell them you did in your coaching that made a difference? So, what does that mean we need to start doing differently in both our own development and in our work as a coach today?

We invite you to choose one area of eco-development for yourself and one simple idea you could take from the various practices we have described and introduce that practice into your work. We have no more time to lose.

Chapter 9

Systemic group coaching, systemic team coaching and working with the wider system

Introduction

So far in this book we have looked at how individual coaching can deliver value beyond the personal development of the individual by bringing a systemic and ecological approach to the coaching process that involves stakeholders and the coachee's wider world. In this chapter we will explore how we can create more value by bringing a systemic approach to both group and team coaching and wider leadership and organizational development.

Peter often asks teams he works with how they could halve the length of their internal meetings and double the value these meetings create. To start the inquiry for this chapter, we might begin with a similar stretch goal:

> How could your organization, or an organization that you provide some form of coaching for, halve the cost in time and money spent on coaching and double the impact the coaching has for individuals, teams, inter-team working, the organization and all its stakeholders?

Let us be clear – we are not advocating that any organization just halves its coaching investment. After all, the organization could then offer coaching to more staff! Rather we invite a radical rethink of what, where and how we do coaching, to deliver much more impact and value. We invite you to address the challenge and write in what you would 'Stop doing', 'Start doing' and 'Continue doing, if you were coaching manager of the organization and wanted to double the impact with half the investment.

Stop:
Start:
Continue:

We have so far suggested that there are many ways coaching can increase its impact and ripple effect by more fully focussing on the needs of the coachee's stakeholders, both in contracting and in the coaching practice. In this chapter we will also show how, through different forms of group coaching, we can both reach more coachees and stimulate peer-to-peer learning and coaching. We will then go on to explore how, by linking individual, team, inter-team, team of teams, organizational coaching and leadership development, we can support change in and between many systemic levels.

Systemic group coaching

There has been a great deal of confusion, both in the literature and in practice between team coaching and group coaching. Group coaching is the coaching of individuals within a group context, where the group members take turns to be the focal client while the other group members become part of the coaching resource for that individual. There is no demand for a common purpose or task for the group members beyond reflective learning, and the members may well have different individual development needs and focus.

In this section we will first explore ways group coaching can be more systemic and less individualistically focussed. We then describe a number of variants and developments of group coaching that deliver learning and value at multiple levels and provide an example of project-based action learning, being supported by an experienced individual and team coach as part of a global leadership development programme that delivers value at many levels of the wider systems.

Whichever approach to group coaching is adopted, it has the potential to both radically increase the number of people benefitting from coaching and broadening possible ways of learning and developing within a coaching context. Group coaching comes in many varieties, not all of which use the breadth of development modalities available, and not all of which are systemic in the way they operate.

We classify group coaching into five types:

1. Individual coaching in a group setting

In this approach the group coach gives time to each group member to explore the issues that concern them. The coach leads the exploration of the presenter's issue or challenge, with little input from the other members and little group interaction, but group members do learn to some extent from watching the coaching of the other members. In her typology for supervision groups. Brigid Proctor called this approach an "Authoritative Group" (2008: 32).

2. Participative group coaching

As in the first approach, the coach gives time to each group member to present a matter of concern or interest, but also invites more participation from the other group members in giving feedback, sharing their parallel experiences, brainstorming possible options etc. This is where an action learning set and a Balint group might sit and Proctor described this a "Participative Group" (2008: 32).

While both approaches 1 and 2 broaden the learning inputs, we see neither as systemic group coaching, whereas the next three types, which can be combined, all bring in systemic elements.

3. Systemic mirroring

This approach draws on the group as an echo chamber where each group member, when listening to the situation presented, will resonate with different feelings to the dynamics they hear. Often individuals will identify with different players in the 'story' presented to them and empathize with different systemic positions. This provides a living laboratory of "wide-angled empathy" (Hawkins, 2019: 74), whereby the systemic dynamics at play in the case can be differentially felt and registered in the group coaching room. At times the presented dynamic can create a parallel process played out in the group, the group beginning to have the conflict that is brewing in the presented organization. This approach builds on the understanding of parallel process which was first written about by the psychoanalyst Harold Searles (1955) and developed in working with supervision and supervision groups (see Hawkins and Shohet, 2012; Hawkins and Smith, 2013, Hawkins and McMahon 2020).

This approach can be enhanced by the coachee asking different group members to listen to their case from different systemic positions, such as: their boss, their team members, their customers, investors, etc. and feedback what they hear and feel from that perspective.

4. Systemic engagement

In addition to using the group as a reflective container for registering the wider systemic dynamics in the cases presented, the group can also be used actively and embodiedly in exploring the case. There are a number of techniques that can be utilized. Among the most useful are:

a) Sculping the external systems in the group coaching room

Sculpting is a method that emerges from the pioneering work of Jacob Moreno (1889–1974) in his development of psychodrama and sociodrama.

Sociodrama is a deep action method dealing with intergroup relations and collective ideologies. The true subject of a sociodrama is the group (Moreno, 1959)

We have further developed the use of this approach in individual, group and team coaching, to explore not just the roles but the systemic dynamics in the coachee's team or organization. Hawkins and Presswell (2018: 254–255) explain this process:

It uses the people in the room as representatives of entities (individuals, groups, principles, goals, etc) within a system and places them in space according to what 'feels true'. In effect, just two factors are in play: each representative's distance from other representatives, and the direction in which they face – whether towards the same point, towards each other or away. Each representative is then asked to report on the thoughts and sensations they experience when taking their place in the sculpt, whilst the facilitator might comment on the representation of the system as a whole.

At the most basic level, getting team members up out of their seats and looking at a problem from (literally) different angles can be energizing and refreshingly new. But there is additional value that comes from teasing a problem apart into its constituent parts and then looking at these in a systemic context. New perspectives are adopted and the relationships between entities (rather than simply the entities themselves) become evident. As a whole system is represented in the room, it becomes immediately apparent how adjusting any one part affects others and, with this, previously unseen implications and possibilities reveal themselves.

b) Systemic constellations

Systemic constellations were developed by Bert Hellinger in the 1970s out of his work with the German perpetrators and victims of World War II and their descendants. Systemic constellations have been developed both in group coaching, coaching supervision (Hawkins and Smith, 2013) and team coaching to help teams explore their own dynamics and collective patterns (see Hawkins and Presswell, 2018; Whittington, 2016). Whittington sees their use in systemic coaching as part of "strengthening the client and freeing them from their stories" (2016: 14).

Hellinger's work (1998, 1999) draws from many theoretical sources; he takes a phenomenological approach, eschewing theory in favour of observing and acknowledging what is experienced in the moment.

The focus is on the individual who explores their issues in the context of a wider system. This may stretch over time and may also include wider stakeholders and abstract elements such as the organization's purpose, values, revenue, performance etc. The coachee places other members of the coaching group spatially and symbolically (in terms of where they are facing and how they are standing seating, kneeling etc.) to represent part of their work system. However, it is also possible to use objects instead where there is not sufficient space. One can use bespoke training tools, or everyday objects, or stones, or draw a picture sculpt (Hawkins, 2017a: 314–315 provides a range of different approaches to picture sculpts). Whittington (2016: 35) uses a metaphor to describe the diversity of the systems involved:

> A useful way of thinking about systems is to think of a white fluffy cloud on a spring day. It's an attractive image but hidden in that cloud are all kinds of

movements, interactions and interdependencies. Its very existence hangs in the balance, vulnerable to change caused by air temperatures, air movement and human intervention. And a small change in any part will affect other parts.

5. Systemic experimentation

Here the group coaching process makes use of the way a parallel is often found between the patterns of the coachee and the situations they bring for exploration and how these patterns of behaviour and response will also show up in how they engage with the group. Most of us have a difference between our narrative self – the stories we tell ourselves and others about who we are and what we are like – and our experienced self –how we experience ourselves directly moment to moment, and how others experience us in the present. Kahneman (2011) and Siegel (2010) show how our narrative self and experiential self are connected to different parts of our brain. The group coach can invite reflections and feedback on the similarities and differences between what the coachee reports about how they are and behave at work, and how they experience themselves and how they are experienced in the coaching group. Here is an example:

COACHEE: "I always hold back from saying what I want to say."
COACH: "How does that show up here in this group?"
COACHEE: "Well I keep thinking of things I could say in response to other's situations but feel others would say them better."
COACH: "Is that what also happens in your team meetings?"
COACHEE: "Yes and I hold back from challenging my colleagues."

As we have shown elsewhere, insight and good intentions are not enough to create sustained change, so the group coach or group members can also invite an individual to experiment with changing their patterns of relating live in the coaching group. Change and learning are both much more powerful when they happen experientially live in the room, and, by using this approach, we can focus on what the coachee can change in the 'here and now' in this group to enable change back at work. Here is a short example.

COACH: "Who have you wanted to challenge here and have stopped yourself?"
COACHEE: "Well I don't want to pick on anyone."
COACH: "Sounds like an old message that stops you from speaking up."
COACHEE: "That is true; well earlier in today's group I wanted to challenge John."
JOHN: "I am happy for you to challenge me."
COACHEE: "You come across so certain and self-sufficient and I wonder whether that might contribute to your team members not stepping up."
JOHN: "Thank you, it is good to know I might be putting people off giving me support."
COACH TO COACHEE: "How did you feel saying that?"

Group coaching can also be carried out when the individuals being coached are all members of the same team. Kets de Vries (2006: Chapter 11) provides an excellent case example of using group coaching with an intact leadership team. In this example the team colleagues also help form the coaching agenda for each other – exploring what the team needed each team member to develop for the team to be more effective. Although group coaching in a team context can be a useful prelude or component of team coaching, it is fundamentally different from team coaching, for in team coaching the primary client is the whole team, rather than the individual team members.

Different approaches to group coaching

Action learning sets are similar to group coaching with members of a set, often between four and seven in number, taking it in turn to bring current challenges to be coached on by the other members of the set and, where present, the set facilitator. In group coaching, often there is more of an emphasis on the individual; and in action learning sets, more of a focus on the challenge being presented but this is not always the case and, in both instances, the focus is on supporting individuals in being the best they can be in meeting their work challenges. While all members may receive learning from bringing individual cases, again there is no demand for a common purpose or task.

Action learning can be understood as a form of group coaching (Thornton, 2016; Hawkins, 2017a). Action learning set facilitators need to undergo training in how to coach the group and enable group members to use coaching approaches to work with their peer colleagues. In Hawkins (2012: 84) there is an outline of how: "over the last sixty years action learning has developed a series of protocols that set facilitators can introduce to support the learning set in acquiring and using. These include

- the principle of shared air-time – everybody gets their equal share of time to bring issues and an equal voice in helping others with their issues;
- active listening;
- avoidance of advice giving and jumping to solutions;
- use of inquiry questions to open up the issue being explored;
- brainstorming ways forward and sharing parallel experiences (but not as solutions);
- helping the issue-holder to arrive at a new way to respond to their issue that they are committed to trying out;
- reviewing what happened when the action was tried out, back at work, at the next meeting." (Hawkins, 2012: 84–85)

Another form of experiential group learning which is used within the health service in both the UK and US is 'a reflective practice group', a process that draws on the work of Balint, (Balint, Gosling and Hildebrand 1966) and his development of reflective practice with doctors. Thornton describes these as "turn-taking, with a focus on one particular member presenting their learning issue at any given moment, for assistance by the group" (2016: 159). They differ from action learning in there being no expectation of every member presenting at each meeting, and there being little interaction between the person presenting their issue and the rest of the group, with members taking their turn to speak. There is limited review and the process requires "careful listening" (Thornton, 2016: 159). In Hawkins (2012: 85–86) there is a short case example by Mary Holland, an external coach from Ireland, on how she had used this approach to help develop a coaching culture across leaders at the European Commission.

The coaching practicum group

Having worked with both learning groups and action learning sets, between 1976 and 1995, Peter began to be interested in creating a form of leadership development that combined the benefits of these learning modalities, with leaders learning the skills of coaching, as well as more effective engagement with peers, staff, and stakeholders. To this end he developed a new approach called 'the coaching practicum group'. Like the action learning set, the coaching practicum comprises a group of four to seven people drawn from different parts of the organization. It is important to create an optimum mix of roles and people in these groups, not only because this has been shown to deliver more effective team learning and functioning (Belbin, 2004), but also because it restricts the likelihood of group members falling into giving advice or trying to solve each other's issues, as they are less likely to know the background or have the technical skills necessary. In Hawkins (2012) there is an example of using this approach in the leadership development across Ernst and Young UK.

Systemic team coaching

Team coaching is currently the fastest growing form of coaching. The 6th Ridler Report found that 58 percent of organizations were using team coaching already and 28 percent are considering introducing it in the next 1–3 years (2016: 34), meaning only 15 percent were not planning to introduce it in the foreseeable future. Systemic team coaching is a dynamic model that brings together the best of coaching praxis over the last 35 years, with the best of team and organizational development from the last 60 years, to create a way of working with a whole team as a living system in relationship to its wider organizational and stakeholder ecosystem.

We should recognize that, even if we only coach one-to-one, sooner or later we find ourselves indirectly working with teams, organizations and wider systems. This is because individual coachees bring not just themselves to their coaching but the dynamics of the teams they lead and work within, the organizational culture they are part of and the wider ecosystems they inhabit.

Systemic Team Coaching is a process "by which a team coach works with a whole team, both when they are together and apart. The aim is to improve their collaboration, collective performance, stakeholder engagement, collective learning and increase the value they co-create with and for all their stakeholders." (see Hawkins, 2017a: 77)

In this definition systemic team coaching is shown as significantly different from traditional team coaching (Level I) and also team coaching that focuses on the team as a bounded system (Level II).

> **Level I: Team coaching** sees the team as created by the individuals within it and focuses on the inter-relationships between the individuals and what the individuals want from the team. Consensus and harmony are highly valued. Individuals and interpersonal relations are the centre of focus and there can be a confusion between individually coaching all the team members and team coaching.
>
> **Level II: Coaching the Team as a System**: sees the team as a living system. Focuses on the team being more than the sum of its parts. Effective meetings, generative dialogue and collaboration are highly valued. The team dynamic is the centre of focus. This form of team coaching often happens on away days and in team meetings.
>
> **Level III: Systemic Team Coaching** sees the team as existing to create value, with and for all its stakeholders. It focuses on who the team is there to serve and the future needs that the stakeholders have of the team. 'Future back' and 'outside-in' engagement are highly valued. The dynamic between the team and its wider systemic context is the new centre of focus.
>
> (Hawkins, 2017: 169–170)

It was to establish this systemic team coaching approach that Peter wrote the first edition of *Leadership Team Coaching* in 2011, with the now widely used "five disciplines model of systemic team coaching."

The Hawkins five disciplines model of team effectiveness

This model is at the heart of systemic team coaching and proposes that to be effective, teams need to have mastered all five disciplines and that systemic team coaches and team leaders need to be able to coach teams both within each discipline and on the connections between these disciplines.

1 **Commissioning:** Are we clear about what our stakeholders are requiring from us? These stakeholders may be the board, the investors, the customers, communities in which the organizations work – so the commission comes from a number of sources and you have to be very careful about the stakeholder/s that you are not noticing. For example, BP didn't realize that the fishermen on the east

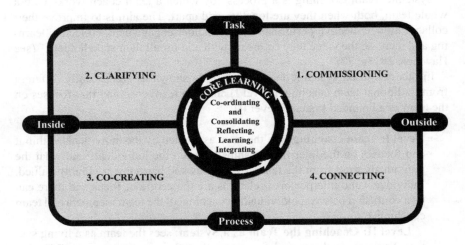

Figure 9.1 The five disciplines of high-performing teams and boards

coast of America were an important stakeholder until it was too late. This is an example of the "13th fairy", which represents the stakeholders we ignore and do not invite to the party, and as a result will come back to haunt us. Commissioning is all about understanding our collective purpose, WHY we exist as a team, our 'raison-d'etre', and this is determined by the stakeholders that we work with.

2   **Clarifying:** Receiving a clear commission from your stakeholders is not enough. A great team creates its own sense of its collective endeavour and asks the questions 'what are we here to achieve collectively that we can't achieve by working in parallel? What are the Key Performance Indicators (KPIs) of our team?' These are not our individual KPIs, but our collective goals and roles. How do we not only run our functions, but contribute to the whole? Clarifying is all about WHAT we are going to do as a team.

3   **Co-creating:** HOW do we work together in a way that is generative? How do we have meetings where we are not just exchanging pre-cooked thoughts, but together we're generating new thinking that none of us had before we came into the room?

4   **Connecting:** Great teams are not just those that have good internal meetings and relate well together. The real value they create is in how they engage and partner externally with all their stakeholders (customers, suppliers, investors, sponsors, communities and the wider environment). It is important that each team member is able to represent the whole team and not just their function when engaging externally.

5   **Core learning:** If a team just achieves being effective in the first four disciplines, it becomes better and better at succeeding in playing today's game.

However, in the world of exponential change every team needs to be growing its capacity to meet the increasing challenges and growing complexity of the future. The team needs to focus on its individual and collective learning. They ask, how can we do more at higher quality with less resources and become more agile and resilient? The team needs to take time out to reflect and pre-flect on its development, to ask how it can grow its collective capacity. Also, how does the team become a source of learning and development for all its members?

Getting the stakeholders' voices into the room

We have explored different ways individual coaching can partner with the coachee and focus on the coachee's stakeholders. This is also crucial for team coaching, where we need to see the team not as our client but as our partner, with both the team and the coach focussing on whom the team serves and what those many stakeholders need.

Peter, after 40 years of coaching many different teams, has stopped focussing on the option of creating 'high-performing teams' and instead partners with teams to help discover 'how they can continually co-create value, with and for all their stakeholders'. This moves away from a fixed end goal or place of arrival, based on what is happening within the team, and provides a dynamic, relational and changing focus on the team co-creating value with and for their stakeholders.

This means that team coaching has to be 'future-back' and 'outside-in' focussed and bring the voice of the future and of the many stakeholders into the coaching room. Peter has distinguished between three levels of involving stakeholders in team coaching:

1   Bringing in data gathered from the many stakeholders.
2   Bringing in the voices of the stakeholders, through stepping into their shoes and speaking as them.
3   Bringing in the live relationship between the team and the stakeholders and coaching this relationship live.

A combination of these needs can be used in the initial contracting with the sponsor and gatekeeper for the team coaching – as well as later when contracting with the whole team and also throughout the coaching process and when re-evaluating progress made.

In Chapters 5 and 6 we described the IDDD process of Inquiry, Dialogue, Discovery and Design. In team coaching these are a necessary beginning phase before a full contract can be developed with the whole team. This we might better label as co-inquiry, dialogue, co-discovery, and co-design.

In team and group coaching, it is particularly important to see contracting as a continuing, crucial element of the work with several phases (see Hawkins, 2017: 88–97). While the initial engagement and therefore the start of the inquiry process could happen with a number of people as previously described, the fuller contract,

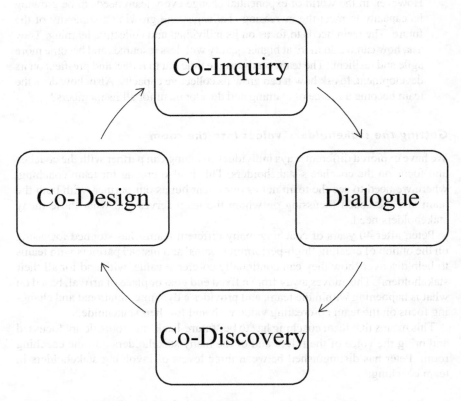

Figure 9.2 The IDDD cycle in team coaching

after the completion of the inquiry process, needs to involve the whole team. Throughout the contracting process it is essential to get the multi-stakeholder voices into planning and execution of the coaching process.

Inquiry stage: initial contract

For the initial inquiry process, after the team coaching request has been made, contracting is likely to include asking some specific questions to gain information. If the team coach then decides to go ahead, the inquiry continues with stakeholders, including team members.

Possible questions include

- What is the reason(s) for seeking team/group development now? What has led to this request?
- What has been tried with this team/group before? What worked and what could have been carried out differently and to better effect?

- Whose idea is the intervention? Are team members involved in this decision and if not, who is getting their buy-in and how?
- Who are the stakeholders of this team/group? What is happening in their worlds that they are requiring this team to step up to? What is talked about openly and what does not get talked about in the team/with stakeholders?
- What is understood by team and group coaching?
- How will we know that the intervention is successful for the team, for the leadership/executive/board, for the team members, for customers and other team stakeholders? What measures might we use?

At this stage, if the organization wants to move forward, it is important to cover more conventional contracting topics too before moving to the next part of the inquiry stage. This will include a discussion on confidentiality – what does the company require of you according to its own rules and procedures? Is that acceptable? How will reporting be done, to whom and by whom? What access will we have to individuals and materials that are relevant? It is important to agree the business terms, including arrangements for postponement/cancellation. Also, to agree the approach that will be taken and the possible events this will include.

The next part of the inquiry phase is critical to the engagement to understand the team better in context and

> is essentially about collecting relevant data and impressions about the team, their performance, functioning and dynamics; the team members and their relationships, and the relationship between the collective team and their commissioners and stakeholders.
>
> (Hawkins, 2017: 84)

This may involve a number of elements, including semi-structured dialogue meetings with team members and dialogical interviews with key stakeholders of the team.

The team coaching inquiry process often also involves some form of questionnaire to elicit perspectives from every team member and a range of external stakeholders. There are a number of useful 360-degree feedback questionnaires for teams such as:

1   The Highly Effective Team Questionnaire, where the team and stakeholders can give and receive feedback on their collective performance in each of these five disciplines (Hawkins, 2017a: 301–304).
2   The Team Connect 360, which can collect and analyze feedback from all team members and a wide range of stakeholders (www.aoec.com/training/team-coach-training/team-connect-360/).
3   Team Diagnostic Survey (Wageman, Hackman and Lehman, 2005) based on the six conditions the authors saw as essential for effective teams. www.team-diagnosticsurvey.com/the-tds/ (see the following case study).

These all provide data about how the team sees itself, how the stakeholders see it and both groups' aspirations for the team. The systemic team coach and the team can jointly explore and use this to co-design the team coaching journey. The questionnaires can be used to evaluate and redesign the team coaching after six months, nine months or a year.

We may also use psychometric profiling tools that help the team understand its diversity.

Hawkins (2017: 89) asks three questions before sharing feedback with the team to ensure a sense of collaborative inquiry is introduced at the outset:

- What do you hope to find in the feedback?
- What do you fear finding?
- What questions would you like the feedback to help you answer?

When the feedback is then shared and explored it allows all members to be active inquirers in discovering the current perceptions and effectiveness of the team, what is required, and the team development needed. To ensure the stakeholders' voice is omnipresent, we use questions similar to those that follow and involve team members in generating their own thoughts based on what they have heard and then inviting them into the roles of the various stakeholders to deliver the challenges back to their colleagues.

The team coaching will be a success for us as individuals if . . .
The team coaching will be a success for us as a team if . . .
The team coaching will be a success for our organization (board, executive team etc.) if . . .
The team coaching will a success for our clients/customers if . . .
The team coaching will be a success for our wider stakeholders if . . .
. . . and so on.

(see Hawkins, 2017: 90)

We will also ask participants to consider how they will continue to involve stakeholders. This could be by connecting with them regularly, inviting their attendance at part of a meeting and by sharing some of the feedback and the work that is being carried out as a result.

Inquiry stage - whole team contract

This takes us into further stages of contracting. The first step is contracting that we will do with the team as a whole; how we will work and be together most effectively. This will range from how we listen and are attentive to each other to how we ensure effective challenge. It is important to run this as a collective dialogue and discovery session to ensure that all members are on board. So, topics may include the use of mobile phones, ensuring each member has equal time to speak and defining what confidentiality will mean for the team. It will also involve considering how we will bring the stakeholders' voice into the room, and when, and how we will feedback to the wider organization. It will consider how we will maintain an external focus and include discussion on the ethical codes we subscribe to.

The second element of contracting relates more specifically to our systemic ways of working. When we meet with the whole team, we contract collaboratively on the outcomes for the team coaching process and for the programme we will use to meet those outcomes, including the implementation of our actions. We will also include an agreement on the continuous involvement of stakeholders and their participation in ongoing evaluation.

Coaching the connections – coaching the relationships, team of team coaching, team on team coaching, coaching critical partnerships

In Chapter 1 we quoted the CEO who said, "I have lots of coaches who coach my people and a lot of consultants who consult to parts of my organization, but that is not where my challenges lie. All my challenges lie in the connections, between people and between the parts." Also, in Chapter 2 we showed how most large global organizations will be employing fewer people in the next 5–10 years, due to digitalization, robotization, AI and outsourcing, yet they all believe they will have to partner with larger and more complex groups of stakeholders. Thus, the challenge for both leadership and for coaching is to move the focus from individuals and what is internal to the organization to the connections and partnerships which are external. Rather than coaching individuals who talk about the relationships, they need to transform so we can move towards spending more time coaching the actual relationship with both parties in the room. This means the coach is able to focus on at least four clients: the two or more people in the relationship, the relationship as a system in its own right and the organization they both work for, as well as the organization's stakeholders.

Where coaching meets organizational development and transformation

Peter has described *Systemic Team Coaching* as "the joint child of coaching and organizational development", but now believes that systemic team coaching and organizational transformation are giving birth to a new level of team coaching beyond the three mentioned earlier, which is described in Hawkins (2017a):

> **Level 1V: Eco-Systemic Team Coaching** sees the team as co-evolving in dynamic relationship with its ever-changing eco-system, with which it co-creates shared value (Porter and Kramer, 2011). Eco-systemic coaching focuses on the interplay between the team and other connected teams (inter-team coaching), the organization's strategy creation involving its wider stakeholders (coaching strategizing processes), developing a team based culture within an organization and across a network of enterprises (coaching networks) or

partnerships that bring people and organizations together in pursuit of a common goal (coaching partnerships).

(Hawkins, 2017: 170)

In Hawkins (2017a: Chapter 10) there is an exploration of the explosion of new opportunities and challenges that require an eco-systemic team coaching approach. These include how we apply systemic team coaching to start-up businesses; innovation and agile teams; edge teams within existing businesses; coaching networks and partnerships between organizations, in and across different sectors; and how we build a 'team of teams' approach that helps teams collaborate between them and to become more than the sum of their parts, rather than being siloed high-performing teams. Examples of doing these things can also be found in Hawkins (2018).

Combining individual, group and team coaching with leadership development

In the Henley Business School research report *Tomorrow's Leadership and the Necessary Revolution in Today's Leadership Development* (Hawkins, 2017b: see Chapter 2), Peter wrote about how too much leadership development is still focussing on creating 20th-century individualistic heroic leaders, rather than 21st-century collaborative leadership. Individual coaching over the last 40 years has greatly helped leadership development move from teaching leadership models to individuals applying these to their own work challenges. It has helped in the move from an over-focus on IQ to also focussing on EQ or the emotional aspects of leadership (Goleman et al, 2002; Goffee and Jones, 2006). For coaching to help create the next revolution in leadership development, it needs to help leaders develop 'WeQ' – collective and collaborative intelligence – and to integrate individual, group and team coaching into leadership development programmes that are based on delivering value, not just to participants but also to the current and future stakeholders of their leadership. This case study, from a global programme of a United States company, brings together a number of these elements, written by our colleague David Matthew Prior.

Organizational client context

The client is a leading American multi-national consumer goods corporation. I delivered one-on-one and team coaching to a team of 12 individuals participating in an action learning project (ALP). Its focus was improving health care in rural sub-Saharan Africa as a core element in a leadership development program.

High potential leaders were nominated by the executive leadership and the program included four two-week modules over a year, including leadership, strategy and design thinking delivered by a US graduate business school. Module I convened in the United States, Module II in Africa and India, Module III in China, and Module IV (final presentation week) in New York. Team members represented a global diversity through country of residence and/or country of origin (Australia, China, India, Mexico, Russia, Slovakia, United States) and functional expertise (customer development, finance, human resources, information technology, marketing and supply chain management). The team was supervised by one internal coach to whom I was accountable as the external coach, and I travelled with the team in the US, Africa and China during the field work of the action learning modules.

Launch in New York: coaching foundations

In addition to team coaching, each member received four one-on-one coaching sessions with me and ad-hoc situational coaching upon request. There was an initial coaching session to debrief each individual team member's 360 and various psychometric reports, to identify developmental leadership coaching objectives. Team activities in Module I focussed on clarifying values, establishing team norms and peer socialization through informal dinners. Following the first module, I asked each team member's direct manager for input on the individual's leadership development needs.

On the road in rural Africa: activating stakeholder inputs

At Module II, I ran a team diagnostic survey (Wageman et al, 2005) based on six conditions: real team, compelling purpose, right people, sound structure, supportive context and expert coaching. This showed the project was well designed and the right people selected. The team's self-assessment was lower in supportive organizational context and I challenged the team on how they would access ongoing stakeholder input from the project sponsors. The team quickly began to map their internal sponsor stakeholder strategy.

The external stakeholder strategy had already been woven into the country field work: the team made home visits with consumers in rural sub-Sahara Africa villages, conducting focus groups with them supported by an African-based research consultancy, team visits to local primary and secondary schools to meet children and to understand educational programs for health care, local distributor and trade visits, meetings with the country ministers of health and appointments with other multinationals who shared commercial and social interests working in Africa. The executive coaching in Module II included informal, on-the-road conversations with each team member to share the feedback and input from their respective managers.

Together in China: intra-team dynamics

Following discussion with the internal coach, team coaching work in Module III included conflict management strategies, using the Thomas Kilmann Conflict Mode Instrument where the team reviewed their individual conflict styles, assessing levels of collaboration and assertiveness. Each participant advocated for their style from different places in the room, allowing them a systemic intra-team view of conflict style pockets and patterns. The team also provided peer feedback using Hawkins' red and green card behaviors (two green cards to identify seen behaviors you want to thank your colleague for; one red card for behavior you have seen that you want your colleague to give up; (see Hawkins, 2014: 287–288). There was resistance from some leaders who considered the task too juvenile for their level and believed that KPIs were more important than applying reflective learning practices. Fortunately, other team members committed to the work by modeling reflective preparation and follow through. This prompted the entire team to find their own way, formally or informally, to deliver the feedback task, resulting in one of the high points of peer development in Module II.

Teaming in between: fostering interdependence

There were virtual, individual coaching sessions throughout the year, and bimonthly virtual team meetings to keep in touch on the action learning project progress, accountabilities and deliverables. I attended most team calls, providing feedback on observed team meeting effectiveness and learning which identified the need to collaborate with increased interdependence during meetings. Members moved from presenting information to providing consultation, to coordination, to joint decision-making and finally to collective work. This provided a transformational shift to higher levels of collective engagement, inspiration and output.

Return to New York: outcomes and learning

The action learning team and project ended with a formal presentation of findings and proposed solutions to the key stakeholders: the organizational executive leadership. Beforehand I conducted a before-action-review (BAR) with the team and completed an after-action-review (AAR) post presentation to harvest the team leadership learning. Each participant had completed a coaching development plan to share with their manager that evaluated progress on initial objectives, outcomes achieved, personal learning and next steps. The project was met with acknowledgment and success by executive leadership.

Programme outcomes benefiting multiple stakeholder groups

- The integrated health care solution was multidimensional and honored the people of rural Africa in what really mattered: living from day to day, access to water and electricity, attachment to the land, connectedness, health and beauty, the importance of tradition and church, economic welfare and entrepreneurialism.
- The action learning team generated a plan that was affordable, accessible and scalable across the regions of sub-Saharan Africa
- The team's strategy included personal touch points and strategic socialization with multiple stakeholder groups, fulfilling the organization's need for whole system integration across countries, divisions, local offices, distributors and customer groups.
- Executive leadership gained further knowledge and perspective about the leadership capabilities of its global talent pool.
- Team members' self-reported learning outcomes in their development plans included: developed a global mindset; improved influence and negotiation skills; built leadership gravitas; learned to shift leading teams from the front to leading from the side and the back; created leadership development value through intra-peer feedback loops; increased listening by slowing down verbal pace and talking less; established a habit of leadership journaling for reflection before action.

Team Coach learning focussed on:

- Calibrating the right amount of external coach involvement with and alignment among organizational stakeholders (i.e. individual team members, managers of the team members, the internal coach, project sponsors and executive leadership).
- Raising the bar in the ongoing assessment and evaluation of coaching effectiveness, progress and learning.
- How to develop the internal and external coach partnership that would optimally serve organizational interests, goals, and value creation.
- Realizing the learning opportunity and process loss of not having had my own coaching supervisor throughout this project. This is more evident to me now as I work with a coaching supervisor and am studying for certification in coaching supervision.
- Appreciating that the successful teams of today and the future will require agile, horizontal teaming that shares collective leadership responsibilities to inspire cross-learning and collaboration.

Conclusion

For coaching 'to deliver value beyond the individual', it needs to be part of a well thought-through coaching strategy built on the future needs of the business and its stakeholders (see Chapter 4). It not only needs to get the stakeholders' voice into the room, but also needs to explore ways of directly coaching the connections between individual clients and significant others. As we have shown in this chapter, it needs to clarify when to use individual coaching, group coaching, team coaching, systemic team coaching and working with the wider eco-systemic approaches.

At the same time, as we are seeing coaching skills re-insourced (see Chapter 1) and coaching increasingly carried out by managers and team leaders as part of 'business as usual'; we are seeing coaching incorporated into other aspects of the collective business. It has become a key part of most leadership and management development programmes. It has also become a key aspect of organizational development and culture change interventions, and at times has been built into acquisition and merger processes.

These are exciting times for coaching, as it reaches out beyond the confidential one-to-one relationship to wider and more complex parts of organizations and businesses. But this requires coaches to be bold, supervisors to be widely trained and experienced, and coach training to broaden its curriculum.

As Bob Dylan famously sings, the times are indeed changing.

Chapter 10

Systemic coaching supervision

Introduction

In this chapter we want to consider how systemic coaching supervision is an enhancement of coaching supervision.

To support our discussion on these questions let's start off with a dialogical inquiry together. Please complete these sentences:

1   An issue I brought to supervision was . . .
2   What I see as the purpose of supervision is . . .
3   My clients (individuals, teams and organizations) would see the purpose of supervision as . . .
4   I have benefitted from coaching supervision and an example of how it has changed my practice is . . .
5   My clients have benefitted from coaching supervision and an example of how they have done so is . . .
6   Wider stakeholders have benefitted from coaching supervision and an example of this is . . .
7   I ensure supervision learning is incorporated into my practice by . . .

What do we mean by coaching supervision?

Reviewing the literature, Turner and Palmer (2019: 2–3) identified supervision as having six common themes:

1   Provides fresh perspectives.
2   Attends to the quality of what we do and ensures safe practice.
3   Attends to how we develop ourselves personally and professionally.
4   Requires us to grow high levels of self-awareness and to work on ourselves, as we are 'the tool'.
5   Has many stakeholders and is about interconnecting relationships, involving systemic work; it is not only about what is created between the coach and supervisor.
6   Is a place to re-source the coach, mentor, leader and supervisor.

This echoes the tripartite model of supervision combining qualitative, developmental and resourcing functions (Hawkins and Smith, 2006, 2013).

Our belief is that supervision plays an essential part in our practice as systemic coaches.

Supervision is not just carried out by the supervisor but by the triangle of supervisor, supervisee and the challenges and lessons that the work and life more generally constantly provide. Supervision can fall into the trap of making the supervisee the client and this can end in the supervisor effectively coaching the coach. Supervision needs to make the work with the coachees and the work brought by and through the coachees, the primary focus.

The growth of coaching supervision

In 2014 we carried out international research on the development and spread of coaching supervision (see Hawkins and Turner, 2017) to see what had changed since the first research on coaching supervision by Hawkins and Schwenk (2006). The section on supervision, with 428 responses, showed that from 2006 to 2014 there had been an increase in the number who regularly receive supervision in the UK, rising from 44 percent to 92 percent (Hawkins and Turner, 2017). Europe also scored highly at nearly 81 percent. For the US and Canada, just under half said they had supervision, suggesting that the state of development of coach supervision is at roughly the same point as the UK in 2006. Other studies have found lower levels of engagement (Passmore, Brown and Csigas, 2017). And in all research, there are caveats: for example, the coaches who take part tend to belong to professional bodies and therefore are more likely to say they engage in an activity that, for some, is a requirement of membership.

Purpose of supervision

Please pause and ask yourself 'Who does supervision serve?'

We include
1   The supervisee/coach and their ongoing learning and development.
2   The supervisor continuing to learn and develop.
3   The quality of the coaching assignments of the supervisee.
4   The current individual, group and team clients of the supervisee.
5   The organizational clients of the supervisee.
6   The future individual and organizational clients of the supervisee, as they continue to develop their capabilities and capacities through reflection and development.
7   The stakeholders of the individual clients, their teams, colleagues, organization, the client's family and community and wider ecology etc.
8   The organizational client's stakeholders – customers, suppliers, investors employees etc.

9 The organization(s) that the supervisee may belong to and their stakeholders.
10 The coaching profession, which itself must constantly learn through reflective practice at all levels within it.

And this is not an exhaustive list, although it may sound exhausting! So how do we collaboratively ensure we are serving all these beneficiaries?

Making the work the primary focus

Already in this book we have shown that to work systemically it is essential to recognize that we as coach are part of any system we are working with, including the relational systemic dyad of the coaching situation which is formed by the coach, the coachee and the work they do together. It is very hard to become aware of the systemic dynamics we are part of and have co-created, and this is one of the reasons why supervision is essential, not just for coaches in training, but throughout the time the coach is practicing. Our view on this is continually reinforced by our own experience of the supervision of our coaching, and from working with supervisors.

We have also already shown that the coach is working in a complex web of nested systems, with stakeholders who have different, and at times conflicting, needs. We both find that in our supervision practice, the issues that are regularly brought by coaches are less about the individual coaching relationship, but about how they appropriately manage the relationship with the sponsoring organization, with the HR purchasers of the coaching, or how to carry out multi-stakeholder contracting and review meetings (see Chapter 5). Turner and Clutterbuck's research (2019), showed how supervisors who work in the executive and business fields believed that just over half of cases brought to supervision (51%) were related in some way to the original contracting with their client(s) (see p64–5).

Here are some generalized scenarios drawn from the many examples we have regularly encountered in supervision. These are true events but we have changed some elements to maintain confidentiality.

> **Scenario 1:** The coach is asked to support the client to deliver specific outcomes in what might be described as performance coaching – based on feedback received from various stakeholders that is considered unsatisfactory. Before the coaching programme has ended, the client is demoted or 'let go'.
>
> **Scenario 2:** The coaching programme has started and seems to be going well, when the phone rings, and it's the HR coaching sponsor. They ask how it is going, what you have been working on, and how engaged is the client in the conversation. They seem quite put out when you mention confidentiality!

Scenario 3: The coach is worried about the client as they seem very stressed and are not sleeping nor eating properly nor able to relax. It's impacting on their performance at work and their relationships outside of work. The coach has committed to keeping confidentiality.

Scenario 4: The client feels they have no choice but to work 16 hours a day or leave their employment which is well paid but highly demanding. The culture is such that 'going the extra mile' is expected. In order to get more balance, to see their family and friends for example, they believe their options are 'stay or leave'. Having heard the client's commitments, the supervisee is struggling to see an alternative too.

Once we widen our perspective and focus on delivering value beyond the individual to a wider circle of stakeholders, the ethical considerations become more complex and multi-level, as can be seen in some of the preceding examples. We will address this issue directly in the next chapter where we will focus specifically on ethics, but in this chapter we will show how coaching supervision itself must not only be built on a systemic foundation, but also attend to developing the capacity to manage complex and conflicting needs in a system which includes the coach, the supervisor and the wider system, and the coaching profession (see Hawkins, 2011c).

In 2011, Peter defined *Systemic Supervision* as based on four pillars:

- **Informed by a systemic perspective**
- **In service of all parts of the system learning and developing**
- **Attends to the client in relation to their systemic context(s)**
- **Includes and reflects upon the coach and the supervisor as part of the systemic field.**

(Hawkins, 2011b: 167)

We see, therefore, that systemic supervision is built on the same principles as systemic coaching. At the heart of systemic supervision is the recognition that we cannot see any system, be it the individual client, the team and organization they are part of etc., without in some way being part of the system we are seeing and understanding. Second, we cannot see the whole of a system we are part of, only the system as it appears in and through our perspective.

This is crucial to understand. Many coaches come to us for supervision, influenced to believe they need to be "agenda-less" in coaching. This is impossible. We all have an agenda – and this does not just come out in which questions we ask and what we choose to pay attention to in a conversation as leader, coach, supervisor etc. Our current and historic contexts, including our family, community organizational culture, ecology, are all nested within us and form how we see and act in the world. We (Peter and I) were talking about a set of Ukrainian 'Russian' dolls I (Eve) have on my shelf and how their history links to my family history, a background that includes fleeing persecution and emigrating to a new world. If the smallest doll represents the individual, then each larger doll represents a systemic level we are nested within. What is harder to comprehend is that the larger dolls are also embedded and nested within the smaller ones. That our family, community organizational culture, ecology are all nested within us and form how we are in the world (see Chapter 3 and Hawkins and Ryde, 2019).

Thus, supervision helps us recognize that our views of the client, the coaching relationship and their contexts are socially constructed and filtered through our own ways of viewing the world, our unique 'mirror' which will be different from everyone else's. The seven-eyed supervision model, first developed in 1985 (Hawkins, 1985) and then developed for supervisors across the helping professions (Hawkins and Shohet, 1989, 2000, 2006, 2012) and within coaching supervision (Hawkins and Smith, 2006, 2013; Goldvarg, 2017) and as part of other models such as the full spectrum model (Murdoch and Arnold, 2013: XXIX), is a systemic supervision model that attends to these systemic processes. It does this by describing three overlapping systems – the coaching system, the supervisory system and the system of the wider system in which both exist.

To work through the first four modes, we invite you to think about a client situation that you have found challenging in the last year, and where you think there's more potential learning from the client situation. Just spend a couple of minutes thinking of the client. It may help to close your eyes and picture them, or to hear the sound of their voice. Pay attention to any feelings that arise in your body.

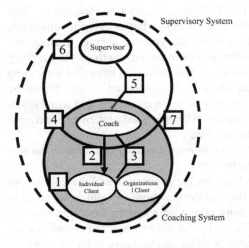

7. The wider contexts
6. The supervisor
5. The supervisory relationship and parallel process
4. The coach for
3. The coaching relationship
2. The coach's interventions
1. The individual client situation. The organizational client situation

Figure 10.1 **The seven-eyed model of coaching supervision**

In **Mode 1**, the supervisor helps the coach describe what happened in the coaching they bring for exploration and to tease out the phenomena of what happened in their story about it, including the coach's reactions. So, whilst thinking of the client, imagine replaying a video or audio of a few minutes of a session. Ask yourself, what did the client look or sound like, how did they walk into the room, where were their eyes looking? What would you have seen or heard or noticed as a 'fly on the wall'? While we are bringing the client into the room, we are also trying to do so devoid of judgements, so we are stripping back to what we saw, heard or felt without interpretation. This can help us pick up elements we didn't notice at the time.

Now we turn to **Mode 2** where the supervisor helps the coach reflect on the interventions they used at the time and other interventions that they were, or are now, thinking about. What intervention did you make? What led to those choices? Might there have been alternatives? Here we help the coach step back and notice our limiting assumptions and widen the possible ways of responding. What are the wildest things the supervisee could do, if there were no consequences? This may release stuckness and help the coach be more spontaneous and creative in their responses.

In **Mode 3**, we invite you to step back from your role in the coaching process and to helicopter up and reflect on the dance that you and the client are co-creating, and how the dance can be shaping the dancers as much as the dancers are co-creating the dance. Who's leading, and who's following? What type of dance is it? Are you in step or out of step? What is the pace, and does it feel like a partnership or as if someone is directing? Doing this can help the coach and supervisor work out what is going on unconsciously in the coach-client relationship but also this may parallel what is happening elsewhere in the wider systems.

Mode 4 encourages the coach to turn their attention back to themselves. How are you showing up differently in this relationship, what is being re-stimulated within you, what are the filters through which you are seeing, hearing and responding to this client? Do they remind you of someone – perhaps the way they look, how they talk, a gesture? Often a client somehow gets us to feel something they are unable to express about their situation. It's important we don't miss the opportunity to bring it to the surface, even if we do so cautiously and with curiosity. The alternative is that the client stays in an unexpressed pattern and 'what we can't articulate we may be doomed to replicate'.

What has this brought up for you? What new information has come to the surface? How might this be useful in the future?

Mode 5 is about the relationship between the supervisor and the coach. Our attention moves from the 'there and then' of the situations brought to supervision to reflect systemically on the supervisory relationship system, how it is developing and evolving and how this is affected by the dynamics of the issues that are brought. What might this tell us of what is going on elsewhere in the system?

In **Mode 6** the supervisor reflects on themselves as part of the supervisory system. Here we offer any reflections tentatively, not as interpretations or judgements, but as data that is in the field that can be inquired into. We may acquire a useful systemic perspective in this mode that helps us understand our 'here and now' experience. For example, in a group supervision situation, members responded to a case with a rescuing stance, wanting to rescue the coach who wanted to rescue the client. It became clear that this was a parallel with the way that the organization operated, avoiding straightforward feedback in the belief that it would protect staff.

In **Mode 7** the supervision work widens its perspective to consider the systemic levels that the client, the coaching and the supervision are all embedded within. It considers both how these are emerging in the work, and also how the work can create value for them. It does this from the same three perspectives: client(s), coach and supervisor (see Figure 10.2).

Mode 7.1 of the client includes their family, their team, function, organization, its stakeholders, the cultures of the sector and places where the work takes place. Modes 7.2. and 7.3, include the coaching policies, frameworks of the organization and the context in which the processes of how this coaching relationship has been contracted are included. Mode 7.4 also includes the organization they work for, where they are in their professional journey, any training programmes they are part of, and professional bodies they belong to. Likewise, Mode 7.5 is the supervisory relationship, while Mode 7.6 will include the organization, trainings, professional bodies, and any accreditation processes of the supervisor.

These are the immediate contexts of the supervision, but as we have shown elsewhere in this book, there are many elements in the larger systemic and eco-systemic levels beyond the immediate direct stakeholders that can impact and

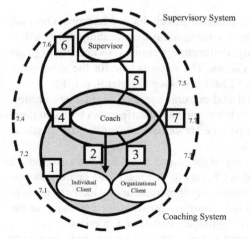

7.7	The wider contexts
7.6	The supervisor's stakeholders
7.5	The context and stakeholders of the supervisory relationship
7.4	The coach's stakeholders
7.3	The context and stakeholders of the coaching relationship
2	The training and context which shapes the coach's interventions
1	The individual and organizational client's stakeholders

Figure 10.2 **The seven perspectives of Mode 7**

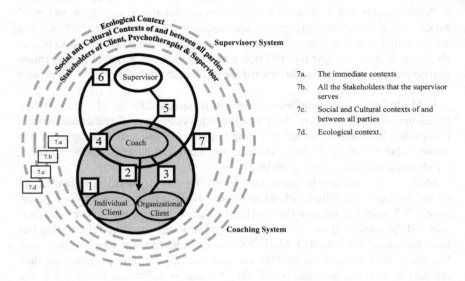

Figure 10.3 The wider dimensions of the seven-eyed model

are impacted by the coaching and supervision. These can be understood to be in concentric circles, like the rings of Saturn, some close to the supervision and coaching and broadening out from there.

In the first ring (7a) is the immediate context of both the coaching and supervision settings, the settings where they take place, the organizational context in which they happen.

In the second ring (7b) we find the different stakeholders who impact and are impacted by the work: the client's family, colleagues and community; the coach's/supervisee's other clients, their family, colleagues, training, community of practice, the profession and their future clients. The same is true for the supervisor. And of course, here we reflect on the "13th fairy" (see Chapter 9, p.138).

In the third ring (7c) are the social and cultural contexts of all three parties, coach, client and supervisor, and the cultural and social differences between them that form the intercultural relationships (see Hawkins and Smith, 2013; Ryde et al, 2019).

In the fourth ring (7d) lies the ecology of the 'more-than-human world', which is shared by all parties, as we showed in Chapter 8. The need for a healthy awareness of the ecosystem is becoming increasingly important and is likely to grow in importance over the next years, as is the mourning for what we are losing as the environment around us becomes more degraded, volatile and in crisis.

Supervision needs to listen and attend to how these wider systemic levels are present, consciously or unconsciously in the work.

The supervisor needs to ensure that these matters are included and not forgotten or ignored when the more obvious presence of the client, supervisee and supervisor are so present and pressing.

Examples from our practice illustrate some of these rings:

- **7b** One of us was worked with a client who was the leader in their field in Europe. Their company was doing everything to keep them from leaving, given that the company's profits were predicated on the client rolling out a multi-billion euro programme. What emerged was their dissatisfaction with their working hours and that they never saw their children apart from weekends. They saw no alternative but to leave prior to the rollout. The coach (one of us) helped them step back and consider their family alongside their profession and colleagues etc. In fact, as you've probably guessed, there were alternatives that minimized the impact on the work with stakeholders, while allowing the client to get home to put their children to bed a couple of times during the week.
- **7c** One of us was working with a male coach who came from a different cultural background. In the culture of this coach, coaches were viewed as authoritative people and men were seen as the dominant gender, taking important decisions regarding work and family. This created challenges for the coach when he was working with female clients, particularly to remember to encourage them to do their own thinking, rather than succumbing to requests for advice.
- **7d** One of us was supervising the coaching process of headteachers in large cities in Asia. Several headteachers were struggling with parents who wanted their children to have more outdoor sports activities while other parents were concerned about the health advice that pollution was too high for the children to go outside during the day. The coach at the same time was being encouraged to fly out to work with each of the schools' senior teams, adding to pollution from travel. In supervision, he became anxious about how his own children in an inner-city school next to a main road were affected, feeling guilty that he was not doing more in his own community.

Our Australian colleague Tammy Turner provided the following case vignette:

I was engaged to supervise a global coaching consultancy providing individual and team coaching to a large organization which was in the news due to its changing operational landscape. As are many industries in Australia, this client's industry is currently going through a Royal Commission investigation and is restructuring accordingly. During professional group supervision, the coaches brought their reflections about the engagement, their coachees, coachees' peers and/or team members and their stresses as a result of the various demands on them to provide their services.

Given the particular case challenges, the supervision sessions extended their reflections to include the mandates coming out of the investigation, the media attention and the general public as elements within the ecosystem, adding perspective to how the changes to 'business as usual' and the societal expectations of them as a large employer impacts their client outcomes. Other lenses we could have explored were how do shareholders and board expectations and/or the employees' interplay with the needed changes? Or the consultancy's and/or the client's expectations of the coaches to be 'successful'? How does the supervisor's bias and/or understanding of the case influence what the coaches focus upon in their sessions? The possibilities are endless and provide a more accurate systemic perspective.

Including these less obvious elements provided a wider perspective for the coaches to view a broader landscape. They reported an ability to more easily stay objective, especially in individual sessions where the pressure by the client to rescue them from feelings of being overwhelmed is greater than they typically would experience. As a coaching team, their ability to be vulnerable with each other has created more team cohesion for themselves and this, in turn, has had a similar impact on their clients.

Contracting for systemic supervision

One of the key foundations to practicing systemic supervision is systemic contracting and here we explore the role of the supervisor, supervisee and peer supervisees, for contracting is always a mutual and collaborative process.

Contracting as a supervisor

When contracting, whether with an individual supervisee or with a group, we hold the four pillars in mind (see p152) and have at its centre a collaborative, co-created relationship. We appreciate that supervisees come with widely different levels of experience both of supervision and of systemic work. So, while we will ask what their aims are for supervision, we will also draw on the pillars to explore their thinking further as appropriate.

The aim is to ensure that we do not see supervision as a one-on-one activity, with the needs of the supervisee being paramount to the detriment of attending to their stakeholders and their systemic contexts. We also need to understand our own roles as part of the system. So, for example, we might include these four questions:

1   "Tell me about you and what has brought you here."
2   "Tell me about who and what your work is in service of. What do those stakeholders currently value and what do they need you to develop and step up to in the future?"
3   "What is the work we need to do together, and how will that create value for you, your practice, your current and future clients and other stakeholders? In

other words, how can we create a future ripple effect and a legacy that continues the benefits?"

4   "What are the challenges you believe you will face in your practice over the next 0–5 years? What would you like this supervision to help you put in place to meet those challenges?"

The role of evaluation is important – and that it is set up right at the beginning of the process, as part of the initial contracting (also see Chapter 5 and 12). To do this systemically we will include questions such as:

- "How will we know our work is meeting the (systemic) needs we've discussed? What do we need to do to ensure this?"
- "When and how will we evaluate?"
- "How will we ensure that our stakeholders have a voice in the outcomes of the work we do?"

From our experience as supervisors and from recent research (Turner and Clutterbuck, 2019) it is lack of attention to contracting that often underpins the issues and challenges brought to supervision. The top themes, seen in Table 10.1, show that having a shared understanding of an assignment is the most significant challenge for both coaches and supervisors and when something goes wrong it is brought to supervision.

So, in drawing on systemic questions, such as those preceding, we are providing a model to our supervisees of the kind of questions they themselves may use when contracting with their clients, both individual and organizational.

Contracting as the supervisee (coach)

As coaches we are all working within systems, regardless of whether we are practicing as executive, organizational, business, career, wellbeing or personal coaches (and so on). When choosing and working with a supervisor, some

Table 10.1 The most significant challenges experienced in contracting

Top 3 themes	Coaches (n = 147)	Supervisors (n = 97)
1	Shared understanding of the coaching assignment between the coach and coachee (62.7%)	Shared understanding of supervision assignment (71%)
2	Quality and clarity of contracting (48.6%)	Relationship between supervisor and supervisee (49.5%)
3	Challenges of three-way contracting; AND coach-coachee relationship (46.5%)	Supervisee's commitment; AND quality and clarity in contracting (29.9%)

questions may be helpful in drawing out whether the systemic approach is one that is used:

1   What is your approach to supervision?
2   Who do you see supervision as in service of?
3   How can we create value for me, my practice, my current and future clients and other stakeholders?
4   How can we ensure, through evaluation, that we are meeting the needs of the stakeholders of my practice and that they have a voice?

Alongside these questions we would expect the contract in supervision to cover a range of areas (Turner and Hawkins, 2019; Hawkins and Smith, 2013):

1   Required outcomes – what are the overall outcomes for our work, how do these bring in the needs of the many systems impacted? How and when will we use evaluation to ensure the work is serving those needs?
2   Practicalities – how often we meet, the agreed fee and payment terms, cancellations.
3   Boundaries – confidentiality, ethical codes, between any roles (are we both associates of the same organization?).
4   Working alliance– what needs to be in place for us to do our best work together, what are our mutual expectations, how will we build trust, what are our learning styles, our desire for challenge and/or support, our hopes and fears?
5   Supervision processes – What models and approaches, if any, does the supervisor use? How do they describe their role against the description of supervision (Turner and Palmer, 2019; Hawkins and Smith, 2006, 2013)? Do they follow a professional body's code of ethics and conduct? What is their data protection policy?
6   Systemic work – What do they see as the purpose of supervision? How do they attend to systems?

Contracting in peer supervision

Peer supervision can be an excellent way to receive and give support, but it can also bring particular challenges, not least around contracting, unconscious bias, collusion, power differentials etc. (Turner, Lucas and Whitaker, 2018; Matile, Gilbert and Turner, 2019). In describing the peer supervision chain of which they are members, Matile et al talk of guiding principles they have established over time. These include

•   Equality between members (no leader/chair)
•   Act as if the sessions are "paid for" supervision, including rescheduling, preparation, feedback and contracting

- Focus on developmental opportunities as supervisor and supervisee to bring value to clients.

(Matile et al, 2019: 175)

Organization's role in coaches having value-creating supervision

Increasingly organizations who employ external coaches are asking them whether they are in supervision (Hawkins and Turner, 2017). However, for many this is just a tick box question. In Hawkins and Schwenk (2006) and Hawkins (2012) we provide a more nuanced way of inquiring into supervision of coaches that considers the impact of the supervision. Building on these we now recommend that the prospective coach is asked:

- Who do you go to for supervision and how often?
- What issues do you typically take to supervision?
- Please can you describe a time when you took an issue to supervision and how it transformed what you did subsequently?
- How have you used supervision to address ethical issues that have emerged in your coaching work?
- What difference do you consider supervision makes to your ongoing practice, and to your stakeholders?

Supervising systemic team coaching of team coaches or team leaders

Peter Hawkins has developed a specific methodology for supervising team coaching (2011, 2014, 2017a).

> This model provides a discipline and framework that ensures the balance of attending to the minimum requisite amount of data that one needs in order to be able to explore the many levels of dynamic (individual, interpersonal, team, organization, wider system, coach relationship with team and team coaching sponsors), before moving on to discover live, what needs to shift in the team, the team coaching relationship and in the coach.

(Hawkins, 2017a: 281)

In this seven-step process, the supervisor starts by asking what is the needed outcome from the supervision (1, contracting), before allowing just one minute for background data (2, context). This ensures that listening to data does not dominate the session. Then the coach explores the team using a picture sculpt (see p. 132–3), drawing images for every team member, the spaces, connections and disconnections between them and for themselves as the team coach (3). They are then invited to stand back and see the collective picture – and look at it through different metaphorical lenses in order to see the whole system, beyond the parts and relationships (4). Next, they draw in the stakeholders of the team, again showing the connections and disconnections with the team (5). Then they can be invited into a role-played dialogue between the team and themselves as the coach, on what is needed going forward and also to speak from the wider systemic needs (6). Finally they commit to what they will do next (7).

Since 2011 we have increasingly found this model useful in coaching team leaders, as one of the most frequent issues that is brought to coaching is: "How do I manage and develop my own team?" At this point coaching morphs into supervision of the team coaching carried out by the coachee.

Overviewing the supervisee's work portfolio

So often in supervision we look at work with clients sequentially, one by one, and some never get focussed upon. Often the clients that are not brought contain important learning. Sometimes as supervisor we ask: "What clients are you avoiding bringing to supervision?" or "Which client work might you regret in the future not having explored?" Also, by this sequential focus on individual clients we may miss the patterns and themes that run through the supervisee's work: for example, what sort of clients (individual or teams) are they drawn to? Are they attracted to certain sectors or types of organizations? Are there themes in the challenges they are experiencing? Are they drawn to play a particular role in their work (for example drawing from transactional analysis; parent, adult and child, see Stewart and Joines, 1987) and what does this mean for their practice?

Eve has developed a model to examine our coaching practice and portfolio more inclusively, rather than through taking individual elements, cases and discussion points and ensuring every client receives some supervisory focus. Eve's supervisees have named it the "Halos and Horns" model (Turner, 2019: 48–51 with supervision examples). It is a powerful group model but is also a useful means of individual self-reflection across our practice and is helpful to clients in looking at their stakeholders and their own teams. It works well for those with an introversion preference and encourages those who have an extroversion preference to develop their reflectivity and take part in journalling (Holder, 2019).

The phrase "halos and horns" refers to an effect that has been written about in relation to selection and recruitment interviews. It suggests that we make quick judgements (possibly due to unconscious bias and counter-transference) about a candidate and then seek out the information that supports our initial view (Turner, 2019). These quick judgements can be linked to appearance, voice, someone they remind us of etc. and unsurprisingly, studies have shown that interviews are not a good predictor of employee performance.

Supervisees have noted that as practitioners we may have the tendency to place metaphorical horns and halos on those we meet. They believe that we need clients who we see as having "horns" to stretch us, even though we may feel we do our best work with those for whom we bring our "halos" out for. So, to use another metaphor, we are caught on the horns of a dilemma and this will be helped by continually seeing and understanding our practice holistically.

Exercise:

I Think of your client list – make a note of your clients' first names or initials in column 1 of a 7-column grid (nothing that identifies them fully). (Table 10.2 – adapt as needed).

II Think of a sentence that sums up how you feel about each client; what physical sensations arise for you, and what images come to mind for them? This might be abstract, or perhaps they remind you of an animal, magical creature, someone from history etc., and add this to column 6.

III Notice what is emerging: sit with it for a while. Are there any groupings between clients, any themes, anything that you are experiencing?

IV Take a moment to consider which clients you might be applying halos or horns to. You can also indicate if you are unsure. Would the organization see the person the same way? Now complete column 2.

V Make a note of any emerging themes in column 7.

VI Taking the themes and any additional data from the halo and horns element, consider what this means for you, your portfolio of clients and for their clients. Share with the group when doing this in a supervision group or with your supervisor when working individually.

VII Are there clients with whom you seem to find yourself drawn to being more parental, adult or childlike or how else do you see your clients (team members)? What is the balance in your relationship with each client and is that the best balance? Complete columns 3 and 4. Note if you or the client end up on the drama triangle (Karpman, 1968) – if so, make a note in column 5 (Stewart and Joines, 1987).

VIII Further questions: Are there particular types of clients you find easier or harder? Are there particular sectors or types of organization you prefer to work in? What does this bring up? Consider what makes a good client (individual or organizational) for you? What makes an effective relationship? What do you notice, when you consider these questions? What might this mean for your practice and your effectiveness as coach, mentor, supervisor, consultant or facilitator?

IX Add any further emerging themes to column 7.

X If the clients had a collective voice what might they say to us? Again, what might this mean for our practice and our effectiveness as coach, supervisor or facilitator?

XI What is your learning edge from doing this exercise? What, if any, implications are there for our contracting and our 'chemistry' sessions – as well as future coaching sessions?

XII Share your thoughts with your supervision group or individual supervisor.

Table 10.2 The Halos and Horns model

1. Client (initials)	2. Brief description— physical sensations I have, image, metaphor, magical creature, historical character, dance we do etc.	3. Halo or horns or unsure (would the organization see them the same way?)	4. Parent, Adult or Child: how I see them and how I see myself in the relationship		5. Parent, Adult or Child: my balance as coach/team leader in sessions with client/team member (e.g. P 25%, A 70%, C 5%)		6. Drama (Karpman) Triangle: do the client or I ever step onto the triangle and become Rescuer, Persecutor or Victim (with us/ others)?		7. Emerging themes
			Me	Them	Actual %	Desired %	Me	Them	

Natasha is an executive coach and trainer who works with senior teams and individuals across a range of sectors and has used this approach with leaders too.

I am coaching a team leader (fairly new into a job in a new company) who feels that he fails to get the team to work together and have real impact. He identified particular individuals who he felt were jeopardizing the success of the team and other members who, although were generally co-operative and competent, were easily influenced by these more powerful figures. This came to a head on a recent away day when one of the more vociferous of his team effectively told him that the team does not respect him as a manager.

I used the halo and horns model with him and asked him to think about how he categorized the individual members of the team from the outset. He had mentally marked some as 'difficult to deal with' or 'unlike me' and realized that he focussed only on their behaviour that upheld that belief but failed to see other behaviour that contradicted the 'horns' category that he had given them. Likewise, those who he had seen as 'most like me' had been viewed through a 'halo' lens. He realized that from the perspective of the team, he had been seen to be giving these 'halo' individuals more of his time and praise. In coaching he thought about ways in which he could re-set the framing of these relationships in a way that would not prejudice him to or against certain team members. He set about having one-to-ones with the whole team and asked a colleague who he trusted to give him feedback about whether he treated team members equally. The team has been collaborating more and is generally much more highly motivated than it has been.

Conclusion

In 2019 Peter and Eve worked with Jonathan Passmore to create the *Henley Coaching Supervision Manifesto* for Henley Business School's Coaching Centre (Hawkins, Turner and Passmore, 2019). It shows how far coaching supervision has progressed but also some of the new challenges for coach supervision to develop further. This includes a need for more research to explore the impact and value creation that is created by the coaching – research not just on the benefits for the coach, but for the many stakeholders their work serves. This document also focuses on the need for greater co-operation between the professional coaching associations to define supervision and its benefits and for coach training organizations to teach trainee coaches how to use supervision and ensure maximum benefit from it.

One of the core elements of coaching supervision is attending to how we manage competing systemic needs that are in and surround the work of the coaching. As coaches we need to constantly expand our ability to engage with the systemic complexity and contending needs, as well as growing our ethical maturity to address the moral complexity that this entails. It is to this endeavour that we now turn in the next chapter.

Chapter 11

Systemic ethics – the door of compassion

Introduction

Through our supervision and research, we understand that ethics can be an area coaches and supervisors worry about. It can bring up notions of right and wrong, good and bad, those binary choices that we are then frightened of 'being on the wrong side of the divide'. We could rewrite the Solzhenitsyn quote

> If only there were evil people somewhere insidiously committing evil deeds, and it were necessary only to separate them from the rest of us and destroy them. But the line dividing good and evil cuts through the heart of every human being. And who is willing to destroy a piece of his own heart?
>
> (Solzhenitsyn, 1973)

for the world of coaching

> If only there were unethical coaches who were abusing their privilege and power for self-interest, and we could divide them from the rest, the ethical coaches. But the line between ethical and unethical practice cuts through every coach and every coaching situation.

In this chapter we will try to address three main areas of inquiry:

1 How do we, as coaches, enable greater ethical maturity in our clients, individual and organizational, and help them in their ethical challenges?
2 How do we as coaches, mentors, supervisors, consultants and leaders manage our own ethical issues?
3 How can supervision, the subject of our previous chapter, help us in developing our ethical maturity and ability to manage those issues?

We would like to engage you in our inquiry and offer these sentences to complete, as a starting point. We have left space for you to record your thoughts and feelings:

1 Ethics can be defined as . . .

2 Ethical behaviour is . . .

3 The work of a coach, mentor, consultant, supervisor or leader (etc.) is in service of . . .

4 I am accountable to them for . . .

5 I exercise my accountability to them by . . .

6 Ethical behaviour in my profession is characterized by . . .

7 Unethical behaviour in my profession is characterized by . . .

8 A complex ethical issue I have been engaged in was . . .

We will now address some of the results of our inquiries into systemic coaching ethics over many years, and you can create a dialogue between your answers and ours and hopefully arrive at a fuller understanding than either alone.

The nature of ethics and our ethical responsibility

In her doctoral research with supervisors Elizabeth Dartnall asked, "What ethical dilemmas have you had to face in supervision and how have you addressed them?" (Dartnall, 2012). Two respondents said that they had not faced ethical dilemmas, with one explaining that this was because none of their supervisees had been involved in unethical behaviour. The interview transcripts suggest that many supervisors equated ethical issues with the emergence of unethical behaviour. For us this is a misunderstanding of ethics which is reductionist and non-systemic.

Many of us will have seen the film *Love Actually* and its core belief that "love is all around". Maybe your view is like ours, that 'ethics is all around' – it is in every conversation, it is part of the fabric of our societies, of being human, of everyday choices. We are making decisions all the time, and they are not always about 'dilemmas'; that's just one facet.

Ethical decision making is influenced by our backgrounds and drawn from so many elements in our makeup, not just "nationality or race but . . . geographical cultures such as countries and regions; social cultures such as race, class, sexual orientation and gender and organizational cultures" (Ryde et al, 2019: 42; Hawkins and Smith, 2013: 297–309). So, in this chapter we take the view that ethical behaviour demonstrates our moral values in action and is the basis of our daily lives and how we relate to others.

Others view ethics as being about making the right choices. At first that seems a broader understanding and highly relevant. However, this can suggest a simplistic approach (the right/wrong, good/bad alluded to previously) which may not help in the complexity we face in making many choices. Eve undertook a university course on ethics and studied many moral approaches from diverse philosophers over the centuries who had different viewpoints and concluded that moral certainty does not exist in an absolute sense and moral standards change over time and across different cultural groups.

We have many codes of ethics, conduct and practice from the leading professional bodies; however, the professional bodies see these as guidance only as they cannot possibly hope to cover the complexity of ethical issues that we meet every day. Only rarely do they include injunctions (such as the ICF, 2019a, paragraph 21 about avoiding any sexual or romantic relationship with a client). Malik points to the responsibility we each have to make our own "moral map," which we can choose to see as "a highly disconcerting prospect . . . or a highly exhilarating one" (Malik, 2014: 344).

The emphasis, to date, has been on individual rather than systemic ethics. We believe that stakeholder contention is at the heart of coaching ethics. What does a coach or mentor have to do to help the client deal with their multi-stakeholder perspectives, which may be seen in the competing demands of a situation?

Hodges and Steinholtz (2017: 20) argue that ethics are innate in humans and believe that we "usually achieve more if we work together with others, using the combined power of our efforts and brains" and that we have an "ethical gene." Boaks and Levine (2017: 68) suggest that while leadership requires followers

> to be able to be motivated to act as group members in realizing shared group goals, the ethical modes of leadership ensure that the followers are not manipulated or deceived into acting this way and in general are not prevented from exercising autonomy.

They also consider it from a multi-stakeholder perspective, talking about consequences of action to both non-members of the group and the parts of the environment that are impacted by the decision. Hawkins (2017c) goes further and argues that leadership only exists when there are leaders, followers and a shared purpose, and all three elements need to frame the ethical appropriateness of what is done.

This suggests that in our role as coach etc. we need to be able to support our client to explore the situations they face so that they can understand and balance their innate sense of what is right with the needs of the context. An example of this can be seen in "Nigel's" case study, which was brought to supervision with Eve and underlines how contracting can be a key component to systemic ethics. What does the supervisor need to do to help the coach, mentor or consultant deal with multiple perspectives, to consider any patterns or themes that may be emerging?

Nigel's case study

In this instance Nigel, who coaches worldwide, was working with a global healthcare system operating in various countries. He had contracted with an individual client and had put in place strong boundaries, having learned from a previous experience where his contracting had been less rigorous. The previous time there had been a challenging situation around whether or not to break confidentiality resulting from potentially life-threating health and safety concerns.

Here Nigel had remembered the concept of the 13th fairy (see p. 138 and 186) and looked at a broad constellation of stakeholders during the contracting. Nigel had posed the questions "Who should we be considering in this discussion?" and "Who have we forgotten?" He then considered with the client "What is the work we need to do?" and "What does a successful outcome look like from the perspective of. . . ?" Doing this thinking, the coachee had brought various stakeholders "into the room"; in this case the stakeholders included patients, families of patients, future generations of medical practitioners and future generations of patients. This systemic approach, which also emphasized the legacy of the coaching, led the client to explore her obligations to the organization she worked for, her profession and her patients. In the end she decided to leave the organization because of concerns about the quality of what was being delivered, raised through this approach, and because she was unable to reconcile her values and the quality standards of the organization. This allowed her to move elsewhere and provide value to stakeholders in this alternative organization and work through her guilt at leaving the unethical issues for others to deal with. In reflecting on contracting now, Nigel describes how he "used to think contracting was something to get out of the way but now I see it as a continual process." His belief is that we neither train in contracting nor discuss it sufficiently.

Nigel's case study may also impinge on another element: what about legality? What if the laws in the country in which you are practicing are being broken? Would the ethical solution be clearer? Passmore and Turner's global research with supervisors (2018) and Passmore et al's European survey of coaches and organizational clients (2017) highlighted inconsistencies in how practitioners deal with ethical concerns. This was true in cases of the law being broken. "The results suggest a lack of agreement about whether this should be reported, even where law breaking involves mandatory reporting of such matters (in some countries) or involves serious criminality" (Turner and Passmore, 2019: 29).

Systemic ethics

Coaches working in organizations, with executives, leaders, managers or teams face complex ethical issues. As mentioned in Chapter 3, coaches need to be in service of at least two clients – the coachee and the organization. Professionally they need to operate within the ethical standards that derive from psychological work with individuals, as well as within the business ethics of the organization, be it in the commercial, public or 'for-benefit' sector. On many occasions the interests of these two clients may be in contention or even conflict. Balancing the needs of these two clients, we would argue, is necessary but not sufficient for systemic ethics, for both the individual and organizational client may be inviting you to collude with serving their local interest at the cost to wider stakeholder needs.

Many ethical codes for coaches focus on protecting the coachee from being exploited by the coach, which is important but just one level of systemic ethics. As coaches we can become entangled in serving, or sub-optimizing, the interests of one part of a system at the cost to the wider systemic levels that this part is nested within. Here we propose five levels of systemic ethics and provide some illustrations for each.

1   **Self-interest** over the interests of the other.

   a)   Using one's professional position to develop a romantic or sexual relationship with the coachee.
   b)   Encouraging the coachee to come on open training workshops you run or have a financial interest in.
   c)   Focusing on them liking you so they give you high scores on the feedback ratings, in order that you receive other assignments.

2   **Dyadic collusion** – Putting the coachee's self-interest over the purpose of the work.

   a)   Often coachees will bring issues of how they can manage their relationships with other colleagues and this can subtly become "help me win my battle or competition with this other 'awful person'."
   b)   Elsewhere (Hawkins, 2011c) we have written about a classic ethical dilemma of a coachee, whose coaching is being paid for by the organization to develop them as a future leader and is asking for reassurance that the coaching is confidential as they want the coach to help them be successful in an interview for a job in another organization, and they have not told their current employer.

3   **Supporting tribalism and sub-optimization of part of the organization**.

   a)   A coachee who ran a regional branch of a large financial organization asked one of us to help him develop a high-performing team which sounded very appropriate. He then went on to say: "I want my team to be the best team on the block, to really standout as best in class."

4   **Organizational exploitation** – This is where, as a coach, you are asked to support the organization's interest over the interests of the wider stakeholders.

   a)   One of us was approached by an international tobacco organization, to coach the team tasked with developing cigarette sales in third world countries where there were less government restrictions on sales and marketing.
   b)   A coach supervisee was working with a mining company, where a regional manager was wanting help in how to manage local community protests about the impact on their local roads and air quality.

5   **Human-centricity** – Here the coach may face situations where human inter-
    ests are being privileged at the cost to the health of the wider 'more-then-
    human' ecology.

    a)   The mining example in 4b, when explored a little deeper, had enormous
         implications for the destruction of local woodland habitats, as well as the
         health of the local river and lake.

These examples could result in possible unethical behaviour. We need to be alert to the
context and what we may fail to ask or to notice. In coaching we can be so focussed
on the immediate, short term and local that we fail to bring in the longer term implications, or the voices of the wider stakeholders including the 'more-than-human' world.

What is ethical maturity and how does it show up?

We see helping coaches develop their ethical maturity as a key role for supervision, in addition to growing their capacity to work systemically. Bill O'Brien, who
was the CEO of Hanover Insurance in the US, writes:

> During my experience as a CEO leading cultural change, I found it necessary
> to constantly stimulate progress in improving both the moral climate of my
> organization and the individual moral maturity of the people within it. When
> one lagged behind the other, the community began to become dysfunctional.
>
> (O'Brien, 2008)

Iordanou, Hawley and Iordanou argue strongly that the key to ethics is not solving
problems but stimulating "the kinds of conversations and conditions that enable
ethical issues to be surfaced" (2017: 3). Carroll and Shaw talk of ethical maturity
as involving elements of "progress, development and growth" (2013: 121).
    As Bachkirova points out, it is the coach (or other practitioner)

> rather than the application of particular techniques or methods, that makes a
> difference in coaching practice. Therefore, coaches have to be aware of their
> own stages of development in order to reflect on their own role in the coach-
> ing process and the dynamics of the coaching relationship.
>
> (2011: 54–55)

In order to achieve ethical maturity, we need to be attending to our own growth and
developing our own self-awareness. Carroll and Shaw define ethical maturity as:

> Having the reflective, rational, emotional and intuitive capacity to decide
> actions are right and wrong or good and better, having the resilience and
> courage to implement those decisions, being accountable for ethical decision
> made (publicly or privately), being able to live with the decisions made and
> integrating the learning into our moral character and future actions.
>
> (Carroll and Shaw, 2013: 137)

At the start of this book we discussed the role of the coach in helping avoid business and organizational disaster with Peter recalling a 2009 lecture when he asked, "What were the coaches doing while the banks were burning in the financial crisis of 2008–9?" More than a decade later ethical complexity and demands have increased. The disastrous effect human activity is having on the environment is growing daily. Digitalization and various types of AI have already raised a new area of ethical complexity (see, for example, DeepMind Ethics & Society, 2019). We live in an even more public world, with a proliferation of social media, and this creates increased risks for our clients and their stakeholders, of any ethically questionable decision or behaviour quickly becoming public knowledge and risking reputation and business loss. Rachel's case study is an example of one such issue a coach brought to one of us in supervision.

Rachel's case study

Executive coach "Rachel" faced the situation with her client "Carla", an expert in her field of safety, whose ideas could potentially save lives if she did her job "properly" as she saw it. Carla had been promoted into a role with considerable responsibility but felt she had limited opportunities to voice her concerns and potential solutions across the organization. Her direct boss had changed twice. She did not know how to create changes in the safety of the practices across the organization, partly because to date there had been no lives lost and previous postholders had indicated everything was in place safety-wise.

Thinking outside-in and future-back, Rachel avoided collusion, either with Carla being critical of the organization or in her occupying victim position. Rachel worked to secure a three-way meeting with the latest boss and to precede this with a coaching session with Carla to rehearse and prepare for the meeting. This helped Carla to focus on her mission and to link it to the organization's, to reconnect the two. The three-way meeting co-created a common, positive outcome and ultimately a safety improvement for the organization.

Underpinning our growth into ethical maturity is our ability to reflect, and our use of supervision and our own ability to self-supervise (see Chapter 10) will play an important part in that. John Heron (1982) points out how all human beings can easily and regularly fall into "illusion, delusion and collusion." Similarly, Bachkirova (2011: 96) warns of the dangers of self-deception which is one of the impediments to maturity we may face. In her research with six very experienced supervisors, many had experienced a variety of manifestations of self-deception among coaches. This included "not noticing ethical dilemmas. . ., forgetting the organizational client. . ., colluding, particularly with powerful or famous clients." As well as internal reasons for this, such as fear or attachment to a personal image of self (like being a 'perfect coach'), there were also external reasons such as a "lack of clarity in terms of standards and accountability, no mechanisms that allow clients to register their concerns; high levels of competition for contracts" (Bachkirova, 2011: 97).

This was alluded to by Peter who described one of the limits of coaching as "the coach's own personal capacity and maturity" and he proposed a developmental model of supervision that is helpful in discussing systemic ethics (Hawkins, 2011c: 285). He draws on the work of Rooke and Torbert (2005), who suggest seven stages of adult development in leaders (see Table 11.1), which particularly show how leaders act under severe pressure or challenge, of which ethics is one example. They found that a correlation between low levels of leadership maturity and below average corporate performance:

> They were significantly less effective at implementing organizational strategies than the 30% of the sample who measured as Achievers. Moreover, only the final 15% of managers in the sample (Individualists, Strategies and Alchemists) showed consistent capacity to innovate and to successfully transform their organizations.
>
> (Rooke and Torbert, 2005: 68)

Having seen this model, where do you think you, as supervisor and/or coach, are on this scale? If we are to support our clients/supervisees to think more broadly and deeply about issues, to develop their ethical maturity, we need to be on our journey too. Is it feasible for us to support growth in others, say to develop their systemic thinking (strategist), if we are still governed by the action logic of being an 'expert'? In 2011c Peter used the example of a supervisor working with a coach's ethical dilemma – the coaching was to support a leadership development process the coachee had been selected for; however, the client wanted the coach to help her prepare for an interview with a new organization without her current employers' knowledge (see column 5, Table 11.1).

Practical tools and methods for ethical reflection and learning

In this section we are drawing on four elements:

1   The use of ethical case studies;
2   The use of codes of conduct and other ethical materials available through various bodies;

Table 11.1 Seven levels of coach maturity (after Torbert 2004)

Action Logic	Motivational driver	Strengths	% Sample profile	Ethical stance on the dilemma –
Opportunist	Survival driven	sees opportunities	5	Most concerned to hold onto client and perhaps continue in their new organization
Diplomat	Avoids overt conflict Approval driven	Good as supportive glue, brings people together	12	Not want to offend coachee or their organization
Expert	Methodology driven	Good as an individual contributor and knowledge provider	38	Will want to follow the 'ethical rules'
Achiever	Goal driven	Outcome focussed	30	Try to serve the interests of both to create a win-win
Individualist	Awareness driven	Can see patterns and how things connect	10	Will look at both the coach-supervisor relationship and at being caught up in the coachee's disconnection between their and the organization's needs
Strategist	Purpose driven	Effective in creating transformational and systemic change in coaching and supervision	4	Will also focus on how to help the coachee confront the dilemma
Alchemist	Non driven	Will help individuals, teams and organizations shift their paradigms and culture	1	Will enable the coachee to transform beyond themselves

3   The use of an ethical decision-making framework;
4   Considerations of our own culture, background and self-reflection and how
     that plays into our ethical awareness and maturity (Ryde et al, 2019; Jackson
     and Bachkirova, 2019).

Case studies

The use of case studies that contain ethical dilemmas is one of the most common ways of exploring ways of working with ethics. Where ethics is considered in training programmes, this is the most likely approach. It is also true of conference sessions. This has the benefit of making discussion interactive but is limited by the choice of scenarios available, especially their systemic nature, and the relatively limited availability and discussion outside of training programmes. Susan's story is included because it illustrates how ethical considerations are 'all around'.

Susan's case study

An example of complexity in contracting was spotted by "Susan" when she was uncomfortable in a four-way conversation involving a new coachee, their line manager and HR. On the surface the coaching was to be a supportive intervention as the coachee had received rapid promotion and it was to help them step up to their latest role, one level below the board. Their boss, a director, talked of needing the manager to take decisions themselves with minimal input and "just get on with things." However, Susan observed a mismatch in how the director then brought up the need for the client to "come and check" anything he decided, something that was making the client unhappy.

In this case Susan was sufficiently concerned to talk with the director about the perceived mismatch. Rather than confront her she asked what she thought about a potential mismatch between what she said and what she expected, and whether it was worth "considering the message you put out to your staff." As a result, the director also decided to have coaching and what emerged was her own unhappiness in her role, one she was close to leaving because of challenges with her own manager, the CEO. In fact, she stayed and quite soon after became the CEO and the company has gone from strength to strength. She puts this down to the intervention from the coach who had picked up the underlying systemic ethical challenge.

Through contracting Susan had picked up a theme of unhappiness that was threatening not just the client and his boss, but also the customers and shareholders who stood to lose two high-performing members of staff.

Here are some further case studies to consider, the first two taken from the chapter on systemic supervision:

- **Scenario 1**: The coach is asked to support the client to deliver on specific outcomes in what might be described as performance coaching, often based on feedback they've received from various stakeholders that is considered unsatisfactory. Before the coaching programme has ended, the client is demoted or 'let go'.
- **Scenario 2**: The coaching programme has started and seems to be going well, and the phone rings, and it's the HR purchaser. They ask how it is going, what you have been working on, and how engaged the client is in the conversation. They seem quite put out when you mention confidentiality!
- **Scenario 3**: The phone rings (again – it's a busy day!) and this time it's the police. They require your coaching notes for a particular client. "They say the client you'd coached has made an allegation against another person which could result in prosecution" (Turner and Woods, 2015: 28). The notes would form part of the investigation.(Also see Turner and Passmore, 2017).
- **Scenario 4**: You are asked to coach a client in a company that works in a sector where you have strong value-based beliefs (depending on your personal stance, this could be a tobacco, gambling, drinks, or coal-mining company etc.). The company are keen to develop their strategy in light of changing perception of their brand and support their leaders in coming up with innovative solutions. Do you take the work?

Discussion: There are no right or wrong answers to any of the preceding scenarios. Nevertheless, our capacity to review and draw learning from however we responded is critical to ethical maturity. How far did we contract and have agreement about some of the issues raised? For example, did we agree a time period with the company and what the consequences were if the coaching met its outcomes or didn't? Did we discuss confidentiality and if so, what did we say in relation to the manager or HR lead contacting us directly and what we would disclose? What might be the benefits of working with someone in a sector that is stretching/challenging for us – developing our own and our potential clients' thinking? Also see the following section on using a tool.

Professional bodies

The professional bodies have considerably increased their activity in ethics in recent years, which may, in part, itself be a response to findings from ethical research that has been carried out, which included involving the professional bodies (Turner and Passmore, 2018; Passmore et al, 2017). There are many examples:

- Case studies are often required in accreditation processes by professional bodies and the ICF has required members to complete an online ethics course since early 2016 before a coach can become credentialed.

- The ICF publishes an annual report on coaching complaints (ICF, 2019b). Other professional bodies like the AC and EMCC also have complaints procedures.
- An ethics working group has been exploring the role of ethical guidelines in coaching supervision jointly led by two bodies, the AC and the AOCS, since 2017; it includes representatives from other bodies such as the EMCC, APECS and ICF. This has resulted in an original research project, which has involved wide discussion on two case studies, to create an interactive guide that will help to 'raise the bar' in terms of standards in ethical practice and support greater ethical maturity and decision making.
- The EMCC launched its own survey into ethics in 2017, for an "EMCC International Provocations Report"(EMCC, 2018). This included real life examples. In 2019 it sought 25 coaches to get involved in what it describes as "ground-breaking research focussed on ethical dilemmas in coaching" (EMCC International Research, 2019).

Ethical decision-making models

There are a number of tools available. Each of the main professional bodies has an ethical code of conduct and practice and the South African coaching association COMENSA ethical code includes a link to an ethical toolkit that aims to help participants make the link between their actions and their core values and beliefs (2019). The ethics working group (AC and AOCS) research project mentioned earlier will publish an interactive guide for coach supervisors (also see Lamy and Moral (2017) and the Medical Coaching Institute Code of Ethics).

We believe that Carroll and Shaw (2013) provide an excellent framework for thinking about ethical activity. They describe six components of ethical maturity, noting that "components are not equal in terms of the tasks and time involved. Situations and stakeholders will demand more from some components than others on any given occasion" (2013: 135).

1   **'Creating ethical sensitivity and mindfulness'**: Creating our 'antennae' to ethics, drawing on our beliefs, values and our self-awareness, actively listening and showing "wide-angled compassion" to all the stakeholders (Hawkins, 2019: 74)
2   **'The process of ethical decision making**: Maximizing choices: free will, accountability and responsibility; conscious ethical discernment and decision making; the influence of the unconscious on ethical decision making': this is where we make a decision about what to do and can see the bigger picture – understanding where our choices have come from (conscious and unconscious influences), be open to possibilities while weighing up what is appropriate in a particular context, including paying attention to the organization's rules and the law of the land.
3   **'Implementing ethical decisions'**: The intention to do what is right, and understanding and working with the space between "knowing and doing" (Carroll and Shaw, 2013: 223)

4   **'Ethical accountability and moral defence'**: When we try to make sense of
what we did we may face challenges from our own defensiveness, our ability
to slightly change facts, to rationalize, to evade responsibility. This begs the
questions: what is "truth"? and whose truth is it?
5   **'Ethical sustainability and peace'**: We need to be able to live by our
decision, and Carroll and Shaw argue that self-compassion and self-for-
giveness are crucial, not to let ourselves off the hook but to accept our
frailty and limitations. It is essential that we continue to reflect and use
this reflection to facilitate our learning from the past. Supervision plays a
role here.
6   **'Learning from experience and integrating new learning into moral
character'**: Carroll and Shaw warn that learning is not automatic. We need
to consider how we can revisit our ethical experiences, so we move from
"information to knowledge, and from wisdom to action" in a way that the
practical knowledge becomes "embedded in who we are" (2013: 261).

Passmore and Turner (2018) developed a similar model specifically for coaching
and coach supervision which they called the APPEAR model (see Figure 11.1). It
built on the model originally described by Duffy and Passmore (2010). The six-
stage model aims to help coach trainers by providing a practical and visual tool to
support coaches and coach practitioners by giving them a step-by-step approach,
covering:

1   **Awareness** – developing our sensitivity to ethical issues through understanding professional codes and our own backgrounds and biases;
2   **Practice** – engaging in actions that develop our practice from journalling to
supervision; being alert to all the influences on how we practice including the
requirements of the organization's regulations and contract;
3   **Possibilities** – considering a range of options when faced with an ethical
decision such as a dilemma;
4   **Extending the field** – considering all the possible sources of support and
information including legal and statutory requirements, and drawing on
the legal support that exists where practitioners have access to professional
indemnity insurance;
5   **Acting on reflections** – here we act on what we have decided but use our
reflective activity, such as our supervision, to review the decision first;
6   **Reflecting on learning** – finally we reflect on (i) the process (ii) the issue and
(iii) ourselves. We hope for new insights that will have developed our ethical
maturity.

Developing our systemic ethical maturity

To develop our systemic ethical maturity we need to cultivate several key capacities that counteract the human tendency to privilege the individual that is present,

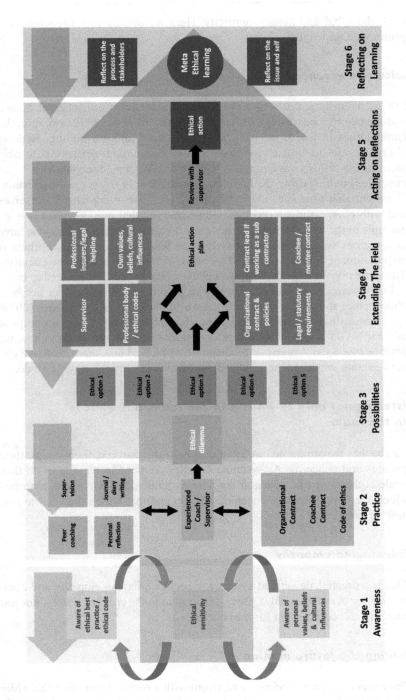

Figure 11.1 Six-stage *APPEAR* ethical decision-making model

Stage 1 Awareness

Aware of ethical best practice / ethical code

Ethical sensitivity

Aware of personal values, beliefs & cultural influences

Stage 2 Practice

Peer coaching

Super-vision

Personal reflection

Journal / diary writing

Experienced Coach / Supervisor

Organizational Contract

Coachee Contract

Code of ethics

Stage 3 Possibilities

Ethical dilemma

Ethical option 1

Ethical option 2

Ethical option 3

Ethical option 4

Ethical option 5

Stage 4 Extending The Field

Supervisor

Professional insurers/legal helpline

Professional body / ethical codes

Own values, beliefs, cultural influences

Ethical action plan

Organizational contract & policies

Contract lead if working as a sub contractor

Legal / statutory requirements

Coachee / mentee contract

Stage 5 Acting on Reflections

Review with supervisor

Ethical action

Stage 6 Reflecting on Learning

Reflect on the process and stakeholders

Meta Ethical learning

Reflect on the issue and self

the local, the tribal and human-centricity. Here we outline four capacities and disciplines we find helpful.

1. Cultural awareness

Ethical maturity requires us to become more aware of our inherent biases, and the assumptions we hold because of the families we were born into, the communities in which we were raised and lived and our culture. Ryde et al (2019) refer to an exercise Ryde uses when training supervisors to help them access "allusive assumptions" (2019: 45). We would recommend it – an example is writing down the first thing you think of in answer to the question: "I assume that time is . . ." or "Challenge is . . ." Having tried it ourselves and with clients and supervisees, we understand that how we answer is an example of the lens through which we see the world. Organizations also have assumptions around time such as: staff can work at their own pace, there is no pressure, or time is limited and we need to work long hours to be effective. The same may be true for what we believe is the purpose of leadership etc.

Our assumptions and beliefs we have absorbed will inform our personal philosophies and thus how we view the world. Jackson and Bachkirova (2019) recommend discussing our philosophy and then how it shows up in the purpose of what we do, and how we choose to put that into our processes in how we practice (the 3 Ps). Argyris and Schön (1974) showed how there is often a gap between our 'espoused theories' and our 'theories in action' or what we do.

2. Listening not only to what is in the room, but what is not in the room

As coaches we are trained to listen deeply to the coachee, their issues, their feelings and concerns. As systemic coaches we need to be able to do this, while at the same time listen through the individual to their world, both that which they bring into the coaching session and that which they fail to see, hear or mention.

3. Wide-angled empathy

This is a practice developed by Peter to focus on having empathy and compassion for every individual, group and system in the coachee's story, not just empathy and compassion for the coachee.

4. Holding the future in mind

Peter was once on a conference platform with a native American tribal elder who spoke of how true leadership began when we made decisions holding in mind the seven generations that come before us, the seven generations that come after us, and all living beings with whom we share this moment in time. In that moment, he realized how narrow and limited is our western perspective on leadership and coaching. Increasingly we bring in the voice of the future, asking what might we regret in two years' time not having addressed in the coaching today; bringing in the metaphorical voice of our collective grandchildren; asking how might this choice appear from the perspective of looking from the 'future-back'.

Conclusion

Let's return to the half-finished sentences we invited you to explore at the beginning of this chapter. We invite you to return to these and explore whether, and if so how, your original answers might have changed through reading this chapter.

In this chapter we have shown how ethical dilemmas are a core element of the work of both coaching and coaching supervision. We can see how the role of the coach and supervisor is not to try and solve the ethical problem but to use the ethical challenge as an opportunity to explore the contending systemic needs that are involved in the situation. By doing this, coaching and coach supervision can help coaches and coachees develop their ethical sensitivity, ethical maturity and systemic thinking, perceiving and being.

One of our core ethical values is that coaching should be delivering value for many stakeholders beyond the individual being coached and that bringing their voice and needs into the coaching room is essential for more ethically mature coaching. Not only do we need to bring in their voice and needs in the contracting phase, as we showed in Chapter 5, throughout the coaching process as we showed in Chapter 6, in supervision as in Chapter 10 through the ethical choices we make, but also in the way we evaluate coaching outcomes and value creation. It is to evaluation we now turn in the next chapter.

Chapter 12

Systemic coaching evaluation – assessing delivering value beyond the individual

Introduction

We agree with the late US Attorney General and Senator Robert Kennedy (1968) that gross national product only measures economic activity and fails to measure everything that makes life worthwhile, such as the health of our children, the quality of education, the beauty of poetry, the strength of our relationships.

Throughout this book we have tried to lay out a comprehensive systemic coaching approach that delivers value beyond the individual coachee, as the sub-title of the book indicates. Some would argue that: "It is all very well having the stakeholders in mind, involving them in the contracting, goal setting and reviewing of progress – but how do you know that this really creates value?" This question may also have occurred to you. It is certainly picked up by other writers, typified by Jones and Underhill, who point out "there is little consensus in the literature regarding the most appropriate outcome criteria for evaluating coaching" (2019: 41).

We realize we cannot duck this question, while recognizing that measuring value creation is a fraught and complex process and the whole area of Return on Investment (RoI) from coaching is a hotly contested space, which we will return to at the end of the chapter.

We have been arguing that in the same way that:

> There is no such thing as a great leader or great executive, only a leader and executive that continuously co-creates greater added value with and for all their stakeholders.

Then the same principle can be applied to the practice of coaching:

> There is no such thing as a great coach, only coaching that continuously co-creates greater added value with and for all the stakeholders of the coaching.

This means that as coaches, or advocates of any system of coaching, be that systemic coaching or any other variety, we need to have ways of looking at, reflecting on, and assessing the added value it creates. Notice we say assessing, not just measuring. Measurement has been captured by, and become the sine qua non, of empirical, materialistic science, where the extreme adherents of this 'religion' of scientism argue, if it cannot be measured, by an objective scientist with no beliefs of their own, in totally repeatable ways, with all other possible agents or influences frozen out, then it is not real. We caricature this to make the point, that measurement in the terms of scientific empiricism cannot be applied to systemic coaching. Empiricism has established its own empire (notice the similarity between the two words!) by capturing not only all physical sciences under its empirical rule but by attempting to colonize all the social sciences as well. We sincerely hope that coaches never work in laboratory conditions where all external forces are frozen out, and that they never aim for conformist repeatability. Jones and Underhill reflect this, writing that "applying a standardized set of outcome criteria across all coachees may not necessarily capture the tailored focus of individual coaching sessions" (2019: 42).

However, that does not mean we abandon all hopes of assessing what makes a difference and what creates beneficial outcomes for coachees (or supervisees), their teams, organizations and wider system of stakeholders. We must do this in rigorous, qualitative and quantitative ways, which recognize that every coaching relationship is unique and that a multiplicity of variables is in play. But this is not scientifically valid, the Empire shouts back! Yes, we reply, but it still can be valid and what's more, it still can be useful and help us develop more value-creating coaching.

So, let us ask you – how do you evaluate the coaching you are engaged in either as a coach, or a coachee, or the coaching you supervise, or manage? How do you assess that the coaching delivers value to people beyond those directly in the coaching relationship? What qualitative and quantitative data do you collect to guide you in making your assessments and evaluation? Who do you involve in the evaluation and at what stages do you do it, how often and in what form (verbally, in writing, through a questionnaire and so on)?

The coaching value chain

A great deal of the literature on coaching has focussed on the inputs into the coaching process: what the coach does, how the coaching is set up, the initial goals and contract, the coach's interventions and tools. Far less time is spent studying the outputs of the coaching process – the new learning, behaviours, competences, capabilities and capacities of the coachee (see Chapter 13 on training, to read more about the distinctions between the three Cs which are acquired through the process). Even studying and rigorously assessing the coaching outputs does not mean we have created value beyond the individual or provided more than "expensive personal development for the already highly privileged" (see Chapter 1). We have to go further and ask: "Do these new learnings of the coachee translate into new behaviours, new ways of relating, new actions back in their workplace?" Some have argued that there is often a delayed effect from the coaching, between the outputs being internalized and integrated by the individual, before they are applied in their workplace (see Spence et al. 2019). This may be true, and should certainly be taken into account, but needs to be balanced by the awareness, that whatever we do not move from cognitive short-term memory into embodied and repeated practice can be easily lost. Both of us worked with the UK's national health service (NHS) national coach register which involved a rigorous three-stage selection process. One of the key questions addressed was "How do you evaluate the effectiveness of your coaching practice?" and in that exploration the issue of long-term benefits was central.

Even if the translation from outputs to outcomes takes place, we still have to ask the question: "Do these new behaviours, ways of relating and subsequent action, create more added value for the team, organization and the wider stakeholders?"

This leads to the following model of the coaching value chain.

The problem with such a linear model is that it implies linear cause and effect thinking, flowing unimpeded in one direction of causation. In reality this is a circular process, with complex influences flowing in all directions. To give a simple example: the outputs and outcomes of one session can feedback and retroact on the coaching inputs and processes of the next session (or should do!). The process is not mechanistic, so the evaluation cannot be either.

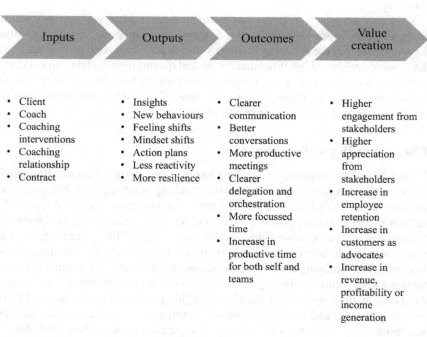

Inputs	Outputs	Outcomes	Value creation
• Client • Coach • Coaching interventions • Coaching relationship • Contract	• Insights • New behaviours • Feeling shifts • Mindset shifts • Action plans • Less reactivity • More resilience	• Clearer communication • Better conversations • More productive meetings • Clearer delegation and orchestration • More focussed time • Increase in productive time for both self and teams	• Higher engagement from stakeholders • Higher appreciation from stakeholders • Increase in employee retention • Increase in customers as advocates • Increase in revenue, profitability or income generation

Figure 12.1 The coaching value chain

This model draws and builds on Kirkpatrick's then ground-breaking work on evaluation of training in organizations, in which he proposed four levels of influence (Kirkpatrick and Kirkpatrick, 1994, 2005). These are:

1 **Reaction** – what participants thought and felt about the training (feedback sheets and satisfaction ratings).
2 **Learning** – the resulting increase in knowledge and/or skills and change in attitudes. This evaluation occurs during the training in the form of either a knowledge demonstration or test.
3 **Behaviour** – transfer of knowledge, skills, and/or attitudes from classroom to the job (change in job behaviour due to training programme). This evaluation, they argue, best occurs 3–6 months post training while the trainee is performing the job. Their main method of such evaluation processes is through observation.
4 **Results** – the final results that occurred because of attendance and participation in a training programme (can be monetary, performance-based, etc.)

Many of the questionnaires we receive after training programmes owe their origins to his model. However, there are issues this model does not address, for example, the many variables that may impact any of these stages and the unique, personal relationship in one-to-one coaching.

It is also similar and different from the "Five Levels of Objectives Model" in Philips et al (2012), which works on assessing the connections between (1) Reactions Objectives; (2) Learning Objectives; (3) Application Objectives; (4) Impact Objectives and (5) ROI Objectives. We understand their stages 1, 2 and 3 as similar to what we term 'outputs', their stage 4 as 'outcomes' and their stage 5 as 'value creation'. As we have shown in earlier chapters, we do not think the objectives can all be formed at the beginning of the process and many are emergent in the processes of both coaching and organizational development. Our approach is distinct from both Kirkpatrick and Philips in emphasizing the creation of value for all parties and all stakeholders and so we will now explore this a little further.

Value creation

In the 1990s the Royal Society for the Encouragement of Arts, Manufactures and Commerce (RSA, 1995) launched a very innovative inquiry process to look at "Tomorrow's Company." This process involved the contributions of members from a very wide variety of organizations across many sectors. In their report they argued that many commercial companies were over-focussed on delivering short-term value to their shareholders rather than sufficiently on delivering value to all their other stakeholders. One of the valuable outputs from their inquiry was the production of a model annual report that could be used by companies to report what they had received and what value they had generated for each of the following stakeholders:

- Investors (taxpayers in the public sector and funders in the 'for benefit' sector);
- Customers (or clients);
- Suppliers and partner organizations;
- Employees (including contractors);
- Communities in which the company operates.

Peter has worked with and developed this stakeholder model both in companies he has chaired as well as in a number of organizations where he has been a consultant. Eve experienced this directly in a meeting in the early 2000s when Peter was coaching the executive team of the BBC and Eve was a senior manager there. Greg Dyke, the then new director-general brought together the BBC's top 100 leaders for the first time. Eve recalls that not only were members of the different divisions split between tables, there was an empty chair at each one, and we assumed someone was late (as usual!). After half an hour, Greg Dyke said that the most important people were now joining the conference room, and several members of the public walked in, one coming to each table – they were there to represent the customers and the shareholders (as each household pays a licencing fee to use BBC services). It was a simple, yet hugely significant and transformative move – bringing the outside in. We then looked to the future.

Peter has added another critical stakeholder group, albeit one that often lacks a human voice to represent it, which is the more-than-human-world of the wider ecology, now under so much threat. Past approaches to community and social responsibility consisted in companies making philanthropic donations to 'worthy causes' from their profits; publishing codes of ethical practice and value statements are now no longer sufficient. All organizations, from whatever sector, regularly need to account for the value contribution they have received from each of these six major stakeholder groupings, as well as the added value they have created for all six groups, human and more-than-human, and consider how they have given back more than they have taken or received in both long-term and sustainable ways. From this work Peter developed the basic stakeholder map (see Figure 12.2), which can be used as a foundation in individual and team coaching, as well as when working with the wider organization.

You will notice that the model has a dark cloud floating to the side, entitled the 13th fairy, the stakeholder we are not noticing, and which will later cause us problems, based on Grimm's fairy story of Sleeping Beauty where the 13th fairy brought the curse because they were not invited to the party.

Michael Porter – a highly influential thought leader in the field of strategy over the last 50 years – with his colleague Mark Kramer, wrote a ground-breaking paper on the need for companies to move beyond the narrow focus on "shareholder value" to one which focusses on creating "shared value" (Porter and Kramer,

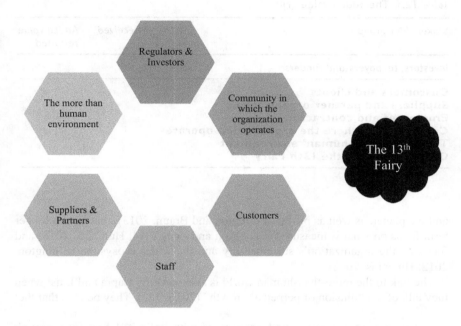

Figure 12.2 The basic stakeholder map

2011). They argued that part of the current economic and global crisis arises from the breakdown of alignment between company goals and social progress:

> companies . . . remain trapped in an outdated approach to value creation that has emerged over the past few decades. They continue to view value creation narrowly, optimizing short-term financial performance in a bubble while missing the most important customer needs and ignoring the broader influences that determine their longer-term success.

They go on to advocate:

> The solution lies in the principle of shared value, which involves creating economic value in a way that also creates value for society by addressing its needs and challenges. Businesses must reconnect company success with social progress. . . . It is not on the margin of what companies do but at the center. We believe that it can give rise to the next major transformation of business thinking.
>
> (Porter and Kramer, 2011: 63)

This has been further developed by the advocates of measuring "the triple bottom-line" (Elkington, 2001); developing "Plan B" corporations that focus on people

Table 12.1 The added value grid

Stakeholder group	Received	Added Value returned
Investors, taxpayers and funders		
Customers and clients		
Suppliers and partner organizations		
Employees and contractors		
Communities where the organization operates		
The 'more-than-human' environment		
Others including the 13th Fairy		

and the planet, as well as profits (Elkington and Braun, 2013); that have a longer term focus on what is measured (Elkington and Zeit, 2014; Hutchins, 2016) and focus on the organization's sustainability and the wider ecosystem (Elkington, 2012; Hutchins, 2012).

The link to the more-than-human world is also made by Capra and Luisi when they talk of the "illusion of perpetual growth" (2016: 353). They believe that the:

> obsession of politicians and economists with unlimited economic growth must be seen as one of the root causes, if not the root cause, of our global multifaceted crisis . . . the goal of all national economies is to achieve unlimited growth, even though the absurdity of such an enterprise on a finite planet should be obvious to all.
>
> (2016: 366)

Mapping received and added value

This approach of accounting for the value received and added value created, can be used with any organization we work for or with, as well as with individuals and teams we coach. In Table 12.1 we have provided a basic framework that can be adapted and built on with the specific client and client system. A third blank column can also be created where the team or individual being coached can write what they can do to both decrease the resources they use and increase the added value they create for all stakeholders (including the 13th fairy!)

Evaluating all along the value chain

One of the most thorough meta-analyses of coaching research was carried out by De Meuse et al (2009). Although they found that there had been an enormous upsurge in papers on coaching in scholarly journals, with English (2006) finding a 300 percent increase in such papers between 1994–1999 and the period

2000–2004; the number of outcome research studies was very small. Most research has been based on retrospective studies, where perceptions of the coaching and progress made were collected mostly from the coaches. There were just a few statistical studies of executive coaching that used pre- and post-coaching ratings, and only a few of these collected data from sources other than the coachee. These other sources that were used included ratings from the coachee's line manager and/or the coach. Unsurprisingly, where multiple perspectives were collected, the coachees rated their improvement through coaching higher than was rated by others. However, for the six studies that met their very strict criteria they concluded:

> executive coaching generally leads to a moderate-to-large amount of improvement in the coachee's skill and/or performance ratings.
>
> (De Meuse et al, 2009: 120)

De Meuse et al (2009) also surveyed ten retrospective research studies and applied 3 of the 4 levels of the Kirkpatrick (1977) model of evaluating training interventions: (a) reactions to coaching, (b) coaching effectiveness (as assessed through change or improvement in skills or performance at the individual level) and (c) coaching impact at the organizational level.

Across the studies surveyed, 75 percent to 95 percent of participants had favourable ratings of their coaching and nearly all studies indicated that the participants' individual effectiveness had improved. One of the most interesting is the study by Parker-Wilkins (2006), where respondents stated that coaching had assisted them on three main competencies:(a) leadership behaviours, 82 percent;(b) building teams, 41 percent and (c) developing staff, 36 percent. Only a small number of studies reviewed looked at the coaching impact at the organizational level. They all reported positive benefits but looked at different impacts: Talboom (1999) looked at the impact of coaching on subordinate absence rates; Anderson (2001) considered productivity and employee satisfaction; and the "When Coaching Measures Up" (2005) survey looked at impact on leadership, management teams and business deliverables. Interestingly in this last study, twice as many respondents (67%) reported an improvement in their personal work/life balance as reported an improvement in business deliverables (33%).

De Meuse et al (2009) concluded that although there is a great deal of evidence that coaching does produce improvements in individual effectiveness, fewer reported that it positively impacted on organizational improvement.

One of the largest pieces of coaching evaluation research was led by Erik de Haan et al, (2014) of Ashridge Business School, UK, looking at "active ingredients in coaching" (2014: 16). It involved coaching pairs of coach and coachee, with both evaluating the inputs and the output benefits from the coaching. There were 1,895 client-coach pairs involved from 34 countries, where both the coachee and the coach completed a separate questionnaire for an assignment, with 3,882 surveys completed (2016: 189).

In a search of the coaching literature in April 2015, de Hann et al found "nine studies that explored the question of which variables within the coaching relationship had impact on coaching effectiveness" (2016: 191). In carrying out their research, they argued that the way forward was for quantitative researchers "to assume that the general effectiveness of helping conversations as convincingly demonstrated in psychotherapy (see, eg, Wampold, 2001; or Cooper, 2008) will also be true in executive coaching" (de Haan et al, 2014: 6). Therefore, they compare "conditions to determine the degree to which various aspects of coaching, the coach, or the coachee have an effect on outcomes" (de Haan et al, 2014: 13). The authors conclude:

> The results show that client [coachee] perceptions of coaching outcome were significantly related to coach and client rated strength of the relationship and to client self-efficacy but are not affected by client or coach personality or even by personality matching. The client-coach relationship mediated the impact of self-efficacy on coaching outcomes, suggesting that the strength of this relationship – particularly as seen through the eyes of the client – is the key ingredient in coaching outcome.
>
> (de Haan et al, 2014: 2)

Research and evaluation models

Leedham (2005) drew on Kirkpatrick's (1977) model for evaluating training interventions in organizations and proposed a pyramid model of carrying out research on executive coaching that shows the connections between coaching inputs at the bottom level, linking to inner personal benefits, to outer personal benefit and from there to business results.

Peter (Hawkins, 2012) built on Leedham's (2005) model of coaching research, which was focussed on individual coaching, to include team coaching and creating a wider coaching culture and their impact on team performance and the organizational culture and from their business results to the creation of value for stakeholders (Figure 12.3).

With regret and the wisdom of hindsight, he now realizes that he put in far too few arrows and all the arrows should have had arrow heads at both ends showing the flows going in all and both directions.

In Hawkins (2012: 173–174) he argued that "more extensive research needed to be carried out on:

a) how a coaching culture can develop coach skills and attributes as well as the coaching processes, and reciprocally be developed by them.
b) how a coaching culture can develop the organizational culture in the required direction.
c) how team coaching influences higher team performance, and business results, and impacts on the organizational culture.

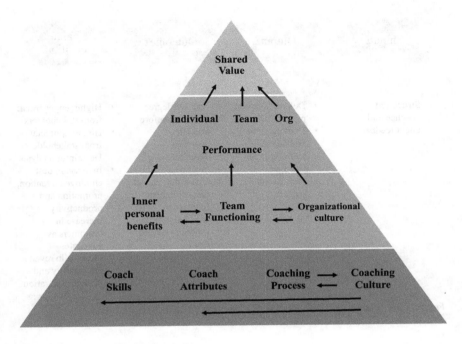

Figure 12.3 The added value grid

d)   how personal coaching impacts on team performance.
e)   how individual, team and organizational performance impact on the creation
     of shared value across the wider stakeholder community."

Evaluation and assessment all along the value chain

If we now return to the coaching value chain, we can list a few of the things we
can assess at each stage of the process from inputs, outputs, to outcomes and value
creation.

We believe it is essential to have both qualitative and quantitative assessment
methods at all four stages, and then develop mechanisms for assessing the connections between them.

Inputs

Most organizations we have worked with – either consulting to them about their
coaching strategy or structure or working for them as a supervisor or external coach – have instituted formal processes for collecting standardized feedback from both coach and coachee on all coaching processes. These processes

Inputs	Outputs	Outcomes	Value creation
• Structured coachee and client feedback	• Delivered action plan • Demonstrable embodied learning in the coachee • New habits repeating	• 360/720 degree feedback before and after coaching • Team meeting measures • Upward appraisal on enablement • Increase in productive time for both self and team	• Higher engagement from stakeholders • Higher appreciation from stakeholders. Descriptor analysis • Increase in best employee retention, promotion and productivity • Increase in customers as advocates • Increase in revenue, profitability and income generation

Figure 12.4 Hawkins 2012 model of coaching research

collect feedback on what was most helpful and unhelpful about the coaching and help both in coach allocation as well as the collective learning of the coaching service.

Outputs

Some of the aforementioned feedback processes also include a section on 'outputs', asking the coachee and the coach to comment on what learning has been acquired and applied back at work. It is important to distinguish between insight learning about what needs to be different, and applied embodied learning that has created new behaviours and ways of engaging back at work.

Sophisticated evaluation processes would then include a question on what it was in the coaching process that facilitated these significant actions.

One of the most important outputs that needs to be tracked is how the individual learning in coaching impacts on team and organizational learning. It is rare that coaches focus on the spread and amplification of the individual learning back at work and ask in coaching: "How could you help others benefit from what you have learned and developed here?" Eve recalls how internal and external coaches were brought together in the BBC to discuss emerging themes from the coaching and action learning elements of their Ashridge leadership development programme (which also involved taught modules), which could then be fed back to the board.

This approach has been used with a number of organizations and is called *Harvesting the Learning* (Hawkins, 2012: 99–101). It has four stages:

1   Bringing together, at regular intervals, the community of internal and external coaches to hear the challenges the organization is experiencing, providing a forum for questions about the organization's strategy and its plan for the development of its business, its organization, culture, leaders and people.
2   Then working with all the coaches in supervision trios (coach, supervisor and observer) on key coaching relationships with managed confidentiality. The observer is given a pro-forma to capture some of the emerging themes in such areas as:

   a)   Clarity and alignment concerning the direction of the organization and what this direction requires from leaders and managers;
   b)   The organizational culture, including the five levels of artefacts, patterns of behaviour, mindsets, emotions, and motivational roots (see Chapter 4);
   c)   Connections and disconnections across the organization;
   d)   Connections and disconnections with stakeholders;
   e)   How coaching is perceived.

Each person has 30 minutes in each role, and there is some time for feedback to the supervisor on their supervision – thus providing additional developmental learning.

3   The three are then asked to look for patterns emerging across the themes collected from the three supervision sessions. We sometimes provide a short input and handout on systemic pattern identification. These patterns are entered onto post-its and posted on different themed flip chart boards. The group are split up into small groups by each themed board and work on clustering the emerging themes, identifying the patterns that connect them, and then feeding this back into the whole group. They are asked to identify the key patterns that enable or block the organization in meeting its strategic and developmental objectives.
4   These enabling and blocking patterns are brought together and a dialogue is facilitated between senior executives and the coaches on these emerging key themes. This can be either at the same event or at a later meeting between the senior leadership team and a representative group of internal and external coaches. Having explored the emerging themes, the dialogue can focus on how coaching can contribute more effectively to the next stages of the organization's development.

This process requires facilitation from a consultant that is not only an experienced coach and skilled coaching supervisor but also one who understands organizational strategy, culture change, systemic dynamics and organizational development. Most importantly, this facilitator needs to translate between the language of senior leadership and the language of the coaching conversations.

This full process for harvesting the learning may sound rather daunting for many coaching communities in the early stages of their development, but simpler forms of the process can be adopted as part of the annual review of the coaching community. In Hawkins (2012: 101–103) there is a case study of such a process with the Electricity Supply Board (ESB), Ireland's premier electricity utility company.

Outcomes

Even fewer evaluation processes evaluate the outcome of these new behaviours and ways of engaging. Some organizations include a 360- or 720-degree feedback (see Chapter 6) on the individual before and after coaching, which evaluates how the coachee's stakeholders are experiencing the changes resulting from the coaching. It is important to carry out a second feedback process just after the coaching, for, as Spence et al (2019) argue, there are many benefits from the coaching that only appear six months or more after the coaching, as new behaviours take some time to embed and be noticed. In contracting, Eve talks with organizational and individual clients about the "delay in shifting corporate memory."

A simpler way of assessing outcome is to build upward appraisal into employee appraisal processes. At the end of each appraisal the employee is asked to give feedback to their boss on the ways they have enabled them to both perform better and to develop and learn in the last period, and the ways they could do this more effectively going forward. Tracking these comments before and after coaching gives clear data on the growing ability of the manager or leader to both manage and develop/coach their staff.

One can also use the Team Contribution Grid (Hawkins, 2017a: 312–313). In this the coachee, before their individual coaching, receives feedback from the team they lead or of which they are a member (or both), on their current value contribution both to and from the team and how this could be developed. They then receive feedback on how this has changed after the coaching has completed.

Value creation

Much has been written about the elements for inputs, outputs and outcomes and ways of effectively assessing them (see for instance Philips and Philips, 2007; Philips, Philips and Edwards, 2012). Much less has been written about the measurements of value creation.

1. Higher engagement with and from stakeholders

To create value, whether you are a commercial company, public sector service organization or a not-for-profit (better termed 'for benefit') organization, the first step in creating value is to achieve greater engagement with your stakeholders, both inside and outside the organization (Corporate Leadership Council, 2011; Rayton, 2012). Often the first group from which we would hope to see increased engagement is the employees.

Clare Chalmers is a leadership development specialist for a large mutual insurance and investment specialist organization. She has been particularly interested in how to make coaching work in organizations. Forty-two of the organization's managers received coaching during 2017 and 2018 concerning the engagement of their team members. All teams whose managers were involved and were in the bottom quartile of performance in the 2017 engagement results moved up by at least one quartile a year later. Coaching has been acknowledged by the board as having an important role to play in the ongoing development of their leaders and the engagement of their teams.

2. Higher appreciation from stakeholders: descriptor analysis

One of the key lead indicators in organizational performance is the way the organization is perceived by all its stakeholders. Many businesses invest a lot of time and money in collecting feedback from employees, customers, investors and other stakeholders and in analysing their press and media coverage. Very few systematically integrate all their data to create a wholistic organizational 360-degree feedback dash board. Multiple stakeholder perceptions, when joined up, provide a valuable intermediate measure of change in organizational performance and value creation. One of the ways we have developed to assist in this process is the "Descriptor Analysis" (Hawkins, 2017: 305–307). This can be carried out informally by asking what words the stakeholders would use to describe the engagement style of the coachee today and what words they would like to be able to use in one year's time. The follow-up feedback can repeat this exercise and evaluate changing perceptions.

One large British financial organization we worked with some time ago wanted to move from being currently seen as 'bureaucratic, British and institutional' to being 'the leading, European and innovative'. It geared its culture change and leadership development processes towards the goal of creating this shift and gradually over the next three years, it was able to see that each of its stakeholder groups was reporting a shift in how they perceived both the organization and its leadership moving towards the vision of how the company wanted to be seen.

The descriptor analysis can then be built into the stakeholder feedback questionnaire before and after individual or team coaching to see if the individual and/or the team are shifting their contribution to the overall culture change and towards more positive stakeholder perception.

3. Retention of best employees, promotion and impact

Measuring employee retention rates is both a gross measurement and can be misleading, as you could be retaining your worst performing employees and still be losing your best staff. It can nevertheless be a useful measure of an organizational benefit from Coaching. Case study E in Appendix 1, from India, shows a reduction in employee attrition from a very high 39 percent down to 12 percent, which is a clear dramatic change.

Some organizations have attempted to measure the retention of their best staff by using a three-by-three scoring grid, which rates all staff on a 1–3 scale for performance and 1–3 on potential for developing to more senior roles. This provides a foundation for measuring whether the leader being coached retains their team members who are in Box 9 (3 on performance and 3 on potential), and other high scorers. It also measures their ability to get improvements in the ratings across their team members and accelerate the readiness for, and achievement of, promotion in their direct reports. This approach emphasizes the key role every manager and leader plays in providing manager and leadership development 'on the job' and focussing coaching on increasing the leader's ability to be successful in this aspect of their role.

4. Increase in customers as advocates

There has been a general move away from measuring customer satisfaction, to measuring customer retention, to measuring customer's advocacy in their 'net-promoter scores', to measuring customer experience and engagement (Clark, Harrington and Myers, 2016). This has been led by some sectors that realize that customers' short-term high satisfaction scores can be misleading. In the car dealership sector, they found that high customer satisfaction at the point of purchasing a car was not strongly correlated with buying their next car from the same dealership. The key influence on customer retention was their experience of how they were related to and engaged by the organization, not just at the time of purchase but afterwards. Increasingly companies are relying on their customers as their 'unpaid sales force', advocating their products and services to family and friends and to promote their products through social media, on sites such as TripAdvisor and Trustpilot (a consumer review website for businesses worldwide). Measurement of the increased percentage of customers actively posting positive recommendations and the decrease in the percentage posting negative comments is a key measure of value creation. We have worked with hospitals by helping them to monitor their letters of compliments and complaints as another customer feedback process that can be linked back to development through coaching.

5. Increase in revenue and profitability

Many organizations that invest in coaching will ask about the 'return on investment', and how spending on the development of their people affects 'the bottom-line'. 'Return on Investment' is traditionally defined as the amount of profit, before tax and after depreciation from an investment made, usually expressed as a percentage of the original total cost invested. A number of writers have used ROI in their studies of coaching and claimed ROI of between 600–700 percent: McGovern et al (2001); Parker-Wilkins (2006) and Anderson (2001).

While he does not use an exact formula, Marshall Goldsmith (2011, online) operates a "pay by results" approach to coaching. At the start of an engagement he asks for agreement on two areas:

- What are the key behaviors that will make the biggest positive change in increased leadership effectiveness?
- Who are the key stakeholders that can determine (six to eighteen months later) if these changes have occurred?

He goes on to say: "We then get paid only after our coaching clients have achieved positive change in key leadership behaviors – and become more effective leaders – as determined by their key stakeholders."

The 6th Ridler Report (Mann, 2016) showed that only 14 percent of organizations measured ROI, little changed from 13 percent in 2007, although 80 percent said they would "value being able to evaluate coaching in this way, were data available" (2016: 20). One organization employing a relevant methodology was E.ON UK. Their first step was to move from employing 54 often single coaching providers to one provider using "a proprietary evaluation methodology which was embedded in the coaching process" (2016: 22). They used three-way meetings in the middle, as well as the beginning and end, of the assignments and questions included achievement of coaching objectives (8.6 out of 10) and coaching making a positive difference to their work performance (8.8 out of 10). The lowest score, for "demonstrate market and customer orientation," was still 7.2. Nick Smith's case study (Appendix 1, G, p256) demonstrates a rigorous evaluated programme over several years.

The 2010 Executive Coaching Survey by Sherpa Executive Coaching in Texas obtained returns from over 200 HR professionals from a wide variety of companies. Of these, 87 percent saw the value of executive coaching as either 'somewhat high' or 'very high'. However, only 18 percent of the HR professionals calculated the ROI on their coaching expenditure, but this was up from 7 percent on the previous year's survey, an increase of over 150 percent.

Return on investment in regard to coaching can be seen simply in the following formula:

ROI as a percentage =

$$\frac{\text{Programme Benefits} - \text{Programme Costs}}{\text{Programme Costs}} \times 100$$

Hawkins (2012: 170) developed a relatively simple way of calculating ROI in regard to coaching following the Sherpa methodology:

1   For every coaching contract, collect the issues addressed by the coaching and for each, estimate the cost of not addressing that issue, or the costed benefit of a performance improvement: e.g. productivity rise in the team £24,000 + reduction in staff turnover £36,000 = Total Benefit £60,000.

2   Multiply by the percentage attributed by the individual coachee or team to the coaching: e.g. the coachee reports that 50 percent of the productivity was directly attributable to the coaching and 20 percent of the reduced staff turnover. This gives us figures of £12,000 and £7,200 = £19,200 for the coaching benefit. More sophisticated measurement would be achieved by asking the coachee's boss and subordinates also to estimate this percentage and average them out.

3   Multiply by the degree of confidence in the estimation say 80 percent = £15,360 adjusted coaching benefit.

4   Subtract the total cost of the coaching = £5,000, which gives a net benefit of £10,360.

5   Then, to calculate ROI, we divide the net benefit £10,360 by the coaching cost £5,000 = 207.2 percent.

There are many weaknesses in the approaches that try and jump to measuring the ROI of their coaching in monetary terms, without first building in a much more rigorous systemic approach at all stages of the value chain. It is often an inexact science, with a great deal of subjective judgement, and driven by the pressure to demonstrate value quickly in purely financial terms. It ignores the many other factors that may have contributed to the value creating improvement. In many cases it only shows an associative connection, rather than a causative link. Michael West, in his work on effective team development in UK NHS hospitals (West, Guthrie, Dawson, Borrill and Carter, 2006; West and Dawson, 2012; West, 2013), first showed that hospitals that had effective real teams had lower mortality rates (an associative link), but then went on to show that those hospitals who then improved the number of their effective real teams saw a subsequent fall in patient mortality rates (indicating a stronger causative link).

We believe that the weakness in nearly all the attempts to measure ROI from coaching can only be overcome if we develop a stronger involvement of stakeholders in:

• contracting and setting the purpose of the coaching,
• reviewing the coaching process,

- evaluation methods of the coaching inputs, outputs, outcomes and value creation, right along the value chain.

Conclusion

In this chapter we have shown that whether you are a coachee, coach, supervisor, manager of coaching, or a leader sponsoring coaching in your organization, it is important that you engage with how you ensure that coaching is creating value right along the value chain. This involves thinking through how the assessment of the coaching inputs connects to the outputs in the coachee's development, behaviours, engagement and actions, to the outcomes these changes create, to the value they create for the full range of stakeholders. We suggest that only by developing these linkages can we address the issue of evaluating return on investment in ways that are more rigorous and well founded.

Evaluation should not be left to the end of the coaching process or just to coach researchers and coach managers. Every coach needs to think about how they build in corrective feedback loops and assessment into every coaching relationship and broadly into their coaching practice.

To do this we need to ask coachees, or have a feedback pro-forma that covers:

1 What did you do differently as a result of your last coaching session? For each difference please fill in answers 2–6.
2 What effect did this have that was different from what you would have done previously?
3 What did this lead to others doing differently as a result of this intervention?
4 What difference did that lead to in the organization?
5 What value did this create for the organization's stakeholders?
6 How did the last coaching session increase your capacity and/or capability as a leader?

Coaching supervision has a 'qualitative aspect' (see Chapter 10) and every coaching supervisor needs to encourage and enable not just personal reflection on the coaching process but on more rigorous assessment and evaluation of the coaching work and the value it creates. This is not just for the immediate parties, but all the wider stakeholders.

Chapter 13

Systemic coach training

Introduction

As we described in Chapter 3, coaching has developed from the world of psychology, psychotherapy and counselling in particular, while drawing on other elements. This was logical at the time when it rose to prominence around 40 years ago, and much of the training has understandably put coaching into that context. But what about for the 2020s? We invite you to begin a conversation with us.

Let's start by considering our own training as a coach:

- What subjects were covered in the coach training?
- What have you encountered in your coaching practice that in retrospect you wish had been covered in your training?
- What elements did you feel well prepared for? Which elements have you felt less well prepared for?
- What has changed/is changing contextually since you were trained?
- If you were designing a coach training, what additional material would you put in place, and what might you remove or change? If you have already designed one, are there any elements you would now like to add, subtract or develop?
- Having read this book, what do you think are additional curriculum elements needed to be a systemic coach?
- How can we better prepare ourselves for the challenges we face as coaches and as human beings?

In this chapter we will explore (a) the global context of coach training,(b) the coach development journey (including a case example),(c) the core curriculum we believe needs to be at the heart of the systemic coach training and (d) advocate the core learning design principles that we believe underpin systemic coach training.

The successful growth of coach trainings around the world

Coach training has developed exponentially in the last few decades. In 2016, the ICF estimated there were 53,000 coaches, nearly twice as many as ten years ago. By now there will be many thousands more. There is also a turnover as coaches join and leave the profession; some leave through retirement, others for commercial reasons, while others join and add to the numbers training now. While not all coaches will have coach-specific training, we can presume most do.

There are literally thousands of courses, some at masters level lasting for a few years, some just a few days, some generic in nature, others specializing in particular fields such as career, executive, relational, health, spiritual, personal, business coaching and so on. The main coaching professional bodies now accredit courses. There are also two global bodies for coach training, Association of Coach Training Organizations (ACTO) and Graduate School Alliance for Education in Coaching (GSAEC). Prices can vary from a few hundred pounds to many thousands. Some will advocate and include supervision, others don't. Some will attend to contracting or ethics in detail and others may do so in a cursory manner or not at all. Some will be run by leading practitioners, some by academics in the field and others will be led by people whose main motivation is supplementing their income, and then we will have mixtures of all in between.

In the 20th century, much of the emphasis in coaching and supervision training was on its scarcity. For several years, courses were mainly available in just a few countries, most of them English-speaking (with notable exceptions such as France, Germany and the Netherlands). This was changing by the turn of the 21st century and coach training is now widely, though not universally, available.

The systemic coach development journey

To be effective in enabling real-time learning and development of another person requires a lifelong commitment to self-development. Not only does this mean acquiring knowledge and skills, but more broadly, developing the whole of one's being. Eve recalls attending a masterclass given by coaching pioneer, the late Sir John Whitmore in 2007. He said, "If you only have time for one piece of development, do it on yourself" (Turner and Palmer, 2019: XXVIII). Personal development is at the heart of professional development.

We believe that training is partially about learning new skills and acquiring new knowledge, but that the core of all training is about the maturation and development of the coach. Many have argued that the most important differentiator in the quality of coaching is the quality of the relationship and the most important aspect of the coach's contribution is their own presence and maturation (de Haan, 2008; Clutterbuck and Megginson, 2011; Bachkirova, 2011; Lawrence and Moore, 2018; Kahn, 2014; Hawkins and Smith, 2013).

Thus the heart of all coach training is the individual developing themselves, as their own cognitive, emotional and ethical maturity (Hawkins, 2011c) are the core of all the coaching they will deliver (Maclean, 2019). Receiving coaching and/or counselling and psychotherapy for oneself is essential for being able to understand the work from the coachee perspective, as well as growing one's own self-awareness, emotional regulation, and relational and emotional intelligence.

Clutterbuck and Megginson (2011, 2010) produced a model of four stages in coach maturation. The four levels are model-based (control), process-based (contain), philosophy or discipline-based (facilitate), and systemic eclectic (enable). They suggest that many coaches start by rigidly applying a coaching model or method, and later progress to greater flexibility, by first being more process-oriented and then in stage three being more based on underlying principles and philosophy. The fourth stage of being systemic eclectic is marked by the coach drawing appropriately on a wide range of ways of being, perceiving and responding. Based on their work with coach assessment centres and training and researching coaches' approaches, Clutterbuck and Megginson (2010: 7) suggest the following are the ways coaches demonstrate they have reached this level.

- They have immense calm, because they have confidence in their ability to find the right tool if they need it.
- Yet they hardly ever use tools. When they do, it is subtly and integrated almost seamlessly into the conversation. Indeed, they allow the conversation to happen, holding the client in the development of insight and steering with only the lightest, almost imperceptible touches.
- They place great importance on understanding a technique, model or process in terms of its origins within an original philosophy.
- They use experimentation and reflexive learning to identify where and how a new technique, model or process fits into their philosophy and framework of helping.
- They judge new techniques, models and processes on the criterion of "Will this enrich and improve the effectiveness of my potential responses to client needs?"
- They use peers and supervisors to challenge their coaching philosophy and as partners in experimenting with new approaches.
- They take a systemic and holistic view of the client and the client's environment and of the coaching relationship and this makes them more sensitive to nuances of the situation and hence to what approaches they can employ.

This echoes our own approach in training and supervising coaches to develop to where their work is not based on tools and methods, but they can work collaboratively and co-creatively with the coachee to discover, through relational dialogue, the development that is necessary. Our systemic approach puts even more emphasis on the last of Clutterbuck and Megginson's points, in coaches developing the capability to bring in more aspects of the coachee's stakeholder world and wider systemic levels, including the ecological.

For systemic coaching, further self-development is essential, beyond that necessary for traditional coaches, for in addition to IQ and EQ (emotional intelligence), it is important to develop WeQ or collaborative intelligence. This includes the capacity to move beyond seeing individuals and individual perspectives, to perceiving the connections between individuals, between teams, and

Table 13.1 The ten steps in embracing greater systemic complexity in coaching

1	Coaching for oneself
2	Coaching a peer
3	Life coaching with an individual
4	Systemic coaching of a manager, leader, executive
5	Group coaching of managers, leaders etc.
6	Coaching a management or leadership team
7	Systemic team coaching of a leadership team in relation to its stakeholders
8	Coaching a team of teams
9	Orchestrating enterprise wide coaching
10	Eco-systemic coaching

between organizations and their stakeholders and finally between the human and 'more-than-human' worlds.

There is a development pathway that many coaches undertake (see Table 13.1), but many stop at one or other places on the journey. This is not wrong in itself, but we would argue there is an urgent need for more coaches to move beyond their current resting place and continue on their development journey to have the capacity to work with more systemic complexity.

In this book we have focussed on steps 4, 5 and 6. Peter's books on leadership team coaching (Hawkins, 2017a, 2018) focusses on steps 7 and 8 and in Chapter 8 we have touched on the urgent need for step 10.

Here is one short example of one of Peter's supervisees, Corine Hines, who describes her own journey and development of a more systemic approach, and the impact it has had on her work:

> I used to think of myself as a leadership coach, helping people in leadership roles be more effective in business. I believe my sessions were personally beneficial to my coachee and useful to their manager. I made sure the goals had a link to the business and did 3 way contracting. I got very positive feedback, and all was fine. However, I often had a question mark in my mind about the value created for the wider teams, the business, and beyond.
>
> I continued my personal development and over the years completed a team coaching course, had supervision with Hilary Lines and business mentoring with Peter Hawkins.
>
> I further developed my understanding of systemic coaching and this significantly changed how I view myself and how I work with my clients.
>
> An example of this is when I recently got a referral from a fast-growing distribution business, with a current turnover of £30 million a year, to offer coaching and training for three of their senior managers. When I met the Managing Director, Tim Goodson at DVS Ltd, instead of focusing on the development needs of the three managers I asked him about the growth plans

for the business, the succession plan (or lack thereof), the culture, and strategy and different stakeholders that the business served.

As the dialogue developed, I gradually became more of a trusted partner, standing shoulder to shoulder with Tim and his team – rather than just an outsourced training resource. What emerged from this meeting was a different way forward. Instead of three, one to one 6-month coaching interventions, we agreed that I would conduct a diagnostic feedback survey with the rest of the organisation.

This has led to working with the whole management team to explore what the 'business of tomorrow needs' from the collective leadership, its culture and how it is structured, and how they can all co-create this. Helping them individually and collectively develop the next stage of their business, instead of just trying to make today's senior managers 'work a bit harder' and 'run a bit faster' and drive the current leadership engine a bit harder with the fuel that is no longer fit for purpose."

Developing the systemic coaching curriculum

Much has been written about the core elements of coach training – and in this book we will outline the core elements that need to be added to these to develop systemic coaches.

The three-legged stool

Coaching over the last 40 years has attracted people who have either come from a business background and become more interested in helping individuals than in pursuing their business and organizational roles or from those with a psychology, counselling or psychotherapy background who are wanting to help relatively healthy people in organizations to become more successful. Many of the former lack the depth of psychological understanding and many of the latter lack the understanding of business, organizational dynamics and systems. Those with organizational backgrounds may also have worked in human relations, or as middle managers, and like those from the people professions have never been in leadership teams, or experienced what it is like to be a senior leader, with the weight of expectation, projection and responsibility bearing down upon you.

In Chapter 4 we introduced the important notion that the craft of business or executive coaching is built on the three-legged stool of:

a) The craft and practice of coaching;
b) Understanding psychology and, in particular, adult development and life stages;
c) Understanding team, organizational and wider stakeholder and systemic dynamics.

Executive coaching needs to stand on these three legs to provide a secure base. This includes principles, models, tools, methods and approaches.

a) **The craft and practice of coaching**. This includes the principles, models, tools, methods and approaches of coaching, but must start with differentiating the role of coach from other roles coaching students may have occupied or are familiar with such as leader, manager, problem solver, teacher, mentor, counsellor, psychotherapist, mediator, consultant, advisor. This centrally involves actively unlearning the often unconscious and automatic habits of engaging and responding that go with these other roles.

b) **Human psychology**, particularly adult development, but also understanding earlier development and how it shows up in adult behaviour, emotional reactivity and patterns of behaviour. Some awareness of mental disturbances is useful, such as addictions, delusional states, narcissism and sociopathic and psychopathic tendencies that coaches might encounter.

c) **Understanding businesses, organizations and systems**. Understanding the various stages in the development of business organizations – from start-up, growth, developing different functions, becoming more bureaucratic, founders leaving or handing over, acquisitions and mergers, bringing in private equity and/or going public with shareholders. It is also important to understand organizational dynamics and organizational change processes. Many of the coaches we supervise have a tendency to look at everything through a personal lens, failing to see that a great deal of what appears personal is an indicator of a team, organizational or system dynamic (Oshry, 1995, 1999; Hawkins, 2018).

Most coaches have a lopsided 'stool', and some lack one of the legs. The role of training is to ensure that all three legs are in place and balanced and to ensure that attention is payed to the battening between the legs and their interrelations in teaching, reflecting on practice and supervision.

The necessary competencies, capabilities and capacities

In Hawkins and Smith (2013), Peter wrote extensively about the need for coach development to integrate three levels: the acquisition of competencies; the development of capabilities and the growth of capacities.

Competencies we see as the ability to utilize a skill or use a tool.
Capability is the ability to use the tool or skill, at the right time, in the right way and in the right place.
Capacity is a human quality . . . rather than a skill and more to do with how you are, rather than what you do.

(Hawkins and Smith, 2013: 151)

Many training programmes have focussed almost exclusively on competencies, particularly those needed for the trainee to become accredited. The limitation of a purely competency-based approach is that having the necessary skills and tools does not necessarily mean that you know how to use these skills appropriately and effectively and how to adapt them for different people, situations and cultures. Competencies are often based on what made yesterday's coaches effective, rather than what will be needed for the coaching of tomorrow. We argue that coach training is a lifetime journey that helps the coach turn competencies into capabilities, through reflective practice and supervision. Also, by focussing on core capacities, these provide the container through which the coach can continually develop new and changing competencies and capabilities.

Systemic coaching competencies

Throughout this book we have shown key tools and methods that we believe systemic coaches need and which can helpfully be covered early in coach training. These include

1　Contracting skills (Chapter 5)
2　Managing the engagement of multi-stakeholders (Chapter 5 and 6)
3　Collecting and feeding back 360-degree feedback (Chapter 6)
4　Collaborative inquiry skills (Chapter 6)
5　Systemic listening skills (Chapter 7)
6　Managing the stages and processes of a coaching session and relationship (Chapter 6)
7　Group and systemic team coaching (Chapter 9)
8　Making good use of supervision (Chapter 10)
9　Understanding ethics and coaching within clear boundaries (Chapter 11)
10　Understanding evaluation and being focussed on outcomes and value creation (Chapter 12)

These competencies need to be built on a solid foundation and embedded in thinking and perceiving systemically (see Chapter 3 and subsequent chapters). This requires the unlearning of linear thinking, entity thinking, seeing everything as 'belonging' to the individual, polarity and dualistic thinking. Without real attention to this unlearning, new competencies and capabilities will be built on the wrong foundations and the coaching will remain instrumental.

Capabilities can only be learned experientially, through action learning. In order to really be capable of good work, the coach or trainee coach needs to be able to prepare to coach someone, coach them, receive feedback, reflect on their work and use this feedback and reflection to deepen their understanding and turn their competencies into capabilities. This learning process can result in a genuine integration. Supervision has a vital role to play in helping the supervisee turn their competencies into capabilities, and to ensure that the capabilities are held within an ever-increasing capacity to work with others with fearless compassion.

In Chapters 5, 6 and 7 we have outlined some of the key competencies and capabilities that we believe are essential for the systemic coach. These include the ability to: contract and recontract with multiple clients and stakeholders; ensure the work is delivering value not just to the individual and their organization (the double client), but the stakeholders of both; listen, not only actively, accurately and empathically, but systemically, hearing what is in the wider field; hear what is said and what is deleted, distorted and denied; move from exploration and insight into embodied change and enable fast-forward rehearsals; and enable coaching development to continue between sessions and beyond the time of the coaching relationship.

Systemic coaching capabilities

Having learned the competencies in the aforementioned areas – developing capabilities comes through practice, reflection and supervision of the coaching process where these competencies are applied. In this way the coach learns how to apply the competencies differentially and appropriately depending on the needs of the individual coachee and the needs of their wider contexts.

Some important capabilities that need to be developed at this stage of the journey include

1   Deepening the coach dialogue through the four levels of engagement (Chapter 7), from addressing issues and problems to exploring patterns of behaviour and then the emotional patterns and the mind-sets and assumptions that drive these patterns.
2   Moving beyond insight and good intentions to create a 'transformational shift' and embodied learning in the coaching room, through using 'fast-forward rehearsals' and other embodied techniques (Chapter 6 and 7).
3   Engaging stakeholder's involvement in all stages of the coaching process and managing conflicting stakeholder needs (Chapter 5 and 6).
4   Effective contracting (Chapter 5).
5   Effective evaluation (Chapter 12).
6   Being able to help the coachee to coach their own staff and their own team (Chapter 9).

'Capacities' relate to one's being, rather than one's doing. They are human qualities that can be nurtured and refined. Capacities can also be thought of in their root meaning of the space we have within us for containing complexity. We have all met people who seem to have little internal space from which to relate to us – and others who carry a seemingly infinite internal spaciousness, which tells us that they are fully present with whatever we feel we need to share or do.

Capacities are not things to be acquired or places to arrive. Each capacity takes our whole life to develop and development is not a uni-directional process. Without attention to our practice and supervision, each of these capacities can atrophy within us, and our effectiveness decline. Development and learning are for life, not just for school. The joy is that there is always more to be learnt.

Hawkins and Smith (2013: 247–248)

Systemic coaching capacities

Hawkins and Smith (2013: 272) list core capacities that we believe need to be part of the continuing lifelong development of all coaches and supervisors. These are, with slight additions:

1   Appropriate leadership
2   Authority, presence and impact
3   Relationship engagement capacity
4   Ability to develop leadership, reflective practice and self-supervision in others
5   Holding one's power and ability to impact
6   Working across difference, transculturally sensitive to individual differences and awareness of one's own cultural history and lenses
7   Ethical maturity
8   A sense of humour, humanity and humility

We believe that to develop as effective systemic coaches these are all important and there are additional capacities we need to develop:

1   **Systemic being and relating**: Having learned about systemic thinking and perceiving early in their training, systemic coaches continually need to develop their capacity in systemic ways of being and relating. In Hawkins (2018), Peter has developed 13 'Systemic Beatitudes' or attitudes of being that are core capacities for systemic team coaches which also apply to systemic coaches.
2   **Ecological awareness**: The capacity to see all human activity as residing in, and supported by, the more-than-human-world of the wider ecology.
3   **Systemic hope**: When confronted with the magnitude of the challenges facing our world, to be able to avoid swinging between despair and heroism, but to hold a wider perspective, in both the dimensions of time and space, and have hope that the wider systems have a greater capacity to bring healing.
4   **Wide-angled empathy and compassion**: The capacity to have empathy and compassion not just for the individual(s) with you in the coaching session, but for every person and organization and system mentioned in their story (Hawkins, 2019). To locate problems, difficulties and conflict, not in individuals or parts of a system, but in the connections, and to coach the connections.
5   **Being a lifelong learner**: The capacity to see every coachee and coaching situation as a new teacher, especially the most difficult ones. This is supported by the capability to continue to use supervision proactively and effectively. This capacity is central to helping clients also become life-long-learners.

6   **Mindfulness and self-reflectiveness**: The capacity to notice one's own fleeting thoughts and emotions, without becoming attached to them, or judgemental of them and to see the systemic dances you are part of, rather than just seeing your dancing partners.

Core principles for training

We believe it is important that to train coaches in systemic coaching, the training itself must be built on systemic principles and demonstrate these in its educational approach.

Lifelong learning

Coaching is not something that can be learned on a short or long coach training programme; it is a craft discipline that one continues to learn throughout one's life. We often use the analogy that the training programme is like the 'base camp' at the beginning of climbing a very tall mountain. 'Base camp' is where you go to become acclimatized, try out the tools, gaze at the mountain and relate it to maps and possible routes, carry out various practice sorties on lower levels of the mountain, study the changing weather, and share stories about past climbs. The deeper learning happens when you are on the mountain, the weather becomes unpredictable, there are ravines not shown on the maps, and unexpected avalanches. Solo climbing of difficult mountains is for the very experienced and/or foolhardy and comes with enormous risks. Teamwork and local guides are highly recommended. This is why we believe that lifelong supervision is essential for all coaches (Hawkins and Smith, 2013; Hawkins, 2018; Turner and Palmer, 2019).

Involves the whole person

We still come across coach trainings that are centred on learning models, tools and methods and that believe if you have a good process model of coaching such as GROW or CLEAR, and have a bank of helpful questions and some popular psychology, you can become a coach. We believe that the main tool the coach brings into the coaching room is their whole self, and it is this whole self that needs to be focussed on, developed and matured (Turner and Palmer, 2019). David Clutterbuck (Clutterbuck and Megginson, 2011, 2010) has developed some helpful models of coach maturity on four levels (see p. 202). In previous writings we (and others) have also drawn on developmental models from counselling psychology (see Hawkins and Smith, 2013: 62–70); vertical models of leadership development (Hawkins and Smith, 2013); and developmental models of ethical and moral maturity (Carroll and Shaw, 2013; Hawkins, 2011c; Laske, 2003; Kohlberg, 1981; Loevinger, 1976). We believe that all coach trainers need to understand maturational stages and use these models to design the stages of their training. In addition, we believe that developmental stages should be taught on coach trainings, so trainees can use these maps to

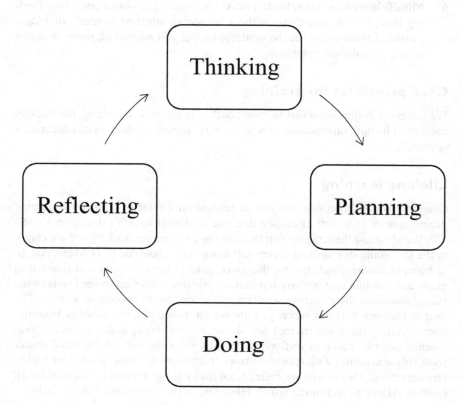

Figure 13.1 Action learning cycle

look both at their clients' maturational journey and also their own, and the relationship between the two.

Cycles of action learning

We follow Bateson (1972) in believing that all important learning is action learning and that "to know and not to act on that knowing is not to know" (Latour, 2017). The acquisition of data is what Bateson calls 'zero learning' –it may be a preparation for real learning, but in itself has little or no value. Like many coaches we have been influenced by the Kolb learning cycle (1971, 1984), Juch (1983), Revans' action learning (1982) and others who have developed approaches to adult learning which demonstrate that learning is richest when it follows a cycle that incorporates several steps: action; reflection on the action; new sense making and theorizing; followed by planning new action. Hawkins and Smith (2013: 153) have simplified the original Kolb cycle and developed the above four stage model (Figure 13.1).

When training coaches, we encourage and guide students and readers to reflect on any new thinking, theories or models, and consider what it means to them and how it relates to their experience and other learning, and then explore ways these new ideas can influence their practice (Thinking into Planning). It is important that, while the learning is in short-term memory, the student takes this learning into 'doing' – coaching their fellow students or clients (Planning into Doing). It is important that this process is followed by reflection, both through feedback from clients and observers, self-reflection and supervision. In supervision the learning from this reflection can inform and reform the thinking (Reflection into Thinking). Then the cycle begins again.

In this way the learning is not 'introjected' (Perls, 1969) and swallowed whole but really chewed and digested and integrated into the student's embodied knowing and understanding of the work.

In a coach's lifelong learning process action learning takes place in many cycles and at different levels. Here are some of the cycles:

- Cycle one, when the student coach is on their initial training, the 'doing' may involve practice coaching in small groups of three. Each has time in the role of coach, coachee and observer. Each 'real play' (not role play) coaching session is followed by structured reflection and feedback. Sometimes trainers will sit in on these practice sessions and provide feedback.
- Cycle two then takes us into practice with volunteers, with structured reflection and feedback and regular supervision. At this stage this will often be received from one of the trainers or a supervisor linked to the programme.
- In cycle three the practice is with actual clients and supervision continues. This is after the completion of initial training but may be part of advanced training.
- Cycle four entails continuous movement around the action learning cycle throughout one's career, still with supervision. It may involve writing about one's work, sharing it at conferences, and/or beginning to train and supervise others. Many of the students on our coach supervision trainings around the world have commented on how training and beginning to be a coach supervisor has developed their coaching practice, even more than advanced coach training. By this stage we have learned to reflect-in-action as well as reflect-on-action (Schon, 1983) – meaning we are bringing our skills of reflectiveness into the moment with our clients during the sessions, rather than doing so only afterwards, whether alone or in supervision.

Kolb (1984) described different learning styles and this has since been developed by others such as Honey and Mumford (1992). Kolb illustrated four styles and a Learning Styles Inventory questionnaire which can be used to determine our particular style:

- Diverging (feeling and watching). Divergent thinkers tend to be sensitive and like to watch and wait before acting. They need to be given time to assimilate new learning.

- Assimilating (watching and thinking). Assimilative learners prefer abstract ideas to relationships and would prefer to learn theory before trying something in practice.
- Converging (doing and thinking). Convergent learners are most at home with technical skills, rather than interpersonal ones, so coaching may not be the best profession for them, but if they can learn by doing, then they are more likely to learn what is needed.
- Accommodating (doing and feeling). Those who have an accommodating learning style prefer to do something immediately, 'hands-on', without having analyzed it, relying on intuition rather than logic.

Most people have a tendency towards one style, but it is important for students and staff to understand that all of us have different learning styles and to allow for that, starting by building on the student's dominant style but helping them to extend it and avoid getting stuck in a short-cut learning loop. It also helps us to be observant of our clients' preferences so that we can help them most effectively.

In Hawkins and Smith (2013: 154), these potential shortcuts are described as:

1   **Fire-fighting or compulsive pragmatic activity**. This is the plan-do-plan-do trap where the motto is: 'If what you plan does not work, plan and do something different'. The learning stays at the level of trial and error.
2   **Post-mortemising**. This is the do-reflect-do-reflect trap, where the motto is: 'Reflect on what went wrong and correct it'. The learning here is restricted to error correction.

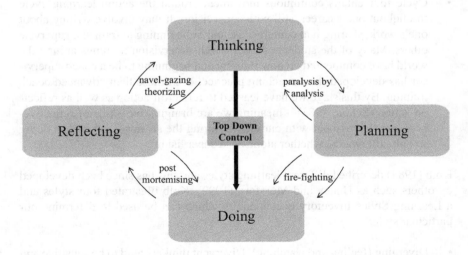

Figure 13.2 Learning cycle shortcuts

3 **Navel gazing and theorizing**. This is the reflect-theorize-reflect-theorize trap, where the motto is: 'Philosophize on how things could be better, but never risk putting your theories to the test'.
4 **Paralysis by analysis**. This is the 'analyze-plan-analyze some more' trap, where the motto is: 'Think before you jump, plan how to do it and think a bit more'. Learning is limited by the fear of getting it wrong or taking a risk.
5 **Totalitarian response**. This is the theorize-do trap, where the motto is: 'Work it out in theory and then impose it on them'.

Using the system of the training and its learning community as a learning laboratory

To provide a systemic training necessitates that we not only attend to the learning needs of each of the individual trainees, but also regularly reflect on the wider system of the learning community. This ensures that we are not just learning about how individual coachee learning and development is embedded in the wider nested systems of their team, function, organization and wider ecosystems but also learning how each individual trainee's learning is nested in the wider systems of the peer learning group, the learning community of trainees and faculty, the stakeholder community of individual and organizational clients (current and future), the wider ever-developing system of the coaching profession and the global interface between the one human family and the wider ecology. By regularly taking time out to attend to the many nested systems of the learning community, we can help trainees develop the systemic muscle of moving their attention from self to other; to relational connection; to group dynamic; to community culture; to wider stakeholder systemic processes and needs; to the wider ecology, and back again. We focus on how every element is both nested in wider systemic levels and these are all nested within each element as well as notice how the systemic dance between the nested systems can be repeated at many levels.

Conclusion

Not only do we believe that coaching needs to develop a new paradigm for the 21st century but that this must start by encompassing the way we educate and train coaches. At the heart of the training must be a recognition of whom coaching serves beyond the individual, and helping the coach learn to be not only client-centred but also stakeholder-centred.

In the same way that we advocate that coaching needs to be partnership-based, we are advocating that it needs to be stakeholder- and future-centred, focussed on creating outcome value for all current and future stakeholders, both human and more-than-human. In this chapter we have outlined how training can not only provide the training necessary for this, but also model a systemic approach in the way the training is structured, developed and reflected on.

Chapter 14

Bringing it all together and responding to the future

Introduction

The core quest of this book has been to answer the challenge of the black frontline manager in Cape Town (see Chapter 1) and discover how we move on from so much 'coaching being highly expensive personal development for the already highly privileged', to coaching delivering value beyond the individual. We live in extremely challenging times, and one of our challenges as the human species is to discover how to live in a globally crowded and interconnected world in partnership with the more-then-human world, recognizing that we are just one small part of a much bigger whole. We need to discover how to reverse what is becoming a 'suicidal' path of eco-destruction; despite all the earth summits and well-meaning plans, human emissions, pollution and destruction of habitats and species are getting worse.

We no longer have the luxury of just spending our time changing the world one person at a time.

We believe that work needs to be based on an ecological ethic, focussed on the interrelationships of humans and the 'more-than-human world' and agree with O'Brien (2008) that

> An enabled ecology means that people, organizational goals, and espoused values are aligned, and that the emotional and psychological aspects of an institution are congruent with the basic, deeper, and higher attributes of human nature. Cultivating this kind of ecology requires a values-based, vision- driven leadership – a careful nurturing of the corporate culture and an acute moral awareness on the part of both managers and individual workers.
>
> (O'Brien, 2008: 3)

We have a very limited window in which to create substantial and global change in our species, or some of the effects of global warming will become irreversible (see IPCC, 2018). In May 2019 experts from 50 countries published a report on biodiversity showing that a million plant and animal species now face extinction within decades, a rate of destruction tens to hundreds of times higher than the average over the past 10 million years. This poses as big a challenge to the world as rising temperatures with a potential loss of plants, insects and other creatures that will affect our food supply, clean water and pollination (IPBES, 2019). In the coaching profession we must ask: "What is it we in coaching can uniquely do that the world of tomorrow needs?" "What is our best contribution to the necessary paradigm shifts in human consciousness and how do we partner with those in other professions that share this concern?"

In this final chapter we will pull together the strands that we have woven throughout this book, of ways that coaching is moving and can move farther, from being self-centred to being stakeholder centred, delivering value to the coachee's team, organization and their many stakeholders and the wider communities and ecology in which their work takes part and is sustained.

We will then address the many ways that coaches are recognizing the privilege of their training and position to make a difference and are applying their coaching expertise well beyond coaching individual managers and leaders.

We will end with a call to action and an invitation to readers to join us in considering what each of us can do to raise our game, to increase our impact both in and beyond coaching and make a greater positive difference in our shared world.

So, in this final chapter we invite you to consider two important questions:

What can you do to increase the value you deliver in your coaching, not just to the individual coachee, but to all their many stakeholders?

What can you do to use the privilege of your coaching training and experience to create a greater beneficial impact in the world?

Shifting the coaching paradigm

We have covered many different aspects of how coaching can become systemic and deliver value beyond the coachee. Here we will summarize and integrate them.

Partner with the coachee

We showed in the early chapters of this book how coaching can move from seeing the individual coachee as the client, to recognizing the double client of the individual and the organization, to a third position of seeing the individual as our partner in the coaching work to deliver value to all the individual's and the organization's stakeholders. This demonstrated how coaching can move from something that is done by the coach, to something that the coach and coachee do collaboratively, along with the third crucial element in the coaching, which is the curriculum of challenges that life is presenting the coachee. We suggest it is the triangle of coachee, coach and context that co-create the coaching process in service of the many stakeholders of the individual and their organization.

Partner with the organization that employs you

Many organizations are moving from focussing simply on 'shareholder value' to how to deliver 'shared value' for all their stakeholders (Porter and Kramer, 2011; Elkington and Zeitz, 2014); not only the investors and funders, the customers and suppliers, the employees and contractors but also the communities and the wider ecology that the organization operates in and is supported by. We believe coaching should actively support this direction, both at the organizational and the individual levels.

When supervising coaches, be they external or internal coaches, if they are coaching three or more individuals in the same organization, we ask them how they are also supporting the organizational learning beyond the learning of the individuals. With small numbers this may be limited as we would ensure nothing is done that would breach the agreed confidentiality with an individual but it is to embed the sense that coaching is a systemic activity and the higher the numbers a coach works with the more themes and patterns can be identified and shared (which would be mentioned in contracting). In Chapter 4 we shared the methodology we developed of 'harvesting the learning', where coaches can individually or collectively reflect and analyze the organizational and cultural patterns that are emerging in their coaching and find ways of feeding these back to the organizational leadership, while preserving confidentiality of individual issues and coachees. We then also described how to facilitate a dialogue between the strategy of the organization and what is showing up about the cultural patterns through the coaching community.

Purpose-led coaching

Stakeholder centred coaching is not just about discovering what your current and future stakeholders want or need from you, using a 'future-back' and 'outside-in' inquiry process but also discovering how coachees can discover and fulfil their deeper and wider purpose. Our initial meetings with individuals wanting coaching includes asking them about themselves and what they are passionate about, what really matters in their life, the positive difference they want to make in the world. Thus, the coaching is facing both ways – what the coachee can uniquely do and what is the purpose out there in the world that the coachee can respond to. We have also shown how individuals and organizations that are purpose led, are more creative, productive and fulfilled.

Contracting to discover the work that the wider world needs us to do

To carry out purpose-led and stakeholder centred coaching requires that we engage with multi-stakeholder contracting; in Chapter 5 we have outlined both the latest research and best practice in doing this. This multi-stakeholder contracting needs to happen not only at the beginning of the coaching assignment but as a regular cyclical process within the whole coaching journey.

Contracting on how we will do it together

Having discovered the work that the coachee, their organization and their world need the coaching to focus on, the coach and coachee need to contract about how they are going to work collaboratively to fulfil this work. In Chapters 5 and 6 we show how this contracting needs not only to cover the practical arrangements of place, timing, costs, work between sessions, confidentiality and other boundary arrangements etc., but also the best ways of collaborating and the different but equal roles of each party.

Bring the wider stakeholders into the coaching room, literally and metaphorically

The voice of the stakeholders should not just enter the coaching room at the times of multi-stakeholder contracting and review but should bring these voices into the coaching process, either directly through shadowing or coaching the coachee live in their engagement with their team or stakeholders, or indirectly through action techniques such as role play, stepping into the shoes and position of the stakeholders, sculpting, constellations etc.

Move beyond insight and good intentions to embodied learning and action

We discovered through our supervision many years ago that the biggest frustration of coaches is when their clients have an 'aha moment' of insight, turn this into an action plan, and then often come back to their next coaching session not having followed through on their planned actions. Often in supervision, the coach then blames or pathologizes the coachee, saying they lacked courage or commitment, or berates themselves for not being 'good enough' as a coach. Instead we encourage them to explore what needs to change about their coaching and way of being to avoid this pattern. There is an old English saying: "The road to hell is paved with good intentions." We need to realize that insight and good intentions are helpful but not sufficient to create sustainable change. Action plans are created with words by the right hemisphere neo-cortex, but change is always embodied. It is really important that we do not stop the coaching at the action planning stage but facilitate moving from words and thinking to embodied action. In Chapter 7 we describe how to carry out 'fast-forward rehearsals' and embodied commitments.

Regularly review our joint work, with stakeholder input and re-contracting

Reviews should not be something that happen at the end of the process, but regularly throughout the process. That way, the coaching partnership can reflect on what has been achieved and how the collaboration is working to fulfil the work agreed on and also how, from the first cycle of coaching, we can improve the second and subsequent cycles. Often the goals and arrangement that are set at the beginning of the work can be upgraded and changed, as together we discover more in the process of the coaching. Coaching itself should be a constant action learning cycle of doing, reflecting, new contracting, new ways of working together and new ways of putting it into action.

Have systemic supervision on our work

We believe it is impossible to do good quality systemic coaching without also having good quality systemic supervision. This is, as we explored in Chapter 10, because we cannot be outside of any system we work with as we become part of all systems we interact with and it is very difficult to see the system we are part of co-creating. As the old Chinese proverb goes: "The last one to know about the sea is the fish." We all have not only blind spots, but deaf spots and dumb spots, things we are not seeing, not hearing and not voicing. Our bodies absorb much more information from the coaching than we are consciously aware of. Much of what we discover remains as what Christopher Bollas describes as the "unthought known," that which we know through our body and in other parts of our brain, that has not been processed by the neo-cortex, cognitive understanding. Supervision can facilitate us stepping off the dance floor of the coaching relationships and see the systemic dance from the balcony, thus being able to process the great deal of information that has been communicated, but of which we are not consciously aware.

Build evaluation into our work, as well as the wider coaching research

It is important that not only are we individually continually learning and developing our work as coaches, but that the coaching profession is collectively learning and developing too, so we are together developing coaching that is 'future-fit' rather than one that is relying on what worked in previous periods of time. In Chapter 12 we explored the need for our coaching evaluation to move beyond feedback on inputs, where we ask the coachee as a customer for feedback on the coaching and the coach. This is what our colleague Jonathan Passmore describes as evaluating "how much the coachee loved their coach!" Evaluation needs to look at the learning and development outputs of the coaching and how these get turned into beneficial outcomes for the coachee's stakeholders, and through this create beneficial value for the coachee, stakeholders, wider communities and the ecology.

Coaching beyond the boundaries of the coaching room – widening the impact

In this book we have mostly focussed on how systemic coaching can create more of an impact through the paradigm shift of working with the individual or the team, not as a client but as a partner, shoulder to shoulder, with them facing the needs of all their stakeholders, discovering what their stakeholders need them to learn, develop and step up to through the coaching. We have shown how the way we engage stakeholders directly and indirectly in contracting, goal setting, feedback, review and evaluation can increase the impact and ripple effect of the coaching to deliver benefits beyond those for the individual and the coach.

However, there are other ways that coaches and coaching can, and are, having a beneficial impact beyond 'delivering very expensive personal development for the already highly privileged' and it is to these that we now turn.

Redistributive coaching

"The history of the twentieth century revolved to a large extent around the reduction of inequality between classes, races and genders" (Harari, 2016: 74), but the short history of the 21st century has seen a rapid and, for many, frightening increase in social inequality. This has been fuelled by many factors, including the rapid growth in house prices, particular in large metropolitan cities; the growth of the underclass, with casual labour, freelancing and zero hours contracts; the growing concentration of capital which creates more wealth for the wealthy; and the concentration of fewer companies such as Amazon, Google and Facebook, which can control value chains and amass data. It is estimated that 1 percent of the world's population own half the world's wealth (*Newsweek,* 14 November, 2017) and may own 64 percent by 2030 based on a projection by the UK House of Commons library (The Guardian, 7 April 2018). In January 2019 the annual Oxfam briefing paper suggested that "Last year 26 people owned the same as the 3.8 billion people who make up the poorest half of humanity" (Oxfam, 2019: 10) a figure that in a year had reduced from 43 people (Oxfam, 2018).

Harari (2016: 75) fears that the growth of inequality will continue, driven by several forces: (a) historically poor countries with low costs of labour could develop through taking on the outsourced manufacturing and production of the richer countries and thus create their own industrial revolution, but with AI, robotization and 3D printing, this route is becoming less available; (b) riches will increasingly go to those who can control and own the data, and labour will be a less needed resource; and (c) the rich will be able to gain greater advantage though the convergence of biotech and infotech providing enhanced health, longevity, education and brain capacity. Harari (2016: 75) writes: "if more money can buy them enhanced bodies and brains, with time the gap will only widen."

Stiglitz (2015) and Piketty (2014) have shown that growing inequality is not just bad for those who become poorer, but also for the so called 'winners', as widening inequality brings with it greater social unrest and instability – the rich have to spend more of the wealth protecting themselves, paying higher taxes for more police, prisons, hospitals and social welfare. Wilkinson and Pickett (2010) observe that as affluent countries have grown richer, there have been long-term rises in rates of anxiety, depression and numerous other social problems.

Unless we as coaches become aware of the social, ecological and political changes that are both around us and we are part of, coaching could contribute to increasing this growing divide. The rich could have their lives and capacity to adapt enhanced further with coaching, resilience practices, yoga, mindfulness, while the under-classes, in both rich and poor countries become more marginalized.

Already in the coaching industry many are waking up to this danger and are taking responsibility for doing something to redistribute the benefits of coaching, moving against the economic tide, which will drive its benefits to the 'already highly privileged'. We are aware of five different forms of action that coaches are doing and could do more of, which we will now briefly explore.

I. Mixed economy

For many years, like many coaches we supervise, train and meet, both of us have operated a mixed economy in our own businesses by offering different fee levels for different sectors and countries where we coach and supervise. We have very different hourly and day rates for the commercial sector, the public sector and the not-for-profit (better termed 'for benefit') sector. We also charge different rates depending on the country where we are working, in person or virtually, that goes someway to recognizing the different national levels of economic wealth.

Increasingly the growth in employment is not coming from the large global corporations but from small start-ups and growth businesses, who have both less time and less money to purchase coaching but have as great, if not greater need. It is estimated that 50 percent of start-up businesses go bust in their first two years of existence, many of them through avoidable mistakes. These companies need a mixture of systemic individual, team and organizational coaching, alongside business mentoring – a mixed skill set that is still in short supply. Some national and regional governments are recognizing this need and provide state provision of leadership development and individual, team and organizational coaching and business mentoring for developing businesses, and Peter has been supervising some of this critical work. Where there is no state help, Peter has found ways of supporting important small business growth by charging them a very low fee, combined with a 'carried bonus' that they pay when they hit certain revenue and profitability targets.

2. Tithing

Charles Handy, a widely published and respected business guru, wrote with great prescience about the growth of portfolio careers. He (Handy, 1994: 185) described how we need to think about four different types of work: (1) paid work, (2) gift work, (3) homework and (4) study work. This is extremely relevant to those working as coaches, who, to be effective, need to be continually developing their skills and capacities through supervision and other forms for reflection and study work; ensuring they have a strong resourceful family and social base to work from to which they contribute through 'home work'; making enough money through 'paid work' that enables them to also have discretionary time for 'gift work' – using their skills to make a beneficial impact on the wider world.

We supervise a number of coaches who tithe or dedicate a percentage (some a tenth) of their coaching time to support causes that cannot afford even reduced-price coaching. Tithing was a process that was used in mediaeval Europe where 10 percent of your produce was taken to support the work of the church, monasteries and nunneries. Tithing now has a much looser but greater possibility, of giving back not just with money but with the skills and capacities that are the harvest of our privilege of education, training and experience, not available to a vast majority.

One example of a collective project that has utilized many coaches' 'gift work' is 'CoachActivism' launched in 2016 – both of us were active members for the first three years (for a case study see Turner and Palmer, 2019: 13–15). This is how Lily Seto describes the launch in Vancouver Island, Canada:

The air was electric as I watched 29 (of 42) participants from our global community literally and figuratively sign onto the Orientation call for our CoachActivism project. Participants on this project are from countries including Canada, the USA, Lebanon, South Africa, Britain, Greece, Portugal, just to name a few! There were the committee members who worked hard and passionately to bring the project to this launch day; there were the trainers who stepped forward to offer training in basic areas that we want to pay attention to when coaching in and around the refugee movement (trauma, ethics, boundaries management, transactional analysis, and cross cultural coaching); there were the six coaching supervisors who stepped up to support the coaches as they coached, and of course, there were the 20 coaches from both Canada and Greece!

The project was to provide free coaching to frontline workers with refugee agencies. The coaches who gifted their time received free supervision from supervisors (including Eve) 'gifting' their supervision time. The supervisors met in a virtual supervision group, which received supervision on their supervision 'gifted' by Peter. Subsequently many coaches and supervisors, including us, have been involved in 'gifting' to "EthicalCoach" (see ahead). There are many examples throughout the profession from people working with prisoners (McGregor, 2015), to the EMCC's Social Responsibility scheme which encourages volunteering within country communities.

3. Diversifying the industry

Although there has been an enormous growth in coaches, coach supervisors and coach trainings throughout the world, the coaching industry is still significantly dominated by white privileged westerners, with North America and Western Europe having by far the largest concentration of trained coaches, followed by other areas of 'European diaspora' (Ryde, 2019) such as Australia, New Zealand, Singapore, and South Africa. Even in these countries it is noticeable how coaching is very 'white' dominated. We have much to do to diversify our own industry and profession. This we believe can be done in three ways:

a) **White Awareness**. We suggest all white coaches include in their training some focus on understanding the cultural history, mindsets, assumptions and privilege that comes with being white, which they carry with them into their coaching and which can become a barrier to effective trans-cultural work, an awareness which serves towards broadening out the profession. Too often trans-cultural training for white people focusses on looking through the binoculars to try and understand other cultures, rather than looking in the mirror at our own taken-for-granted ways of perceiving, thinking and being. Ryde (2009, 2019) provides a useful model of working through the necessary stages of white awareness.

b) **Actively opening the doors to greater diversity**. Barbara Walsh who wrote case study C in Appendix 1, from South Africa, recognized that the whole coaching business in South Africa was dominated by white coaches, supervisors and trainers in a country where white people only make up 8.9 percent of the population (2011 census) but have politically and economically dominated for centuries. They are setting up a programme for all their white full-time coaches to mentor a young black internal coach working within an organization, to help them accelerate their own development and contribution to the coaching community in South Africa.

c) **Taking coaching to countries that need it but cannot afford it**. Ben Croft, founder and President of WBECS, the largest virtual conference and training community of coaches, in 2017 launched EthicalCoach, supported by a number of founding Coaches including Peter (www.ethicalcoach.org). The first large scale initiative got under way in 2018 in Ethiopia in which Eve and her colleagues through her learning organization for supervisors' the Global Supervisors' Network (GSN, 2019) have been involved, gifting time and skills.

"The Ethical Coach vision was initiated in Ethiopia. By introducing NGO leaders from non-government/civil society organizations to the power of coaching, the goal is to support them in their quest to make a substantive difference in the lives of millions of children and families in need. The journey began with the Ethiopian NGO Leadership Coaching Summit in October 2018 and the launch of a coaching programme that engages teams of coaches, comprised of world-class international coaches together with local coaches, in supporting the efforts of NGOs serving some of Ethiopia's most vulnerable populations. The entire programme is designed to foster local sustainability and is being evaluated through a rigorous assessment process that will allow best practices and case studies to be developed for replication around the world" (Ethical Coach, 2019).

One of the supervisees Peter trained and worked with, Trevor Waldock, has gone from being a coach and coach trainer in London, to leading leadership programmes for young leaders across Africa (www.emerging-leaders.net). They describe their work as follows:

There is no sustainable change anywhere in the world without good, strong and effective LEADERSHIP in any area of personal, community or national life. We bring leadership training to everyone, because we believe EVERY-ONE IS A LEADER. . . . and it will take leadership to achieve all 17 of the SDG from now until 2030 (Sustainable Development Goals). It takes leadership to get more girls into school worldwide. It takes leadership to stop gender-based violence in your community or get yourself tested for HIV/AIDS. It takes leadership to repair broken relationships, or claw ourselves out of debt, change the things that aren't working in our lives and keep hold of our life-pen, to write our own unique story. It takes leadership to face and climb impossibly high walls that challenge us at different stages of life. It takes leadership to achieve goals for our families and save for a better future; leadership is about taking initiative and living courageously. It takes leadership to see and take responsibility for what we want to change in our communities, to fight for justice and equality and to stand up for the weak and vulnerable. All this is leadership. . . . Our training equips people to:

- LEAD their lives proactively and to release their potential
- LEAD their teams,
- LEAD their finances and
- LEAD a project to benefit others.

4. Focusing coaching on the future benefit makers

A number of coaches we have mentored and supervised have decided to become more choiceful in where they work and who they support. One switched from well-paid coaching in large global oil and gas businesses to coaching small renewable energy start-ups and growth businesses. Other colleagues have decided to continue working with carbon, mining and tobacco industries, but only where they can coach the parts of the industry that are working towards a changing purpose, for example working with a major tobacco company on a post tobacco future, and helping a major oil company on how it moves beyond carbon-based energy. Prishani Satyapal – based in South Africa – has been using her coaching skills to work with the Pope's commission on mining. Paul Lim in Singapore has focussed his pro-bono efforts on coaching frontline teachers in schools, who have the responsibility for preparing the next generation to cope with the challenges we are leaving them.

5. Awakening the profession

Much can be done and needs to be done to further awaken ourselves, our colleagues, the coaching professional associations and the wider public to the challenges of our times and to discover how we can be part of the solution and stop being part of the problem. It is not uncommon for us to attend coaching conferences that are primarily internal dialogues between privileged, mainly white, middle-class coaches talking to other members of the privileged world. Peter has actively encouraged coaching conferences to have on the platform CEOs who are critical of coaching, young millennials who are finding new ways of networking coaching, social activists and those from non-privileged groups. We are aware of a real effort being made to include more people from non-white backgrounds and we hope that together we can accelerate these small seeds.

We also encourage all the coaching professional bodies to see their members not as their customers, but as partners in moving the profession forward, beyond expensive personal development for the already highly privileged to being part of shifting collective consciousness – to be future-fit for the challenges that now face us.

John Whitmore, one of the founders of Performance Coaching, and Hetty Einzig, author of *The Future of Coaching*, were both central figures in the "Be the Change Initiative".

Hetty describes the work of this movement as:

> Be The Change Initiative (BTCI) seeks to inspire, catalyse and support committed action in the areas of environmental sustainability, social justice and spiritual fulfilment. We see these issues as one not three and frame the crises facing humanity as our greatest opportunity for change. We believe that humanity faces the greatest ecological, social and economical crises in history. Our modern culture, with its over-consumption and over-exploitation of humans and nature, has led us into an impasse. We address these crises through offering educational and transformative workshops and by building a connected passionate community of people who stand for this vision of a sustainable, just and fulfilling human presence on Earth. At the heart of this work is the Be The Change Symposium. We believe that in order to create long term systemic change we need to change our collective story from that of an Industrial Growth Society to that of a life-sustaining civilization, this is the essential adventure of our time.
>
> (www.bethechangeinitiative.org)

One of Peter's supervisees, Alison Whybrow, who has also contributed many publications to the coaching arena, decided to make one of her contributions through the Pachamama Alliance, whose purpose is:

> empowered by our partnership with indigenous people, is dedicated to bringing forth an environmentally sustainable, spiritually fulfilling, socially just human presence on this planet.

Our unique contribution is to generate and engage people everywhere in transformational conversations and experiences consistent with this purpose. We weave together indigenous and modern worldviews such that human beings are in touch with their dignity and are ennobled by the magnificence, mystery, and opportunity of what is possible for humanity at this time.

We are here to inspire and galvanize the human family to generate a critical mass of conscious commitment to a thriving, just and sustainable way of life on Earth. This is a commitment to transforming human systems and structures that separate us, and to transforming our relationships with ourselves, with one another, and with the natural world.

(www.pachamama.org/about/mission)

Alison has found other contributions to make too. In a personal communication to us she described how she chairs a residents' association for her street – one of whose core objectives is about reducing climate impact and is campaigning for street trees locally and is one of the coaches who has marched with Extinction Rebellion (the global environmental movement which espouses nonviolent civil disobedience to compel government action on the climate emergency). So rather than contributing to one thing – it's about integrating the planetary perspective at the heart – putting it at the core of all engagements and interactions from local to global; it's extending from the relationships we hold in our families and as neighbours to the frame used in coaching engagements and gentle challenges to the wider profession with the opportunity to bring facilitation skills to programmes specifically designed to support people to transition towards awareness and actions that will be part of the emerging, generative human earth story.

In the following case study, coach Dr Josie McLean shares her work with a local authority in Adelaide, South Australia, inspired after she heard John Whitmore talk in 2003 about global unsustainability. She became involved with the Pachamama Alliance and describes moving through stages of depression and grief for humanity and our planet as she watched signs of the sixth mass extinction, social disintegration and environmental destruction roll by, seemingly little noticed. Work often meant air travel for blue chip companies. She writes, "I was now aware of ecological footprints, and our global unsustainability and yet I was travelling around with no regard to it. One incredible woman, whom I met, observed: 'You must have an incredibly large carbon footprint!'" This led to Josie repositioning her practice to serve people working within local councils to serve and nurture sustainable cities and communities and to doctoral research and the case study below.

City of Marion case study

Between 2009 and 2012, I undertook an emergent, systemic action research for my doctoral thesis: "Embedding Sustainability into organizational DNA: a story of complexity." The central question was to understand and trace the nature and dynamic of a paradigmatic shift within an existing organization (McLean, 2017).

This is a brief overview of the impact systemic organizational coaching may have within organizations that are a part of our global sustainability challenge – and contributing to the solution.

Many authors have identified that for us to be sustainable, a paradigm shift is required from operating enterprises according to the received management wisdom to being an enterprise that perceives the world through the lens of complexity (or living systems).

Perceiving through the lens of living systems focuses attention on interdependence and fuels an intrinsic motivation of people within the organization to nurture its environment: people and planet. This occurs due to the recognition that the organization's success is interdependent with the success of the community and the natural environment within which it exists.

I began working as a coach and consultant with middle managers and staff within CoM (City of Marion) as we delivered leadership development programmes that shared and explored the principles of living systems within the context of managing people and leading change. The programmes were all delivered by engaging participants to raise their awareness and sense of responsibility to do things differently. By 2011 my firm had worked with approximately 120 employees or 27 percent of the 450 employees.

Between 2007–2011, five industry awards acknowledged CoM's success at nurturing a human environment that enabled the best from people – in their organization and within their communities. Despite this growing success, the CEO believed it was possible to do more to be "a leader in the delivery of The Community Vision" for a sustainable city. After six months of contracting discussions, we agreed how I could do my doctoral research within CoM.

I enrolled a small and passionate group of employees to join me as co-researchers. Together we met fortnightly for two hours, over approximately two years, during which time we defaulted to a group coaching approach to explore what CoM would be like if it were a sustaining organization (Dunphy, Griffiths and Benn, 2007). As the group coach, I asked questions employing the lens of living systems. These discussions eventually took me throughout the organization as group members linked me to their teams and other teams creating an informal network of relationships and conversations. Also, I returned to the executive team from time to time to share information that influenced feedback loops within the organization. I worked within the organization viewing it as one living system that comprised nested subsystems of other living systems (business units, teams and individuals).

At the end of the action research period in early 2012, it was possible to trace many important changes from the subtle changes within the research group members' ways of being. For example, group members catalyzed deep dialogues about previously taken for granted activities: a Central Business District development planning conversation turned into a Central People District conversation that impacted the Elected Members' strategic planning forum.

The most potent indicator of the paradigmatic transformation, however, is the transformation of the organization's strategic planning process and the format of its plan, its vision and organizational DNA. During the research period, the CEO and Director responsible for strategic planning, were intent on finding ways to engage everyone, employees and community, in the vision of sustainability. There was a great deal of excited energy and inquiry into this challenge. The enacted strategy became engagement with the vision story and the values embedded in the vision. Two years later in 2014, a new strategic plan format emerged. The strategic plan had transformed from the traditional format, to a new one page plan that described a vision of wellbeing: economically, environmentally and individually and the values that were most important in that vision (see Figure 14.1).

The 2040 vision is a description of how people want to experience life when the organization is sustaining itself and its community. The strategic plan is to develop and implement projects that nurture the six values identified around the vision: Livable, Valuing Nature, Engaged, Prosperous, Innovative, Connected. The new strategic plan format is an important indicator of the paradigmatic shift because:

1   It features the integration of the previous four pillars of sustainability (separate parts) into an integrated vision of wellbeing with different facets that are interdependent (a hallmark of perceiving living systems).
2   Interdependence means that the system is inherently unpredictable and uncontrollable as the feedback loops interconnect. Given this, it is not

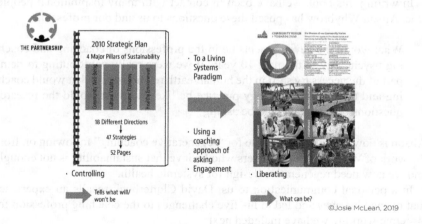

Figure 14.1 Transformation of the strategic planning process and plan format (McLean, 2018)

possible to determine the physical form of the vision in 2040 or even identify concrete goals over that timeframe; however, we can say how we want to experience life in 2040 (Wells and McLean, 2013). In this sense, the 'plan' shifts from controlling what is to be done, to liberating possibilities for what can be done.

3   Direct links from the new strategic planning process and format were traced back to a joint envisioning activity with the research group and executive team in 2010.

While the transformed and transforming strategic planning process emerged, the City of Marion won another award – Australian Sustainable City 2013.

In Chapter 8 we mentioned the work of many colleagues who are convening and training coaches to become active in increasing climate change consciousness and ecological responsible action.

These and other movements are drawing coaches who want their work to have a wider impact on fundamental social change and realizing that their training in systemic approaches to coaching provides them with useful skills and awareness they can bring to these movements.

We invite you the reader to think which of these approaches you could use to increase your beneficial impact in the wider world, beyond the individuals, teams, organizations and their stakeholders you currently help. To ask the question: "What can you uniquely do, that the world of tomorrow needs?" – based on the unique privileges of education, experience, trainings, skills, network etc. that you combine.

In writing this book we have been in contact with many inspirational people. One, Alison Whybrow has posed these questions to us and our profession:

What would the developments be in the professions of coaching and coaching psychology in the next 10 years if we were really contributing to being part of the necessary shift in the human/earth relationship; what would coaching and coaching psychology practice be like and what would the research questions be that we would be asking?

Alison is now working on a frame for "regenerative coaching" following on from the work of Wahl (2016) and others who believe that sustainability is not enough, and we now need regenerative design for systemic health.

In a personal communication to us, David Clutterbuck recalls an experience that opened his eyes and led to his five challenges to the coaching profession for systemic working we have included next.

Several years ago I was asked to support the UN Climate Change team in Ghana in a mentoring project aimed at countering the churn amongst environmental champions, both in the Agency, but more importantly amongst government officials and politicians. It would have been easy to breeze in, stay at a 5-star western style hotel and learn little or nothing. Instead, we spent the entire time within the local culture – with the sole exception that I was given a set of cutlery. This was their world, their environment and I was there to learn as much as to teach. And so it was that I learned how rare and precious printed books were, which led me to organize a case full of second hand volumes for the schools my hosts' children attended. The connection between literacy and positive climate action – so obvious now – would not have occurred to me without this partial immersion. I am grateful.

So, David's five challenges to us and our profession are:

1   How do we help coaches to take responsibility not only for the client in front of them, but for the multiple systems that client influences and is influenced by?
2   Virtual coaching helps to reduce the carbon footprint of coaching. Yet to do virtual coaching well requires a high level of coaching competence, well beyond that of the average coach. So, do we simply accept that a high proportion of virtual coaching will be of poor quality?
3   It is not normally considered to be a coach's role to offer moral judgements to their clients. But where do we draw the line between moral responsibility and moralizing?
4   We now have a forum, at which the three main professional bodies in coaching sit together to achieve professional alignment. How can they have a collective voice on the wider issues of society, humanity and environmental impact?
5   How can we enable others to take responsibility if we do not show compassion for them (and for ourselves)?

The coaches' never-ending development journey

As we have stressed throughout this book, the main instrument that the coach uses is their own self, and for this instrument to be effective it needs constant development. We need to sharpen our saw (Covey, 2004), hone our relationship skills, expand our wide-angled empathy, (Hawkins, 2019) increase the depth of our compassion, and increase the range of our systemic thinking, perceiving and being.

Our development needs to include integrating, developing, and expanding our sense of self, to integrate and find coherence between our many selves. One of the most fundamental integrations is between our 'narrative self' and our 'experiencing self' – the story we have about our self, originating in our left hemisphere neo-cortex, and how we experience our embodied self in each and every moment. Often our narrative self is also divided many ways: there can be the story we tell ourselves and the story we relate to others; the story about ourselves we tell our family, the story we tell when we are going for a job, and the story we tell a prospective new partner. Then there are the stories that others tell about us. Often our life is restricted by living with a historic narrative we have accepted about our self. Coaching, counselling, psychotherapy, supervision and other forms of dialogical reflective development helps us rework our narratives and become self-authoring in a way that does not reduce our many-sided selves to one single narrative but provides meaningful connection and coherence between each one.

In developing our self in such dialogical reflective processes, we are increasing the capacity to reflect on the many different aspects of our self, from a place of inner witness. We learn to increasingly respond to situations with greater sense of choice, rather than react emotionally. This comes from the ability not just to see the others in a situation but to see ourselves in context and witness our reactions, rather than act from them. Wilber (2006) describes this as the process by which increasing amounts of the 'I' that is perceiving and reacting to the world, becomes the 'me' which the 'I' can see. Thus, he describes all development as 'envelopment'.

In developing our self, we also recognize that our life is embedded in many layers of context that in turn become part of our internal text. We develop relationally, first within and then with our mother, then others. We become part of a family with its own unwritten and spoken rules, ways of relating and being. We grow up within different tribes – people like us – this may be extended families, or local communities, our school, sports club or other wider ways of belonging. These in turn are contained within shared cultures, which may be regional, national, religious or ethnic, which share language, both verbal and non-verbal, ways of being and perceiving the world, beliefs and shared mind-sets. Beyond the cultures that divide us, all homo sapiens are part of one species, which has evolved over many millennia on this earth and shares distinct species characteristics. This species has, in very recent history, become more globally interconnected, much more numerous and even more exploitative and damaging of the rest of our shared ecology than ever before.

Thus, in the coaching room are many selves, for the coach and the coachee are both nested in many systemic levels and these larger systems are nested within them. Both coachee and coach bring into the room their individual self, relational self, family self, tribal self, nationalist, religious, ethnic self, global human self and our ecological or eco-self. We are not just systemically nested within our family, culture and ecology but they are also deeply nested within us, in every fibre of our being, the way we live, move, talk, hear, feel and see the world and think, as well as the way we construct our narratives.

The work in coaching is not only to separate and find our own unique identity, but to re-own each of these widening aspects of our extended self; to own, not only our personal history, but those of our families, communities and culture. Only through this process can we each find our belonging, our rootedness, and a fullness of participation in the world, which is both out there, but also intimately within us. It is through dialogical exploration with another that we regain a participatory consciousness, and a life of grace and gracefulness (Bateson, 1979; Reason, 2017). Through this process we find the ever-widening path to a fuller life in our eco-self, where the ecological environment is part of us and there is a two-way flow of caring and being cared for.

For a coach to help a client on this journey, they too must have walked and be walking this path. Their training needs to involve not just understanding individual human psychology and development, but embracing relational, systemic and ecological perspectives. We need to learn how to participate with our clients intersubjectively, not just as two individualized subjective beings, but as two people, each deeply embedded in their family, community and cultural life-worlds – two people who are each just small parts of a much, much, larger evolving ecosystem.

We need to learn not just how to deepen our empathy and compassion for each individual client, but to develop what I (Peter) have termed 'wide-angled empathy' – that is empathy for every individual, organization, system and being in their story and the connections between them (Hawkins, 2019: 74). So often coaches experience such empathy for the client, that they begin to react against the others in the client's narrative, seeing them through the client's eyes. This can easily lead to confluence and even collusion with the client or the playing out of Karpman's (1968) drama triangle of client as victim, others in their story as persecutors and coach or supervisor as rescuer, which can become a self-perpetuating cycle, kept turning by all three parties. It is also possible we might view the client as persecutor and align with their team, seeing their direct reports, for example, as victims.

'*Wide-angled empathy*' also needs to be extended, so we can empathize not just as another individual, but we can meet their family, tribal, national and cultural self from those levels within us, with what we now term '*deep-level empathy*'. This involves finding the family, tribal, community or cultural self within you than can empathize with those levels in the client. Without these we remain an outsider, struggling to empathize but caught in external judgement.

Our work is to learn to go even beyond '*wide-angled*' and '*deep-level empathy*' to '*eco-empathy*' where we find the natural responsiveness and compassion to all aspects of life, not from our separate self, but from being part of the connected web of life. It is from this place that judgemental morality drops away, and we acknowledge all life as part of us and ourselves as just a very small part of a much bigger ecological world. Coaching is not only a lifelong learning and development journey, but at heart it is a spiritual practice.

We started this book with the story of the young black frontline manager in Cape Town, South Africa saying that executive coaching sounded like "very expensive personal development for the already highly privileged." Throughout this book we have offered our response to this challenge, drawing on the work of many colleagues and fellow travellers.

We have achieved a great deal in coaching in the last 40 years, but now so much more is required if we are to use the potential of coaching to go beyond expensive personal development of the already highly privileged and make the fullest contribution that is needed to meet the many great challenges of the 21st century.

Appendix

Case studies of systemic coaching from around the world

Introduction

By now we hope that from the many examples we have included you will already have a sense that systemic coaching is happening widely, rather than being the name Peter and Eve have adopted for their way of doing coaching, a new brand along with many others in our crowded marketplace. In Chapter 3 we showed how we were part of a growing movement and named just a few of the fellow travellers on this journey.

In this Appendix we wanted to include further stories and case studies from colleagues around the world, who we have invited to offer their experience, from within their culture, of how they are delivering systemic coaching that delivers value beyond the individual. First, we offer a few reflections to link these rich pictures of practice to some of the theory, models and processes outlined elsewhere in this book.

As you read these case studies, you might also notice the connections they make for you, the patterns within them and between them, the ways they illustrate what has gone before in this book, and the ways they challenge what has been said or offer a different perspective.

They have been particularly chosen from contrasting places and cultures in the world: Australia, China, France, India, Mexico, South Africa and the UK. You might inquire into how you think the culture of both the context and the writer shows up in the story.

Reading to gain maximum learning from case studies

To get maximum value from these case studies we would encourage you as the reader to engage with these case studies dialogically; that is as if you are in a generative conversation with the authors. Whether you are a coach, coachee, trainee coach or coach supervisor, we would invite you, as you read these case studies, to reflect on the following questions (perhaps writing your answers down either as you go along or when you have finished reading them all):

1 What did the coach and coachee do that you could learn from?
2 What methods and tools did they use that you might find useful in your work?

3   What do you glean from the cases about their way of being and engaging with the client that you could draw from?
4   How did the coach contract with the individual and organizational client?
5   How did the coach and coachee bring in other stakeholders to the contracting, coaching and evaluation? What more might they have done (accepting that the brevity of the cases may mean some elements that did happen may have been omitted by the authors for space reasons)?
6   How did they engage with the wider systemic levels and bring a focus on these into the coaching engagement?
7   What stakeholders (including the wider ecology) might have been ignored or not seen in this coaching work and how might you have brought them in?
8   Was there anything the coach and coachee failed to do (or didn't have space to include details of) that with the wisdom of hindsight you would have liked to have done in their place?
9   If you had one curiosity or piece of advice for the author(s) what would it be?
10   How does that advice to the authors also apply to you and your work?

You might also like to apply some of the models and methods from Chapters 6 and 7 and the evaluative measures mentioned in Chapter 12 to the coaching work in the case study, which might provide other indications of both what this work did achieve and what further progress you would encourage if you were supervising the coach or doing further work with this client. For example:

Applying the seven-eyed coaching model to the cases (see pp. 35–37 and 153–157)
Applying four levels of engagement model to the cases (see pp. 89–92)

In Chapter 14, we discussed several aspects of how coaching can become systemic and deliver value beyond the individual, summarizing it in these ten points:

1   Partner with the coachee
2   Partner with the organization that employs you
3   Purpose-led coaching
4   Contract to discover the work that the wider world needs us to do
5   Contract on how we will do it together
6   Bring in the wider stakeholders into the coaching room, literally and metaphorically
7   Move beyond insight and good intentions to embodied learning and action
8   Regularly review our joint work, with stakeholder input and recontract
9   Have systemic supervision on our work
10   Build evaluation into our work, as well as the wider coaching research

As you read through the cases you might note how these show up. There are eight case studies. Three reflect coaching done on a one-to-one basis and these are first, from Julie in China, Michel in France and Barbara in South Africa (case studies A to C). We then have four which involve working with individuals across teams or with teams or both: Tammy in Australia, Ram and Preeti in India, Ingela in Mexico and Nick in the UK (case studies D to G).

Conclusion

This Appendix has provided a series of systemic coaching case studies drawn from a variety of countries; a wide range of types of organizations including manufacturing, pharmaceutical and public service; and different types of individual and organizational clients working individually, in teams and across whole organizations.

We have also included case studies and vignettes in other chapters:

1   A case study on teams from David Matthew Prior in the US in Chapter 9.
2   A case study on sustainability from Dr Josie McLean based on a public authority in Australia in Chapter 14.
3   Vignettes from Giles Hutchins, Catherine Gorham, David Jarrett, Sarah McKinnon and others, some written anonymously, illustrating many of the themes we have introduced.

We have also described some methods for maximizing your learning from reading case studies systemically:

- How to look at a coaching relationship, through our 'varifocal lenses' considering:
  - o   The coaching relational system
  - o   The individual (and the coach) bringing their family, team, community, function and organizational, cultural and ecological dynamics embedded within them into the coaching
  - o   The need to serve at least two clients – the individual and the organization
- How to view the coaching process in each of the case studies through the seven-eyed coaching and supervision model (see Chapter 10).
- How to view the coaching through the Hawkins and Smith (2018) 'four levels of engagement' model.
- How to reflect on the relationship between the coach and the coachee and how this developed over time.
- How then to reflect on how you might have handled the challenges and needs of the coaching differently if you were coach, coachee or coach supervisor.

Case study A: the story of Lee (and Eric) and 'eagle eyes' from Julie Zhang, China

It was mid-December in Shanghai. Early in the afternoon, Lee and I met in a coffee shop close to his office for a casual talk after completing his coaching journey. Amidst the cheerful Christmas carols, we settled into our chairs close to the window. Outside, snow was falling. Lee was in a relaxed mood, sipping coffee and appreciating the snow outside. Finally, it was time to celebrate after striving through another year.

"Congratulations for your great achievement this year!" I started the conversation. "Thank you! I am so glad that my team achieved 15% increase of after-sales revenue and maintained the gross margin." He went on, "I really appreciate your coaching that has supported me through these two years to cultivate better ways of collaborating with my boss and peers and develop my team."

My thoughts flew back to two years ago when I facilitated a few strategic planning workshops to help Lee's company, a leading European heavy machinery manufacturer, to define a new business model to better compete in the Chinese market. After-sales was then identified as the new growth engine. Lee was at that moment promoted from a senior machine salesperson to lead the after-sales team, reporting directly to the CEO, Eric, a French gentleman who relocated to China a year ago. To help Lee transition into his new role, leadership training was offered and followed by individual coaching.

The first round of coaching aimed to embed the insights and learning from training courses to his daily leadership practices. With six one-on-one sessions contracted, we started off with a quick meeting together with Eric for input on expectations, followed by sessions focussing on his new identity as a leader, leadership styles and key skills such as delegation, motivation, feedback etc. There was limited involvement during the course from Eric and other key stakeholders.

Around six months later, we were happy to see that Lee had made a mindset shift from an individual contributor to a manager, letting go of work that defined his previous success, putting focus on getting his team members to perform better, and consciously exercising the newly learned managerial skills. To allow him to further practice and embed these skills, we agreed to discuss further needs of coaching in half a year.

Time flew by. I heard that market situation was tough, sales were not picking up as expected and his team seemed to have rather low morale. I could feel the anxiety from Eric when he mentioned, "I can't believe why he does not seem worried, and not eager to act on changes I suggested." The tension was growing between them. So, I suggested continuation of the coaching, and this time with a more systemic approach.

"Look at that snowflake on the umbrella!" Lee's voice pulled my thoughts back. "Wow, amazing!" I marveled at the natural beauty as well as his keen observation. "Eagle eyes!" We almost said in one voice and laughed. This was Eric's pet phrase. "Remember when we first started, how I struggled to answer your questions such as 'What did you notice in your team's reaction? How do you think they may think and feel?' Eric was right that as a leader I need to develop all my senses. Thank you for allowing me additional time outside the coaching session to observe my team and collect their feedback. I can then make better choices and reflect on my approach. It also helped me tremendously when you offered me your observations and feedback during shadow coaching sessions in the second phase. I noticed that I had still missed so many verbal and non-verbal clues around me. I was all in for the 'doing', with little awareness on 'being'. Your feedback helped me to discover my blind spots. It is much more efficient than our initial sessions in the first phase."

"Thank you for acknowledging that." I probed, "Tell me more about what you find particularly helpful in the second phase compared to the first."

"Well, the 360 survey is the first thing coming to my mind. After being in my role for around one year, it is great to have some concrete feedback from my boss, peers and subordinates. I am glad that we had that three-party meeting with Eric and talked it over. Before that I really felt being torn apart by two opposite forces."

Lee was caught in a cultural conflict. Eric was not in agreement with Lee's approach to communication and leading. He expected Lee to be very direct in giving negative feedback, take quick actions with low performers, and show great passion in front of his team. In a nutshell, Lee needed to be as French as possible to lead his Chinese team.

I facilitated their discussion to surface the culture differences. Together, Eric and Lee discovered how different they are in communication, use of energy, control of emotions and decision making. Lee learned how to appreciate Eric's direct and sometimes confrontational communication style. It could help to clarify the problems and uncover the root causes. Eric also realized that he needed to be more considerate to his Chinese colleagues who care about 'losing face' in front of others, and Lee's more diplomatic approach can be appropriate in a Chinese team environment. By going deeper beneath their behavioural patterns in a quest for beliefs and values, they were both pleasantly surprised that they actually shared common values, such as passion for excellence, persistency, fairness, and etc. These values became solid ground for them to strategize ways to meet each other's needs and adapt to each other's styles. Lee had his new coaching objectives that are aligned to major stakeholders' expectations. Eric committed to change as well, and they both agreed to be each other's support system.

"Again, shadow coaching is very powerful," Lee continued. "It served the development of my team as well when you sat in our team meetings and reviewed the process with us." I smiled. "Thank you for being so open and inviting me to give you real-time feedback right at the team meeting." In fact, his team became very open and participative once he committed to change from his directive approach to a more participative one. They had a wonderful discussion right on the spot about how to improve the way of having weekly meetings.

With shadow coaching, I was no longer only relying on what Lee brought into the coaching dialogue. I could be in the situations real-time with him, replaying the process, provoking him to think both 'inside-out' and 'outside-in'.

On my way back, I concluded two powerful learnings from Lee's engagement. Using three-party meetings aligned expectations from his sponsor and other major stakeholders, and providing shadow coaching sessions offered quickly a wealth of data about the environment, organizational culture and the key stakeholders, the system the coachee works in.

Case study B: the story of Hélène, the marketing director, from Michel Moral, France

During my professional life, I have always been interested in the systemic aspects of situations. So, when I started coaching in 2002, I introduced a session on the systemic representation of the client context in all my coaching journeys. In 2005, I decided that this particular session would be the first one. For this, I usually draw a 'systemic sketch' with the client on a paper board. This representation is enriched during the coaching mission and I give it to the client at the end of the journey.

When I have several clients in an organization, those sketches illustrate the systemic structure of the whole. In the case that I am relating here, I had already noticed that this particular organization suffered not only from a silo mentality but also from conflicts between horizontal layers of management.

My client, Hélène, was the marketing director of a product line worth 2 billion euros income per year. Her manager was the marketing executive, himself a member of the board. Her key business objective was to establish the weekly volumes to be manufactured and stored and to get the approval of the general manager on her numbers. The difficulty was to reach an agreement between all the stakeholders who fiercely defended their own objectives.

Her request for the coaching was to manage her time such that she would not be exposed to the risk of burnout. During a three-way contracting meeting her line manager added an objective on conflict avoidance.

The systemic sketch done during the first session showed that, in order to fulfil her mission, she had to relate with most of the functions of the enterprise: sales, manufacturing, purchasing, logistics, finance and HR. During this first session, she described at length her daily nightmare, which she compared to plate spinning in a circus: the need to reach an agreement with different functions which did not have the same objectives, accounting systems and references for the same products. Her relationship with the persons in charge in the functions was awful. This was replicated in the relationships of her team members with their counterparts in the functions.

The systemic sketch was a shock for her: she realized that there was a lack of a common language and understanding between the different

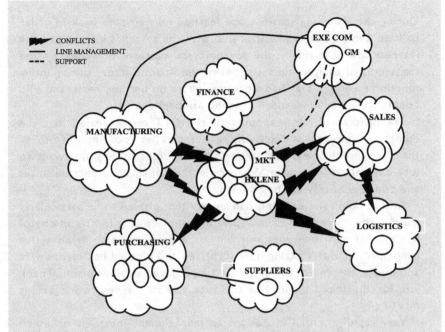

Figure A.1 The systemic sketch

functions and layers within the company. For instance, the production function was talking 'part numbers' and costs, while the sales were talking 'models' and revenue. Her first decision was to create a kind of conversion table, but the IT people refused to automate it because it did not comply to their strategy.

At the beginning of the second session, the alliance between the two of us was very strong: I was the one who helped her to understand the functioning of the system.

At that point, I decided that my strategy for this particular coaching mission would be to:

1   Focus on the management of her emotions when she is in relation-ship with someone else. I would use the role play and reverse role play techniques to work on this.
2   Continue to explore the functioning of the system and the cor-porate culture. For this, I sent her a cultural transformation tool (CTT) called the IVA questionnaire.

During the following sessions she learned how to step back in order to have a more relaxed relationship with the system's players and she learned how to highlight the psychological patterns or games (in the transactional analysis sense) between the various actors during inter-function meetings. This had a positive effect on her and her team, who could finally work in a more peaceful atmosphere.

Examination of her responses to the CTT test revealed that the company's culture was extremely resistant to her coordination efforts: the silo mentality was too strong and each function did not want to lose any part of its power. When reflecting on this she became upset and considered leaving the company.

At that point, she suddenly had an idea that proved to be particularly fruitful: she invited her counterpart in manufacturing to attend one of her management meetings, not only as a guest but also as an active participant. It was amazing how surprised and pleased her invitee was and said at the end of the meeting: "I discovered another planet. Thank you for the trip. I would like to invite you to my next management meeting."

Very rapidly, mutual invitations to management meetings occurred between all the functions. New processes were established by the stakeholders and responsibilities were distributed differently.

Due to homeostasis, strong resistance emerged from the IT, HR and finance functions, which raised arguments about confidentiality, collusion and disrespect of the corporate strategy. Eventually, the general manager supported Hélène's position and her recommendations, which were incorporated into the processes of the company.

Exploration

A lot of tools, techniques and models exist to work on the systemic aspects of an individual coaching situation and we have seen two of them in this case: role play and CTT. In terms of theory, we are in the field of complex adaptive systems in which understanding of relationships and behaviours of the actors is not enough to predict the functioning of the whole. In these systems the collective mutation comes from the self-organization of individuals.

But the mutation can occur only if the initial conditions are such that it is possible. An analogy would be that a forest can burn only if it has been dried up by hot weather and wind (contributing factors). If the favourable initial conditions are there, then one match is enough to light the fire.

The role of the coach is to assess if initial conditions are such that simple actions can initiate the mutation. If they are not, then the coach's work is to enable the necessary contributing factors.

How would the coach assess the initial conditions and consider possible coaching actions? Well, supervision is the place where such reflection can occur if the supervisor has enough knowledge and experience working with complex systems. Developing such skills in both coaches and supervisors requires appropriate training and I personally work on designing training programmes for this purpose.

Case study C: the story of Talia and the outsourced team in a consultancy business from Barbara Walsh, South Africa

The organizational client is a well-known multinational consultancy, where I have worked with many individuals and teams across its South African region since 2011. My first engagement with the business unit was to coach a senior manager, 'Yousef' in preparation for his promotion into an executive role.

'Talia' reported in to Yousef and was a senior manager brought in from one of the company's Eastern European offices for her specific expertise in managing large call centre environments. Her complex task was to take over the entire customer services call centre operation of a large retailer, an important client for the consultancy, including the employment of the call centre's managers and agents and integrate them into an existing internal team. Talia had a team of seven managers reporting to her and the retailer was implementing a turnaround strategy, which created additional pressure.

Contracting initially was with Talia herself. Coming from Eastern Europe with its strong culture of compliance, she was finding it difficult to cope with the dynamics and culture she encountered in South Africa. Resistance from new and existing team members, combined with internal politics, power games, racial innuendos and perceived sabotage, alongside the requirements and demands of the retail organization left her feeling anxious and overwhelmed. Although considered a high performer by her company, she had lost confidence in her ability to lead, felt she had to micromanage everything, and was extremely stressed.

The next level of contracting was with her sponsor, Yousef. The disconnects within the team and between the team and its leader were having a strong negative impact on their service levels to the key stakeholder and its customers. The objectives of the management team needed to be clearly defined and evidence of performance achievement clarified. Trust needed to be built between the team members and new behavioural norms established supporting a culture of respectful, open, honest and timely communication. Yousef wanted Talia to become an 'influential leader' to this diverse and scattered team.

Talia and I also met with their HR business partner, 'Grace' to gain further insights. Talia distrusted Grace, whom she felt colluded with the 'other camp'. Grace expressed her concern for the team dynamics and the inability of this team to collaborate with other internal teams and felt that Talia should develop greater accountability within her management team.

Besides regular conversations Talia had with both Yousef and Grace respectively, Talia and I met together with both of them mid-term and towards the end of our work to get their insights and feedback. Contracting, obtaining feedback and re-contracting with other stakeholders was largely conducted by Talia throughout the coaching.

The complex situation reflected disconnections at many levels: two very different cultures had been merged into this one management team, with no preparation. The 'newcomers' from the retail company were expected to adapt quickly to the consultancy's fast-paced, demanding culture and were experienced by their new colleagues as 'soft', unfocussed and obstructive. One of the incoming managers felt she should have been given Talia's role, and appeared to undermine her leadership.

With significant problems of its own, the retailer, their key stakeholder, needed to be able to trust the consultancy to deliver. Meanwhile other teams in the consultancy relied on this team meeting its objectives to deliver their own objectives. The disconnects meant crisis management with nobody working effectively.

Talia needed an effective, coordinated and collaborative management team rather than spending her time handling drama and trying on her own to pre-empt crises.

We began by building the relationship between Talia and myself. Using Karpman's Drama Triangle (Karpman, 1968) as a situational map for exploring relational dynamics alongside a framework for distinguishing between fact and assumption (see Chapter 4) and reframing techniques (see Chapter 5), Talia learned to turn 'absolutes' into questions and shifted into a more self-empowered position. As she stepped 'out of the dance and onto the balcony'(Heifetz and Linsky, 2002), she was able to get a clearer perspective on where the real disconnections were and which she should prioritize.

Stakeholder mapping helped Talia identify where she needed to build stronger relationships. She accepted the limits of her influence and needed to learn to locate the problem in a connection which did not exist yet rather than in an individual.

Using role play and stepping into shoes of key stakeholders (see Chapter 5 and Walsh (2014)) and an empty chair to represent other perspectives, Talia was better able to sense what might be going on for others and practice her next engagements with them (see fast-forward rehearsal, Chapter 5). This helped her develop unexpected empathy for situations others found themselves in and significantly changed her perspective. This was transformational and some of Talia's most troublesome relationships improved significantly.

Talia learned to lead by asking questions, rather than by telling and expecting things to be done her way. Through holding silence she encouraged answers to emerge from the team, combining the experiences of both teams in a process of co-inquiry. While uncomfortable initially, this led to some surprising discoveries as there were the first honest conversations; the team members expressed their understanding that they needed each other to be successful individually for the consultancy to be successful and for the client to be successful — together they were more than the sum of the parts.

Talia and her team were encouraged when their improved performance metrics were appreciated by their key client. At the same time other senior managers commented on the change as they collaborated better towards common goals.

Talia glowed as she gave me feedback from her family, who felt she had 'come back' to them. She was applying her learnings in her family context as well and was able to coach her young adult children as they transitioned into "a South African way of life".

Towards the end of Talia's coaching programme an unexpected crisis resulted in a decision to disband the team. Although Talia found herself facing another challenging, emotional situation, she held her ground and navigated resourcefully through the process. Yousef reflected that he "not only valued but very much respected the way she handled herself and worked through this exceptionally difficult process."

Talia was subsequently offered another role in Europe and our coaching relationship ended. The following is adapted from an email I received from her four months after her redeployment:

"I was given a project that had a Customer Satisfaction score of 3/10 (unstable). This is a huge client and it was critical to get things right quickly. . . . Working with the team and just putting in the basics turned this around so that within two months we were achieving between 6 and 8/10 and had stabilized the project . . . I was nominated for an award given to people that go above and beyond for their client and for the company. I believe I am in a space that works, and I have made the right steps to get alignment and deliver the outcomes. A collective one goal. I listened, I learned, and I have applied. It works."

Was the initial project successful? It depends on what is being measured. Some of the initial outcomes were not achieved. The real success was in the emerging realization that the structure and some roles did not support the objectives, which prevented the necessary connections. A clear case for change to achieve more productive outcomes going forward became apparent.

The art of collective inquiry is probably the most important skill of a systemic coach. We don't have the answers and neither does our client, but somewhere in the system are the necessary clues. Working 'future-back' and using the 'Three Horizons model' (Sharpe, 2013: – see pp 5–6 and p97) brings many perspectives to strategic goals. Prioritizing stakeholder expectations and needs (outside-in) helps focus the individual, team and organization on how to generate the most value. From the whole, working back to the parts helps identify the next steps.

As a coach, our flexibility to work with both what is, and what is emerging, helps embed this for the clients we work with – be they individuals, teams or multiple teams within the organization and beyond. The ability to co-inquire, diffuse drama and connect creates partnership, enabling resilient changeability and systems that thrive.

Case study D: the blind spot of being in service to create a better future, from Tammy Turner, Australia

Introduction

I approached this engagement confidently expectant. It was a sector I cared about and where I had experience. The organization was interested in an 18-month project to develop the culture through team and individual coaching. The coachees were intelligent and intrinsically motivated. The coaching team we brought together was both experienced and had an eclectic range of skills and personalities to enhance the client experience. I felt elated to be engaged in this dream project, and this false bravado added to my initial blind spots. I am grateful that the complexity of this assignment was pivotal in understanding my leadership, sharpening my ability to contract and broadening my perspective about ecosystems.

Section 1 – context

After tendering, we were interviewed by the general manager of strategy, heading up the cultural and leadership change initiative. We discussed their issues, their requirements-gathering process and who comprised their executive leadership team as well as the team and individual coach matching process. Both the client and our coaching team were excited to be part of the organizational mission to advance their industry by collecting research within a knowledge-sharing platform and become a centre of excellence. Their employee survey indicated that the agency's vision provided intrinsic motivation and employee engagement. We took this conversation, cultural data gathered by the client and their final tender at face value. The signed contract became our formal agreement for their requirements and how the project commenced.

More straightforward elements included working with individual executives and their 'teams' to devise an enhanced reporting infrastructure leading to increased project funding and engaging the entire executive 'team' around a shared mission and purpose. Team coaching was proposed to foster knowledge sharing between executives and ultimately across the industry. An early blind spot was defining the executive as a 'team'. Due to the tender language and compounded by our unconscious bias for them being a team, we responded to the tender using Hawkins' criteria "Level I: Team coaching sees the team as created by the individuals within it and focuses on the interrelationships between the individuals and what the individuals want from the team" (Hawkins, 2017a: 180).

When we embarked on coaching the executive, we witnessed this intact team operating like a group: individuals feeling more part of a team with their reporting managers than their executive peers. Our blind spot was illuminated when we began working with their managers and teams. Organizational key performance indicators supported the 'teams' acting more like a group:

- The executive did not call themselves a 'team'.
- Most staff members were independent contractors or on secondment from other agencies, creating monthly turnover double that of other agencies.
- The chief executive officer's contract had recently been renewed for another 2 years. Most members of the executive had only been there for less than a year.
- An entire division was tasked with adhering to stringent contractual reporting elements, when neither the board nor the industry itself had relevant examples from which to draw these metrics. Individuals were not sharing data interdepartmentally, much less reporting their learning in a consistent format.

These combined factors indicated that original project timeline and milestones were unrealistic, unless we could engage members to build "consensus and harmony . . . and interpersonal relations are focused on" (Hawkins, 2017a: 180). As a result, we implemented individual coaching with a team objective of "What is my contribution to being part of the leadership imperative needed to achieve our mission?" As coaches we were heady with making a difference. To avoid being enmeshed into the system of 'making a difference' each coach had their reflective practice and coaching supervisor familiar with team coaching.

Section 2: uncovering and working with blind spots

Dilemmas great and small arose, including: Do we only use environmentally responsible furniture in our offices? What projects should be funded? Despite changing policy agendas, how do we stay relevant?

Despite strong individual acumen and aptitude, catalyzing the brightest ideas between various inter and intra groups to share their learning and meet the agency mission to advance the industry was difficult. At the executive level, this was compounded by scrutiny of an overseer board whose members changed regularly and by political shifts in the federal government.

Nearly every decision taken needed data, sign off or multiple points of view. As external coaches we saw their blind spot around individual and collective accountability. It was endemic within the ecosystem: individually as a contributor; within a project group as a team leader; within governmental regulation and/or a legal binding contract with an external partner. Using accountability as a lever for change was a provocative motivator for the team. During team coaching sessions we introduced typical questions such as:

- What is important to each individual? The group/team? The project?
- How do they measure their progress?
- How do they capture and share their learning?
- What happens when things go wrong?

These created opportunities for a coach to contract with an individual, the group or team and/or team members with each other. As the engagement cascaded through the organization, these questions became scaffolding for a process which could be used between departmental groups, within the multi-organizational 'think tank' project teams and/or with external and internal stakeholders involved in a single complex project.

As coaches, we thought we were merely facilitating their internal dilemmas, helping them to solve their own problems. And yet each coach was an element in the accountability ecosystem and subject to its lure of power, being of service and/or providing expertise, rather than remaining curious and creating learning opportunities. There were multiple examples of our team exhibiting the same behaviours as those we were witnessing. During an individual coaching session, the people and culture executive wanted to use session time to discuss return on investment (ROI) metrics linking coaching to decreased staff churn. During a team coaching session, a team coach had a personality clash with one of the executives and was triggered into a defensive stance, creating a power struggle not dissimilar to the one the executive had been having with an external partner stakeholder where negotiations had gone poorly. As project lead, I had difficult conversations with the client sponsor and CEO about multiple team coaching last minute scheduling changes and late invoice payments.

Section 3 – conclusion and recommendations

Through coaching supervision a similar process of questioning to uncover the 'parallel processes' we were being drawn into gave us an observer lens with which to gain perspective. Our coaching biases such as "we're only coaching, so we're not responsible, the client is" were highlighted as collusions.

Including us as an element within the system of change, with responsibility to openly share appropriately during team coaching sessions, was encouraged. These factors allowed us to recontract that we were part of the organizational learning and share our experiences and failures as opportunities for growth. Together these factors provided more consistent sharing, vulnerability and openness as reported by coachees and coaches.

Despite my coaching experience, like our client, I was often drawn into problem solving. I learned that providing perspective is different from providing a solution because I'm not tied to the outcome. This allowed me to engage the coaches and the executive team at various junctures to offer feedback or encouragement, by being an observer and also part of the system. I reflected that the simplest questions are elegant, and foundations to a psychological contract. Without effectively clarifying the project detail or adding a consulting discovery phase into the initial contract, I learned that addressing issues as early as they become apparent creates clarity, a more respectful business relationship and more reciprocal way in conducting business for both parties. The desire to be part of something greater is innately human. The ebb and flow of how we shape the ecosystem and the ecosystem shapes us, as well as my desire to be of service, provides me an exciting ongoing opportunity for development.

Case study E: creating organizational practices in engagement, dialogue and sociability through systemic alignment of information, team and self, Ram S. Ramanathan and Preeti D'mello, India

Background

This case study is of an Indian multinational company in engineering and automobile products with 100,000 personnel, predominantly male, with 20 global locations, achieving 12 percent growth annually.

The author, Ram S Ramanathan, was an external coach and supervisor to some of the coaches. The co-author, Preeti D'mello was the programme architect and internal supervisor coach within the company.

The company had faced what was considered alarming attrition in the group of direct reports to the senior leaders of around 39 percent. Research linked these exits to poor supervisory relationships with an absence of psychological safety, arising from transactional leaders who were not creating meaningful interpersonal dialogue with their direct reports.

Despite acceptable financial growth, the company CEO was concerned about sustained long-term performance. He felt that organizational culture and leadership needed to develop new mindsets and behaviours with enhanced awareness based on meaningful dialogue. The CEO initiated coaching for the top 300 leaders to learn, value and engage in generative conversations integrating their own psyche with their workplace ecosystem. He nominated the leaders for developmental coaching and was convinced that the company would serve all their stakeholders better by helping the leaders to discover their purpose, even though the head of HR feared that this might lead to people exploring opportunities outside the organization.

Systemic coaching framework and structure

Four coaching summits were held where leaders articulated organizational needs and emergent goals creating a common understanding and ownership of what the organization required in order to sustain and transform. Through this the company developed a systemic coaching framework aligning organizational goals with individual and team requirements and then identified individuals and teams agreeing to align with these needs. The HR team, as sponsor, coordinated confidentiality agreements formally with both nine external coaches and nine executive leaders and their team members. This was informally conveyed to all related stakeholders. Coaching as a concept was new to India and the organization and the HR team agreed with the coaches that they would build trusting contact with their clients before focussing more fully on behavioural transformation to minimize anxiety about the coaching. The coach would create a partnering of generative listening, curious questioning, developmental feedback and building multiple perspectives.

Organizational goals centred on recommendations from a leadership study on attrition at senior leadership levels, especially on creation of psychological safety and better interpersonal relationships. Team goals and individual goals were left to coaches to co-create and report back on. Leaders made visible their business deliverables as action learning projects and reported progress through the lens of their evolving self. The projects, ranging from building collaboration to increasing revenue, supported the team goals. Individuals, with coaches to support them, developed goals based both on their personal values and what was needed to support team and organizational goals.

The coaching process spanned six months and involved six hourly individual coaching sessions and two team coaching sessions of eight hours for each team.

Coaches and teams used supporting information such as the leadership study on attrition, a leadership style survey, a self-awareness survey and a personal scorecard with all individuals, as well as oral 360 feedback through coachees speaking to their supervisor, team members, peers, family and friends to understand how they were perceived. Many breakthroughs were reported during this time with teams speaking openly and requesting an altered approach to management and being honest about work/life balance or family time.

Evaluation metrics

Before, during and after coaching, the HR team measured the effectiveness of the process by the shift in personal development, repeating the leadership style survey, self-awareness survey and personal scorecard. In addition, attendance and participation in coaching sessions were monitored, documented and reviewed, and there was little absenteeism and only through business need.

Quantitative and qualitative evaluation outcome

Measurements done a month after the completion of coaching showed an increase in self-awareness by 17 percent. In leadership style measurement: business focus increased by 23 percent; people focus by 20 percent; result orientation by 15 percent; social relationships by 19 percent; participation by 15 percent; and readiness to coach by 81 percent, with leaders keen to sustain the impact.

The company found through studies six months after coaching was completed an increase in productivity of 27 percent and a reduction in staff attrition of more than two-thirds, from 39 percent to 12 percent. Qualitatively, the company found that there were fewer meetings or they were of shorter duration, enhancing effective professional interactions across the company. The leadership culture became more aligned with the worldwide digital revolution and there was greater ownership, with each team autonomously designing its own practical and measurable action plans, tracking mechanisms, deadlines and verbal and written commitments.

Insights gained from feedback, testimonials and self-reporting

The systemic process created curiosity and excitement, surfacing consensus on developing self, team and system, allowing transformation of the workplace culture and performance. Action learning projects contributed significantly. Focusing on results allowed for collaborative ownership and alignment between "what I desire as a leader and what the organization needs to grow."

The coaching process of building client contact before exploring the context allowed coachees to become bridges, mirrors and co-inquirers, leading to conscious transformational action, creating greater consciousness of the teams and collective organization.

This transformation was hard work and the system, despite enthusiasm, surfaced its shadow of resistance in weaving personal and team development at the workplace. A common question leaders asked was "why is a developmental intervention required" and "why me"? Coaches addressed this as a part of the cultural context, generating rich reflective conversations on recent organizational experience, growing to meet future organizational context.

A dilemma that was anticipated, that occurred and was accepted was the exit of some leaders after coaching resulting from greater awareness of personal purpose and their understanding this was not the right organization for them.

Recommendations

Learning through this process leads us to these recommendations for our future projects and to our readers.

At the individual level, coaches need to address clients' values and beliefs before addressing the outer world of organizational objectives. At the same time the approach needs to be systemic to help client mindset to empower and risk, exploring a new way of being and doing with the larger organizational goals in mind.

At the team level, creating psychological safety through open conversations is key to personal exploration and stepping out of one's comfort zone. In addition, setting clear goals supported by system structure integrated with the meaningful meta goal of work/life balance.

At the organizational level, action learning projects are important to implement changes and experience individual and collective impact.

In addition, coaches need to have organizational experience, team coaching skills and the ability to build trust and empathy with their clients, establishing clear goals and action orientation. Clients need to be selected on the basis of willingness to make sustained behavioural changes, and matched appropriately with coaches, which was done through chemistry meetings.

The process needs to be simple, expressed in practical language and tools, rather than as complex ideas for making coaching-driven insights accessible and effective. It needs to be systemic, empowering individuals to build and expand their mindset as teams take emotional risks towards exploring new ways of being and doing to produce organizational outcome.

Summary

An impactful and transformational systemic coaching process resulted in heightened awareness of individuals and teams. As the HR chief rightly feared, some executives left the organization to seek more favourable spaces to further their own goals and careers. The company's meta goal was built upon its Indian roots of family orientation through creation of emotionally bonded workplace communities integrated with the life beyond the workplace.

Case study F: the story of a company turnaround from Ingela Camba Ludlow, Mexico

Five years ago, I sat down with the owner of a mobility company. He was interested in a proposal based on a particular coaching model that included interacting with many levels of his company. His father had started the company 50 years earlier and now the second generation was managing the business. His particular objectives at the time were to regain market leadership and ensure customers received higher quality service. Recent company efforts focussed on employee development and succeeded in reaching the highest loyalty levels across the industry.

The company was composed of directors, managers and frontline employees that interacted vertically. The first task at hand was to form a leadership team that would direct, communicate and build strategies together. This team had never collaborated as such, despite several interactions that were part of their everyday tasks.

The most valuable elements of the programme were the individual coaching conversations and the team coaching sessions with the complete leadership team. Initially, individual coaching focussed on who they were, their history, what they liked most about their work and what was difficult to cope with. This individual reflective space was critical to strengthen their being as a person, working through uncertainties and reservations, also to help them resurface their own aspirations and the necessary challenges they faced. This was critical in preparing them to honestly and courageously contribute within the collective conversations. Then we had similar dialogues as a team. This allowed the team and myself to discover their collective aspirations and values, their common purpose, in the complex network composed of personalities, rules and beliefs with their own particular dynamic. This also provided the benefit of gauging the temperature of a system that seemed overall fit and healthy.

A critical finding for the owner and his closest directors was that the company was composed of microsystems, each one with its own rules and alliances that did not interact freely with others, similar to medieval feuds, protected but walled. Interestingly, loyalty and compromise had a heavy weight in the origin of the current status quo. The teams were so engaged in working out the best possible way to respond to their close environment needs, that they were unable to see what was going on beyond what they believed was their area of responsibility.

Most of the rules were focussed on detecting any anomalies in the process, and despite the evident conflicts this generated between departments, nothing was done to prevent it. The coaching work was needed across all departments and middle and upper management levels.

Three questions were critical throughout this process:

- What is it that you have to do?
- Who are your clients and stakeholders?
- What are the implications of your own work and ways of operating for the different people in the company?

Interestingly, after these conversations began to take place, people that affected the system the most felt there were no possibilities to do things differently, believing that their loyalty to 'the company's' old ways prevented any change. Comments such as: "we have been a very successful business for years. . . . Why change?"; "I need people from the other departments to understand the importance of my work so they can comply with what I request from them for administrative controls," were very common. Once engaged in the process, the leadership team was the one that generated the change that impacted the most. Challenging the status quo was always felt as a threat. I especially remember being challenged during the first sessions by one manager who was two years away from retiring, protesting about why he needed to make friends at work (this was his way of interpreting collaboration at different levels). After less than a year, this same manager had the most profound changes in his team and in business results. He became the best advocate for the process and a great role model for the rest of the team. When he was retiring he had this inexplicable feeling that he continued to be the same as he always had been but he felt different about it. He was right. He stopped thinking as himself but more as a part of a dynamic living system.

Two elements were very important throughout the process that involved coaching conversations across many different levels and teams. The first one was that every single day that I met them involved at least one meeting with the leadership team and the second was that in every conversation, despite the immediate issue at hand, there was awareness on how their work affected the work/efficiency/life of others, whether the conversation was individual, within a department or across departments.

After five years, the programme efforts proved to be highly successful, generating meaningful results in the following areas:

a) Business – Achieved the highest quality of the service to customers in a way that was sustainable over the years in contrast to prior to the start of the process, when consumer service results had deteriorated. Consumers' expectations had changed and the company had previously been unable to respond to this market change. There was a genuine surprise in the teams that despite their best efforts they were not able to meet consumers' expectations. As a result of the programme, customer satisfaction levels had improved, achieving record levels (97% consumer satisfaction in sales from an initial 80%) and becoming the benchmark for the industry.

b) Overall team dynamics leveraged the following key values:

- Trust. The continuous interactions across functions and levels allowed trust to grow as part of the culture. This became a virtue in many areas: to share findings and ideas, to be open and solve conflicts or anticipate potential conflicts and encourage individuals to ask for help or even better, to create new possibilities.
- Flexibility. The willingness to modify or change what is required. This allowed directors and managers to make decisions in a faster way as the business required.
- Empathy. The possibility to consider how life and work looks from other team's perspectives and take action towards this new vision.

These are all interconnected values. The challenge for the coming years will be to strengthen these new capabilities and capacities.

As a recommendation, it is critical to identify the key individuals that will be crucial for the success of the programme. Individuals who must participate in key decisions and help generate awareness across the organization.

Finally, all this work considered the interconnecting systems of the organization, the various levels of employees, the stakeholders and the customers. The big next step we need to focus on is to generate awareness on how to positively interact in a larger system considering the environment and the community.

Case study G: providing a worldwide coaching service to a global company, from Nick Smith, UK

A global product company changed its CEO and wanted to look at how they could most effectively outsource the executive coaching of their top 200 leaders worldwide. The incoming CEO had challenged the HR team to explain the value created by their previous attempt to run their own coaching 'bench'. HR were clear that outsourced coaching would need to deliver several benefits and create explicit value for the budget allocated through:

- Consistency of 'coaching' globally
- Alignment with the leadership principles used by HR in other development activities
- Alignment between the individual needs of the coachees and the organizational needs of the company
- Transparency of cost and an ability to provide some qualitative analysis of the value that had been added

To satisfy these needs and provide value-add raised significant challenges for the coaching supplier, we had to:

- Discuss and harmonize with the company how they would internally manage who was eligible for coaching and the criteria to apply
- Set up and manage a global group of external senior executive coaches
- Set up ways of evaluating the coaching benefits
- Find the best way of feeding back to the organization the cultural themes noticed by different coaches globally

What will be the purpose of the coaching?

As Stephen Covey (2004) suggests, we needed to start with the end in mind. The company wanted the coaching to link personal development with organizational development. So, we decided that leaders needed to create a business case to access coaching as well as articulate why coaching rather than another development would be most effective. Each business case was developed with the leader's HR business partner and signed off by the coachee's line manager, which made the development explicit and alerted the line manager that behaviour change was being attempted. This created a clear purpose for the company to support leaders in adapting to the business' changing circumstances so leaders would develop the concomitant changes needed in leadership behaviour. The company therefore takes responsibility for who comes forward for coaching and for setting the purpose.

Setting up the global executive coach bench

It was not practical nor desirable to have everyone coach in the same way, so we created a common, core coaching approach that whatever their training, the coach would embrace. These five standardized strands were:

- Linking personal and business goals
- Working with assumptions, not just feelings and behaviours
- Creating fast-forward rehearsals in the session to embody new behaviour
- Using the data in front of the coach more than the reported data from outside
- Working with the systemic and the intra-personal

We already had a good spread of coaches from past work, so their on-boarding was fairly straightforward. To build our resources in particular regions we sought other experienced coaches through our network. Candidates were asked to complete a semi-structured questionnaire and to read about the five core approaches. Each coach then had a one-hour virtual session during which the lead coach fed back whether they would be asked to be part of the bench, and, if so, in what circumstances we might consider using them. It was important to be clear with our feedback to the new coaches, so that we modelled the sort of coaching we expected of them.

To provide ongoing support the coaches were offered an hour's supervision session during each coaching contract, and a yearly review of what has worked well and what improvements might be needed.

The coaching process

The service offers two potential coaches and the coachee selects their coach after a short chemistry meeting; the chosen coach then receives the coachee's agreed business case. As part of the contracting process, the coach holds a three-way meeting with the coachee and their line manager to agree on the behavioural change that is needed. Both then rate the coachee against the agreed changes: how they rate them now and where they would need to be rated for the coaching to be deemed a success. There is an initial contract for 14 hours, although this can be extended if signed off by the company.

Around halfway through the coach and the coaching supervisor have a one-hour supervision session to provide support for the coach and allow the service to keep a quality check on the coaching. At the end the coach is encouraged to hold a further three-way meeting when they go over the initial changes that had been agreed and these are re-rated in the light of the coachee's current behaviours. This provides some quantitative and qualitative assessment of change brought about through coaching. Whenever possible, coachee feedback is also obtained to put on the company intranet to contribute to developing a coaching culture in the company.

Creating organizational learning from across all the coaching activity

Every year or so, we create an organizational review including these elements:

- With HR, we construct a semi-structured questionnaire that looks for patterns of behaviour and broader systemic patterns that have been coached during the previous year. We ask coaches to compare this company's executives and their issues with other executives from other companies they have worked with to gain a broader sector comparison. We also add in one or two specific questions HR might need feedback on (for example what impact new leadership standards had).
- When the data is returned, the supervisor draws out the broad themes, making sure personal confidentiality of the coachees is not compromised.
- These themes are sent to the coaches for sense checking and two conference calls are arranged to cover all time zones.
- At each conference call the task is not to revisit the original data but to develop our understanding of what is happening

through building on this data together. Further pattern analysis is collected.

- The supervisor then amends the initial themes and creates the learning review for HR, often accompanied by a debrief meeting between supervisor and HR lead.

Value-added coaching activity

Over an eight-year period, the company has been able to:

- Track its coaching spend.
- Begin to quantify the impact of its coaching.
- See where the uptake of coaching is happening.
- Receive insights as to the issues facing its senior leaders.
- Support its leaders to embrace the changing leadership challenges in its turbulent business environment.

The reports of the shift in executive behaviour that the coaching has encouraged is more specific. Through answering questionnaires, we receive coachee and line manager feedback on where positive impact had been created. Regularly the coaching service received evaluations of eight or nine out of ten (90% of respondents) for the quality of its coaching across the regions. Eighty-six percent of coachees felt they achieved their major goals set at the initial three-way contracting meeting. The business impact and performance improvement attributed to coaching included

- Better and improved conflict resolution outcomes within and beyond the company.
- More significant uptake of business opportunities by certain leaders.
- A significant and complex project was achieved with much better support from colleagues.
- One coachee's PDP showed their individual business contribution had significantly increased in comparison with before.
- Some coachees achieved significantly better leadership of team as measured by annual staff survey feedback.
- Leaders' improved development of their staff has resulted in a knock-on improvement in team delivery at lower levels.

Conclusion

When coaching is properly embedded in the business strategy of a company and where it is supported by an understanding of the systemic needs of the business, the value-add for coaching of individuals is high. It delivers for the individual, their teams and the overall business. It also alerts the business to its environment and its stakeholders through the strategic focus held by the coaches in relation to their coachees.

References

Abrahms, D. (1996). *The spell of the sensuous*. New York, NY: Random House.

Adshead-Grant, J., Hathaway, A., Aspey, L. and Turner, E. (2019). Supervision in a thinking environment. In E. Turner and S. Palmer (Eds.) *The heart of coaching supervision-Working with reflection and self-care*. Abingdon: Routledge.

Alexander, G. and Renshaw, B. (2005). *Supercoaching*. London: Random House Business Books.

Anderson, M.C. (2001). Executive briefing: Case study on the return on investment of executive coaching. Retrieved 1 November 2019 from www.metrixglobal.net

Argyris, C. and Schön, D.A. (1974). *Theory in practice: Increasing professional effectiveness*. San Francisco, CA: Jossey-Bass.

Argyris, C. and Schön, D.A. (1978). *Organizational learning: A theory of action perspective*. Reading, MA: Addison Wesley.

Assagioli, R. (1993). *Transpersonal development*. London: Thorsons.

Association for Coaching (AC, 2019). Recognized leader as coach. Retrieved 1st November 2019 from: https://www.associationforcoaching.com/page/RLaCDetails

Attenborough, D. (2018). The people's address to the United Nations. Retrieved 1st November 2019 from https://unfccc.int/sites/default/files/resource/The%20People%27s%20 Address%202.11.18_FINAL.pdf

Atwood, G.E. and Stolorow, R.D. (1984). *Structures of subjectivity: Explorations in psychoanalytic phenomenology*. Hillsdale, NJ: The Analytic Press.

Balint, M., Balint, E., Gosling, R. and Hildebrand, P. (1966). *A study of doctors*. London: Tavistock Publications.

Bandler, R. and Grinder, G. (1979). *Frogs into princes: Neurolinguistic programming*. Utah: Real People's Press

Bateson, G. (1972). *Steps to an ecology of mind: Collected essays in anthropology, psychiatry, evolution and epistemology*. London: Paladin, Granada.

Bateson, G. (1979). *Mind and nature*. Glasgow: Fontana/Collins.

BBC. (2018). Making the BBC a great workplace for women. Retrieved 1st November 2019 from http://downloads.bbc.co.uk/aboutthebbc/insidethebbc/reports/gender_equality_ recommendations_2018.pdf

BBC. (2019). BBC coaching-A guide to coaching and the skills involved. Retrieved 1st November 2019 from https://canvas-story.bbcrewind.co.uk/sites/bbc-coaching/

Belbin, M. (2004). *Management teams: Why they succeed or fail*. London: Heinemann.

Berry, W. (1983). *Standing by words*. San Francisco, CA: North Point Press.

von Bertalanffy, L. (1928). The history and status of general systems theory. *The Academy of Management Journal*, 15(4), 407–426.

Bion, W. R. (1970). *Attention and interpretation*. London: Tavistock Publications.

Bird, J. and Gornall, S. (2016). *The art of coaching*. Abingdon: Routledge.

Blakey, J. and Day, I. (2012). *Challenging coaching*. London: Nicholas Brealey Publishing.

Bluckert, P. (2006). *Psychological dimensions of executive coaching*. Maidenhead: Open University Press.

Boaks, J. and Levine, M.P. (Eds.). (2017). *Leadership and ethics*. London: Bloomsbury Academic.

Bohr, N. (1934). *Atomic physics and human knowledge*. New York, NY: John Wiley & Sons Ltd.

Bohm, D. and Nichol, L. (1998). *On creativity*. London: Routledge.

Bollas, C. (1987). *The shadow of the object: Psychoanalysis of the unthought known*. London: Free Association Books.

Boulton, J.G., Allen, P.M. and Bowman, C. (2015). *Embracing complexity: Strategic perspectives for an age of turbulence*. Oxford: Oxford University Press.

Bresser, F. and Wilson, C. (2006). What is coaching? In J. Passmore (Ed.) *Excellence in coaching*. London: Kogan Page/Association for Coaching.

Brown, B. (2013). *Daring greatly*. London: Penguin Books.

Bucke, R.M. (1901). *Cosmic consciousness*. New York, NY: Dutton & Co.

Bunker, K.A., Hall, D.T. and Kram, K.E. (2010). *Extraordinary leadership: Addressing the gaps in senior executive development*. San Francisco, CA: Jossey-Bass.

Cairo, P.C. and Dotlich, D.L. (2010). On the other side of the divide-How leaders must lead in the post-boom era. In K.A. Bunker, D.T. Hall and K.E. Kram (Eds.) *Extraordinary leadership: Addressing the gaps in senior executive development*. San Francisco, CA: Jossey-Bass.

Caplan, J. (2003). *Coaching for the future: How smart companies use coaching and mentoring*. London: Chartered Institute of Personnel and Development.

Capra, F. (1996). *The web of life: A new scientific understanding of living systems*. New York, NY: Anchor Books.

Capra, F. (2002). *The hidden connections*. London: HarperCollins.

Capra, F. and Luisi, P.L. (2014). *The systems view of life: A unifying vision*. Cambridge: Cambridge University Press.

Capra, F. and Luisi, P.L. (2016). *The systems view of life: A unifying vision*. Cambridge: Cambridge University Press.

Carrington, D. (2019). School climate strikes: 1.4 Million people took part, say campaigners. *The Guardian*, 19 March. Retrieved 1st November 2019 from www.theguardian.com/environment/2019/mar/19/school-climate-strikes-more-than-1-million-took-part-say-campaigners-greta-thunberg

Carroll, M. and Shaw, E. (2013). *Ethical maturity in the helping professions*. London: Jessica Kingsley.

Castelloe, M.S. (2018). Coming to terms with ecoanxiety. *Psychology Today*, 9 January. Retrieved 1st November 2019 from www.psychologytoday.com/gb/blog/the-me-in-we/201801/coming-terms-ecoanxiety

Centre for Transpersonal Psychology. (2019). Transpersonal psychology. Retrieved 1st November 2019 from http://transpersonalcentre.co.uk/index.php/transpersonal-psychology

Clance, P. and Imes, S. (1978). The imposter phenomenon in high achieving women: Dynamics and therapeutic intervention. *Psychotherapy Theory, Research and Practice*, 15(3), 1–8.

Clark, M., Harrington, T. and Myers, A. (2016). Promoting excellence in customer management: Emerging trends in business. *Journal of Emerging Trends in Marketing and Management*, 1, 119–129. ISSN 2537–5865

Clutterbuck, D. and Megginson, D. (2005). *Making coaching work: Creating a coaching culture*. London: Chartered Institute of Personnel and Development.

Clutterbuck, D. and Megginson, D. (2010). Coach maturity an emerging concept. *The International Journal of Mentoring and Coaching*, VIII(1), December.

Clutterbuck, D. and Megginson, D. (2011). Coach maturity an emerging concept. In D. Brennan and L. Wildflower (Eds.) *The Handbook of knowledge-based coaching: From theory to practice*. Chichester: John Wiley & Sons Ltd.

Clutterbuck, D., Megginson, D. and Bajer, A. (2016). *Building and sustaining a coaching culture*. London: Chartered Institute of Personnel and Development.

CNN (2019). Teen activist tells protesters demanding action on climate change: We need to do this now. Retrieved 30th October 2019 from: https://edition.cnn.com/2019/09/20/world/global-climate-strike-september-intl/index.html

Cohen, Z. (2019). Personal email communication to Peter Hawkins and Eve Turner, September 2019.

COMENSA. (2019). Ethics toolkit for coaches and mentors. Retrieved 1st November 2019 from www.comensa.org.za/information/ethicsread

Cooper, M. (2008). *Essential research findings in counseling and psychotherapy: The facts are friendly*. London: Sage Publications.

Cooperrider, D. and Srivastva, S. (1987). Appreciative inquiry in organizational life. In *Research in organizational change and development*, Vol. 1, pp.129–169. Stamford, CT: JAI Press.

Cooperrider, D.L. and Whitney, D. (1999). *Appreciative inquiry*. San Francisco, CA: Berrett-Koehler Communications.

Corporate Leadership Council. (2011). *Driving performance and retention through employee engagement a quantitative analysis of effective engagement strategies*. London: Corporate Leadership Council.

Covey, S. (2004). *The 7 habits of highly effective people*. London: Simon and Schuster.

Cox, C. (2019). The climate change coaches. Retrieved 1st November 2019 from https://www.climatechangecoaches.com

Csikszentmihalyi, M. (1999). *If we are so rich, why aren't we happy? American Psychological Association*, 54(10), 821–827.

Dartnall, E. (2012). *Supervisors' perceptions of the impact of supervision on therapeutic outcomes: A grounded theory study*. Doctoral Dissertation City University, London.

David, S., Clutterbuck, D. and Megginson, D. (2013). *Beyond goals: Effective strategies for coaching and mentoring*. Farnham: Gower Publishing Limited.

DeepMind Ethics and Society (DMES). (2019). Retrieved 1st November 2019 from https://deepmind.com/applied/deepmind-ethics-society/

de Gues, A. (1997). *The living company*. Harvard, MA: Harvard Business School.

de Haan, E. (2008). *Relational coaching*. Chichester: John Wiley & Sons Ltd.

de Haan, E. and Kasozi, A. (2014). *The leadership shadow: how to recognise and avoid derailment, hubris and overdrive*. London: Kogan Page

de Haan, E., Burger, Y., Grant, A., Dini, S., Eriksson, P.-O., Man-Mul, A., Mannhardt, S., Penninga, S., Van Abbe, M., Van Boekholt, M., Van der Heide, J., Van Elst, C., Van Gorp, J. and Voogd, M. (2014). A large-scale study of executive coaching outcome: The relative contributions of relationship, personality match, and self-efficacy. Ashridge, VU, Amsterdam. (personal communication to participants)

de Haan, E., Grant, A.M., Burger, Y. and Eriksson, P.-O. (2016). A large-scale study of executive and workplace coaching: The relative contributions of relationship, personality match and self-efficacy. *Consulting Psychology Journal: Practice and Research*, 68(3), 189–207. American Psychological Association. Retrieved 1st November 2019 from http://dx.doi.org/10.1037/cpb0000058

De Meuse, K.P., Dai, G. and Lee, R.J. (2009). Evaluating the effectiveness of executive coaching: Beyond ROI? *Coaching: An International Journal of Theory, Research and Practice*, 2(2), 117–134.

Diamandis, P.H. and Kotler, S. (2014). *Abundance: The future is better than you think*. New York, NY: Free Press.

Downey, M. (2003). *Effective coaching: Lessons from the coach's coach*. 2nd edition. New York, NY: Thomson Texere.

Duffy, M. and Passmore, J. (2010). Ethics in coaching: An ethical decision-making framework for coaching psychologists. *International Coaching Psychology Review*, 5(2), 140–151.

Dunphy, D., Griffiths, A. and Benn, S. (2007). *Organizational change for corporate sustainability: A guide for leaders and change agents of the future*. 2nd edition. Abingdon: Routledge.

Earth Overshoot Day. (2019). Past Earth Overshoot Days. Retrieved 1st November 2019 from: https://www.overshootday.org/newsroom/past-earth-overshoot-days/

Edelman. (2013). Good Purpose 2012 Fifth Global Consumer Study. Edelman. Retrieved 1st November 2019 from https://www.edelman.com/research

Einzig, H. (2017). *The future of coaching*. Abingdon: Routledge.

Elkington, J. (2001). *The chrysalis economy*. Oxford: Capstone.

Elkington, J. (2012). *The Zeronauts: Breaking the sustainability barrier*. London: Routledge.

Elkington, J. and Braun, S. (2013). *Breakthrough: Business leaders, market revolutions*. London: Volans.

Elkington, J. and Zeitz, J. (2014). *The breakthrough challenge: 10 Ways to connect today's profit with tomorrow's bottom line*. San Francisco, CA: Jossey-Bass.

EMCC. (2011). Commercial coaching agreement. Retrieved 1st November 2019 (for members) from www.emccouncil.org/uk/

EMCC. (2018). Coaching and ethics in practice: Dilemmas, navigations, and the (unspoken). 3rd Provocations Report, April 2018. Retrieved 1st November 2019 from https://www.emccbooks.org/book-contents/provocations/april-2018-coaching-and-ethics-in-practice-dilemmas-navigations-and-the-unspoken

EMCC International Research. (2019). Ethical dilemmas in coaching. Personal communication to all EMCC members, 20 March.

Eriksson, K. (2011). *Executive coaching: Diverse stakeholder perspectives and a model for agreed procurement procedures*. Abridged version. Submitted for the award of Doctor of Philosophy at the University of Derby, unpublished.

EthicalCoach. (2019). *EthicalCoach: Ethiopia initiative*. Henley-on Thames: Henley Business School and EMCC. Retrieved 1st November 2019 from https://ethicalcoach.org/ethiopia/

Ferrucci, P. (1995). *What we may be (the vision and techniques of psychosynthesis)*. Wellingborough: Thorsons.

Firman, J. and Vargiu, J. (1977). Dimensions of growth. *Synthesis Journal: The Realization of the Self*, 3–4(1), 60–120.

Fredrickson, B. L. and Losada, M. (2005). Positive affect and the complex dynamics of human flourishing. *American Psychologist*, 60, 678–686.

Friedman, T. L. (2005). The World is Flat. London: Penguin Books.

Friedman, T. L. (2008). Hot, flat and crowded. New York, NY: Farrar, Straus and Giroux.

Friedman, T.L. (2012). Thomas Friedman on 'Connected to Hyperconnected. Huffington Post video. Retrieved 2nd November 2019 from https://www.huffpost.com/entry/thomas-friedman-connected-to-hyperconnected-_n_1878605?fbclid=IwAR2V3w9l1VP3c6-ZqhAxMPikqfRxs_FY5bTWI8jwbhD5hkgbE_hJdi0TE-U

Ghemawat, P. (2012). Developing global leaders. *Mckinsey Quarterly*. Retrieved 1st November 2019 from www.mckinsey.com/global-themes/leadership/developing-global-leaders

Global Supervisors' Network. (2019). Virtual professional network. Retrieved 1st November 2019 from www.eve-turner.com/global-supervisors-network/

Goffee, R. and Jones, R. (2006). *Why should anyone be led by YOU?* Boston, MA: Harvard Business Review Press.

Goldsmith, M. (2008). *What got you here won't get you there*. London: Profile Books.

Goldsmith, M. (2011). Our "pay for results" executive coaching process. Retrieved 1st November 2019 from www.marshallgoldsmith.com/articles/our-pay-for-results-executive-coaching-process/

Goldsmith, M. and Silvester, S. (2018). *Stakeholder centered coaching*. Cupertino, CA: Thinkaha.

Goldvarg, D. (2017). *Supervision de coaching*. Buenos Aries, Argentina: Grantica.

Goleman, D., Boyatzis, R.E. and McKee, A. (2002). *Primal leadership: Realizing the power of emotional intelligence*. Boston, MA: Harvard Business School Press.

Graves, C. (1974). Human nature prepares for a momentous leap. *The Futurist*, April.

Grof, S. (1975). *Realms of the human unconscious*. New York, NY: Viking Press.

The Guardian. (2018). Richest 1% on target to own two-thirds of all wealth by 2030. Retrieved 1st November 2019 from www.theguardian.com/business/2018/apr/07/global-inequality-tipping-point-2030. 7 April 2018.

Hall, K. (2018). Coming home to Eden: Animal-assisted therapy and the present moment. *The British Journal for Psychotherapy Integration*, 14, 53–63.

Handy, C. (1994). *The empty raincoat: Making sense of the future*. London: Hutchinson.

Harari, Y.N. (2016). *Homo Deus: A brief history of tomorrow*. London: Harvill Secker, Penguin Random House.

Hardingham, A., Brearley, M., Moorhouse, A. and Venter, B. (2004). *The coach's coach: Personal development for personal developers*. London: Kogan Page.

Hawkins, P. (1985). Humanistic psychotherapy supervision: A conceptual framework. *Self and Society: Journal of Humanistic Psychology*, 13(2), 69–79.

Hawkins, P. (2004). A centennial tribute to Gregory Bateson 1904–1980 and his influence on the fields of organizational development and action research. *Action Research*, 2(4), 409–423.

Hawkins, P. (2005). *The wise fool's guide to leadership*. Winchester: O Books.

Hawkins, P. (2011a). *Leadership team coaching: Developing collective transformational leadership*. 1st edition. London: Kogan Page.

Hawkins, P. (2011b). Systemic approaches to supervision. In T. Bachkirova, P. Jackson and D. Clutterbuck (Eds.) *Coaching and mentoring supervision theory and practice*. Maidenhead: Oxford University Press.

Hawkins, P. (2011c). Building emotional, ethical and cognitive capacity in coaches-A development model of supervision. In J. Passmore (Ed.) *Supervision in coaching*. London: Kogan Page.

Hawkins, P. (2012). *Creating a coaching culture*. Maidenhead: Open University Press.

Hawkins, P. (2014). *Leadership team coaching*. 2nd edition. London: Kogan Page.

Hawkins, P. (2017a). *Leadership team coaching: Developing collective transformational leadership*. 3rd edition. London: Kogan Page.

Hawkins, P. (2017b). The necessary revolution in humanistic psychology. In R. House and D. Kalisch (Eds.) *The future of humanistic psychology*. London: Routledge.

Hawkins, P. (2017c). *Tomorrow's leadership and the necessary revolution in today's leadership development*. Henley: Henley Business School.

Hawkins, P. (2018). *Leadership team coaching in practice*. 2nd edition. London: Kogan Page.

Hawkins, P. (2019). Resourcing-The neglected third leg of supervision. In E. Turner and S. Palmer (Eds.) *The heart of coaching supervision-Working with reflection and self-care*. Abingdon: Routledge.

Hawkins, P. and McMahon, A. (2020) Supervision in the Helping Professions. 5th edition. Maidenhead: Open University Press

Hawkins, P. and Presswell, D. (2018). Using embodied interventions in team coaching. 2nd edition. In P. Hawkins (Ed.) *Leadership team coaching in practice*. London: Kogan Page.

Hawkins, P. and Ryde, J. (2020). *Integrative psychotherapy: in theory and practice; A relational, systemic and ecological approach*. London: Jessica Kingsley.

Hawkins, P. and Schwenk, G. (2006). *Coaching supervision*. London: CIPD Change Agenda.

Hawkins, P. and Schwenk, G. (2011). The seven-eyed model of coaching supervision. In T. Bachkirova, P. Jackson and D. Clutterbuck (Eds.) *Coaching and mentoring supervision*. Maidenhead: Oxford University Press.

Hawkins, P. and Shohet, R. (1989). *Supervision in the helping professions*. Maidenhead: Open University Press.

Hawkins, P. and Shohet, R. (2000). *Supervision in the helping professions*. 2nd edition. Maidenhead: Open University Press.

Hawkins, P. and Shohet, R. (2006). *Supervision in the helping professions*. 3rd edition. Maidenhead: Open University Press.

Hawkins, P. and Shohet, R. (2012) *Supervision in the helping professions*. 4th edition Maidenhead: Open University Press.

Hawkins, P. and Smith, N. (2006). *Coaching, mentoring and organizational consultancy: Supervision and development*. Maidenhead: Open University Press/McGraw Hill.

Hawkins, P. and Smith, N. (2013). *Coaching, mentoring and organizational consultancy: Supervision and development*. 2nd edition. Maidenhead: Open University Press/ McGraw Hill.

Hawkins, P. and Smith, N. (2010). Transformational coaching. In E. Cox, T. Bachkirova and D. Clutterbuck (Eds.) *The complete handbook of coaching*. London: Sage Publications.

Hawkins, P. and Smith, N. (2014). Transformational coaching. In E. Cox, T. Bachkirova and D. Clutterbuck (Eds.) *The complete handbook of coaching*. 2nd edition. London: Sage Publications.

Hawkins, P. and Smith, N. (2018). Transformational coaching. In E. Cox, T. Bachkirova and D. Clutterbuck (Eds.) *The complete handbook of coaching*. 3rd edition, pp. 231–244. London: Sage Publications.

Hawkins, P. and Turner, E. (2017). The rise of coaching supervision 2006–2014. In *Coaching: An international journal of theory, research and practice*, Online, pp. 1–13. Retrieved 1st November 2019 from www.tandfonline.com/eprint/AxfVpA6637y9DYX2jg42/full

Hawkins, P., Turner, E. and Passmore, J. (2019). The Manifesto for Supervision. Henley-on-Thames: Association for Coaching and Henley Business School. Retrieved 1st November 2019 from https://www.henley.ac.uk/articles/the-manifesto-for-coaching-supervision

Heffernan, M. (2011). *Wilful blindness: How we ignore the obvious at our peril*. London: Simon and Schuster.

Heifetz, R. and Linsky, M. (2002). *Leadership on the line: Staying alive through the dangers of leading*. Boston, MA: Harvard Business School Press.

Heisenberg, W. (1958). *Physics and philosophy*. New York, NY: Harper Torchbooks.

Hellinger, B. (1998). *Love's symmetry*. Phoenix, AZ: Tucker and Theisen.

Hellinger, B. (1999). *Acknowledging what is*. Phoenix, AZ: Tucker and Theisen.

Heron, J. (1982). *Empirical validity in experiential research*. London: Sage Publications.

Heron, J. (1996). *Co-operative inquiry*. London: Sage Publications.

Hodges, C. and Steinholtz, R. (2017). *Ethical business practice and regulation: A behavioural and values-based approach to compliance and enforcement (Civil Justice Systems)*. Oxford: Hart Publishing.

Holbeche, L. and Springett, N. (2004). *In search of meaning in the workplace*. Horsham: Roffey Park Institute.

Holder, J. (2019). Creative forms of reflective and expressive writing in coaching supervision. In E. Turner and S. Palmer (Eds.) *The heart of coaching supervision: Working with reflection and self-care*. Abingdon: Routledge.

Honey, P. and Mumford, A. (1992). *The manual of learning styles*. Maidenhead: Peter Honey

Huffington, C. (2006). A contextualized approach to coaching. In *Executive coaching-Systems-Psychodynamic perspective*. London: Karnac Books Ltd.

Hunter, M.R., Gillespie, B.W. and Yu-Pu Chen, S. (2019). Urban nature experiences reduce stress in the context of daily life based on salivary biomarkers. *Frontiers in Psychology*, 4 April. Retrieved 1st November 2019 from https://www.frontiersin.org/articles/10.3389/fpsyg.2019.00722/full

Hutchins, G. (2012). *The nature of business: Redesigning for resilience*. Totnes, Devon: Green Books.

Hutchins, G. (2014). *The illusion of separation: Exploring the cause of our current crises*. Edinburgh: Floris.

Hutchins, G. (2016). *Future-fit*. CreateSpace Independent Publishers.

ICF. (2016). The 2016 ICF global coaching study. Retrieved 1st November 2019 from https://coachfederation.org/app/uploads/2017/12/2016ICFGlobalCoachingStudy_ExecutiveSummary-2.pdf

ICF. (2019a). ICF code of ethics. Retrieved 1st November, 2019 from https://coachfederation.org/code-of-ethics/

ICF. (2019b). *Ethical conduct and compliance report*. Lexington, KY: ICF. Retrieved 1st November, 2019 from https://coachfederation.org/app/uploads/2018/08/2017EthicalConductandComplianceReport.pdf

Intergovernmental Panel for Biodiversity and Ecosystem Services (IPBES). (2019). The global assessment of biodiversity and ecosystem services: Paris, 6 May. Retrieved 1st November 2019 from www.ipbes.net/

Iordanou, I., Hawley, R. and Iordanou, C. (2017). *Values and ethics in coaching*. London: Sage Publications.

IPCC. (2018). Special report: Global warming of 1.5 °C, October. Retrieved 1st November 2019 from www.ipcc.ch/sr15/

Ismail, S. (2014). *Exponential organizations: Why new organizations are ten times better, faster, and cheaper than yours (and what to do about it)*. New York, NY: Diversion Books.

Jackson, P. and Bachkirova, T. (2019). The 3Ps of supervision and coaching-Philosophy, purpose and process. In E. Turner and S. Palmer (Eds.) *The heart of coaching supervision: Working with reflection and self-care*. Abingdon: Routledge.

James, W. (1902). Varieties of Religious Experience: A Study in Human Nature. The Gifford lectures at the University of Edinburgh, 1901-1902. Accessed 1st November 2019 2019 from https://www.globalgreyebooks.com/varieties-of-religious-experience-ebook.html

Jaworski, J. (1998). *Synchronicity: The inner path of leadership*. San Francisco, CA: Berrett-Koehler Publishers, Inc.

Jones, R.J. and Underhill, B.O. (2019). Mastering evaluation. In J. Passmore, B. Underhill and M. Goldsmith (Eds.) *Mastering executive coaching*. Abingdon: Routledge.

Juch, B. (1983). *Personal development: Theory and practice in management training*. Chichester: John Wiley and Sons.

Jung, C.G. (1966). *Two essays on analytical psychology*. 2nd edition. London: Routledge.

Jung, C.G. (1969). *Synchronicity: An acausal connecting principle*. Princeton, NJ: Princeton University Press.

Kagan, N. (1980). Influencing human interaction-eighteen years with IPR. In A.K. Hess (Ed.) *Psychotherapy supervision: Theory, research and practice*. New York, NY: John Wiley & Sons Ltd.

Kahn, M.S. (2014). *Coaching on the axis*. London: Karnac Books Ltd.

Kahneman, D. (2011). *Thinking fast and thinking slow*. London: Penguin Books.

Karpman, S. (1968). The drama triangle. Retrieved 1st November 2019 from www.karpman dramatriangle.com/

Keats, J. (1970). *The letters of John Keats: A selection*. Edited by R. Gittings. Oxford: Oxford University Press.

Kegan, R. and Lahey, L.L. (2009). *Immunity to change*. Boston, MA: Harvard Business Press.

Kennedy, R. (1968). Speech at the University of Kansas, March 18.

Kelly, K. (2016). *The inevitable: Understanding the 12 technological forces that will shape our future*. New York, NY: Viking Press.

Kets de Vries, M.F.R. (2006). *The Leader on the Couch: A clinical approach to changing people and organizations*. San Francisco, CA: Jossey-Bass.

Kilburg, R.R (2000). *Executive coaching: Developing managerial wisdom in a world of chaos*. Washington, DC: American Psychological Association.

King, M.L. (1964). *Methodist student leadership conference address*. Lincoln, Nebraska. Retrieved 1st November 2019 from www.americanrhetoric.com/speeches/mlkmethodisty outhconference.htm

Kirkpatrick, D.L. (1977). Evaluating training programmes: Evidence vs. proof. *Training and Development Journal*, 31(11), 9–12.

Kirkpatrick, D.L. and Kirkpatrick, J.D. (1994). *Evaluating training programs*. San Francisco, CA: Berrett-Koehler Publishers, Inc.

Kirkpatrick, D.L. and Kirkpatrick, J.D. (2005). *Transferring learning to behavior*. San Francisco, CA: Berrett-Koehler Publishers, Inc.

Klein, N. (2014). *This changes everything-Capitalism vs climate*. London: Allen Lane.

Kline, N. (1999). *Time to think*. London: Cassell Illustrated.

Kline, N. (2015). *More time to think-The power of independent thinking*. 2nd edition. London: Cassell Illustrated.

Kline, N. (2019). Eleven innate breakthrough questions: Time to think collegiate meeting, London, January.

Knights, A. and Poppleton, A. (2008). *Research insight: Coaching in organisations*. London: Chartered Institute of Personnel and Development.

Kohlberg, L. (1981). *Essays on moral development, Vol. I: The philosophy of moral development*. San Francisco, CA: Harper & Row.

Kolb, D. (1984). *Experiential learning: Experience as the source of learning and development*. London: Prentice Hall.

Kolb, D.A., Rubin, I.M. and McIntyre, J.M. (1971). *Organizational psychology: An experimental approach*. New York, NY: Prentice Hall.

Laing, R.D. (1965). *The divided self: An existential study in sanity and madness*. Oxford: Penguin Books.

Laing, R.D. (1967). *The politics of experience and the bird of paradise*. Harmondsworth: Penguin.

Laloux, F. (2014). *Reinventing organizations*. Brussels: Nelson Parker.

Lamy, F. and Moral, M. (2017). Stretching ethical dilemmas-A creative tool for supervisors. Presentations, Oxford Brookes Supervision Conference, May and EMCC Research Conference, June 2017.

Landsberger, H. (1958). *Hawthorne revisited. Management and the worker: Its critics, and developments in human relations in industry*. New York: Cornell University.

Laske, O. (2003). Executive development as adult development. In J. Demick and C. Andreoletti (Eds.) *Handbook of adult development*, Chapter 29, pp. 565–584. New York, NY: Plenum/Kluwer.

Latour, B. (2017). *Facing Gaia: Eight lectures on the new climatic regime*. Translated by C. Porter. Cambridge: Polity Press.

Lawrence, P. and Moore, A. (2018). *Coaching in three dimensions: Meeting the challenges of a complex world*. Abingdon: Routledge.

Laybourn, L., Langton, L. and Baxter, D. (2019). *This is a crisis: Facing up to the age of environmental breakdown*, February. London: IPPR.

Leakey, R. and Lewin, R. (1996). *The sixth extinction: Biodiversity and its survival*. London: Orion Books.

Lee, A. (2013). Welcome to the Unicorn Club: Learning from billion-dollar startups. *Tech crunch*. Retrieved 1st November 2019 from https://techcrunch.com/2013/11/02/welcome-to-the-unicorn-club/

Lee, R.J. (2016). The role of contracting in coaching: Balancing individual client and organizational issues. In J. Passmore, D. Peterson and M. Freire (Eds.) *The Wiley-Blackwell handbook of the psychology of coaching and mentoring*. Chichester: John Wiley & Sons Ltd.

Leedham, M. (2005). The coaching scorecard: A holistic approach to evaluating the benefits of business coaching. *International Journal of Evidence Based Coaching & Mentoring*, 3(2), 30–44.

Loevinger, J. (1976). *Ego development*. San Francisco, CA: Jossey-Bass.

Lovelock, J. and Margulis, L. (1974). Atmospheric homeostasis by and for the biosphere: The gaia hypothesis. *Tellus*, 26(1–2), 2–10.

Lovelock, J. (1979). *Gaia*. Oxford: Oxford University Press.

Luthans, F. and Peterson, S.J. (2003). 360 degree feedback with systemic coaching: Empirical analysis suggests a winning combination. *Human Resource Management*, 43, 243–256.

MacLean, P. (2019). *Self as coach: Coach as self*. New York, NY: John Wiley & Sons Ltd.

Malik, K. (2014). *The quest for a moral compass*. London: Atlantic Books Ltd.

Mann, C. (2016). *Strategic trends in the use of coaching*. 6th Ridler report. London: Ridler & Co. Retrieved 1st November 2019 from www.ridlerandco.com/ridler-report/

Marshall, G. (2014). *Don't even think about it: Why our brains are wired to ignore climate change*. New York, NY: Bloomsbury.

Maslow, A.H. (1962). *Towards a psychology of being*. New York, NY: Van Nostrand.

Maslow, A. H. (1968). *Toward a psychology of being*. 2nd edition. Princeton: D. Van Nostrand Company.

Matile, L., Gilbert, S. and Turner, E. (2019). Resourcing through a peer supervision chain. In E. Turner and S. Palmer (Eds.) *The heart of coaching supervision: Working with reflection and self-care*. Abingdon: Routledge.

Maturana, H. and Varela, F. (1998). *The tree of knowledge: The biological roots of human understanding*. Revised Edition. Boston: Shambhala Publications

May, R. (Ed.) (1961). *Existential psychology*. New York, NY: Random House.

May, R. (1969). *Love and will*. New York, NY: W.W. Norton.

McGovern, J., Lindemann, M., Vergara, M., Murphy, S., Barker, L. and Warrenfeltz, R. (2001). Maximizing the impact of executive coaching: Behavioral change, organizational outcomes, and return on investment. *The Manchester Review*, 6(1), 2–10.

McGregor, C. (2015). *Coaching behind bars*. Maidenhead: Open University Press.

McLean, J.J. (2017). *Embedding sustainability into organisational DNA: A story of complexity*. Ph.D. thesis, The University of Adelaide, Adelaide. Retrieved 1st November 2019 from http://dx.doi.org/10.4225/55/5b21f318e7939

McLean, J.J. (2018). People, planet and profit: Facilitating change through coaching. ICF Bengaluru Coaching Conclave. Conference keynote presentation, Bengalura, India.

McLuhan, M. (1964). *Understanding media: The extensions of man*. New York, NY: Mentor.

Mead, M. (1949). *Male and female: A study of the sexes in a changing world*. New York, NY: William Morrow.

Meadows, D. (2008). *Thinking in systems*. White River Junction, VT: Chelsea Green Publishing.

Moreno, J. (1959). *Psychodrama Volume 2: Foundations of psychodrama*. New York, NY: Beacon House.

Morgan, G. (1986). *Images of organization*. London: Sage Publications.

Murdoch, E. and Arnold, J. (2013). *Full spectrum supervision*. St Albans: Paloma Press.

Newsweek. (2017). The 1 percent now have half the world's wealth. Retrieved 1st November 2019 from www.newsweek.com/1-wealth-money-half-world-global-710714, 14 November, 2017.

Naess, A. (1987). Self-realization: An ecological approach to being in the world. *The Trumpeter*, 4(3), 35–42.

O'Brien, W.J. (2008). *Character at work: Building prosperity through the practice of virtue*. Mahwah, NJ: Paulist Press.

O'Neill, M.B. (2000). *Executive coaching with backbone and heart*. San Francisco, CA: Jossey-Bass.

Oshry, B. (1995). *Seeing systems: Unlocking the mysteries of organizational life*. San Francisco, CA: Berrett-Koehler Publishers, Inc.

Oshry, B. (1999). *Leading systems: Lessons from the power lab*. San Francisco, CA: Berrett-Koehler Publishers, Inc.

Oxfam. (2018). *Reward work, not wealth*. Oxford: Oxfam International. Retrieved 1st November 2019 from https://www-cdn.oxfam.org/s3fs-public/file_attachments/bp-reward-work-not-wealth-220118-en.pdf

Oxfam. (2019). *Public good or private wealth? Briefing paper*. Oxford: Oxfam International. Retrieved 1st November 2019 from https://oxfamilibrary.openrepository.com/bitstream/handle/10546/620599/bp-public-good-or-private-wealth-210119-summ-en.pdf

Parker-Wilkins, V. (2006). Business impact of executive coaching: Demonstrating monetary value. *Industrial and Commercial Training*, 38(3), 122–127. doi:10.1108/00197850610659373

Parlett, M. (2015). Future sense: Five explorations of whole intelligence for a world that's waking up. Kibworth Beauchamp, Leics: Matador.

Passmore, J. (2016). Introduction. In J. Passmore (Ed.) *Excellence in coaching*. 3rd edition. London: Kogan Page.

Passmore, J., Brown, H. and Csigas, Z. (2017). *The state of play of coaching and mentoring*. EMCC.

Passmore, J. and Turner, E. (2018). Reflections on integrity: The APPEAR model. *Coaching at Work*, 13(2), 42–46.

Perls, F. (1968). *Gestalt therapy verbatim*. Moab, UT: Real People Press.

Perls, F. (1969). *Ego, hunger and aggression: A revision of Freud's theory and method*. New York, NY: Random House.

Peterson, D.B. (2010). Executive coaching: A critical review and recommendations for advancing the practice. In S. Zedeck (Ed.) *APA handbook of industrial and organizational psychology: Vol. 2: Selecting and developing members of the organization*. Washington, DC: American Psychological Association.

Peterson, C. (2013). *Pursuing the good life*. Oxford: Oxford University Press.

Philips, P.P. and Philips, J.J. (2007). *The value of learning: How organizations capture value and ROI and translate them into support, improvement and funds*. San Francisco, CA: John Wiley and Sons.

Philips, P.P., Philips, J.J. and Edwards, L.A. (2012). *Measuring the success of coaching: A step by step guide for measuring impact and calculating ROI*. Alexandria, VA: ASTD Press.

Piketty, T. (2014). *Capital in the twenty-first century*. Cambridge, MA: Belknap Press,

Pomerantz, S. and Eiting, J. (2007). Drawing lines in the sand: Ethics in coaching, contracting, and confidentiality with commentary. *International Journal of Coaching in Organizations*, 5(1), 94–102.

Porter, M.E. and Kramer, M.R. (2011). Shared value: How to re-invent capitalism and unleash a wave of innovation and growth. *Harvard Business Review*, 89(1-2), January-February, 62–77.

Prigogine, I. and Stengers, I. (1984). *Order out of chaos: Man's new dialogue with nature*. London: Heinemann.

Proctor, B. (2008). *Group supervision: A guide to creative practice*. 2nd edition. London: Sage Publications.

Rayton, B. (2012). *The evidence employee engagement task force "Nailing the evidence"*. Bath: University of Bath School of Management.

Reason, P. (2017). *In search of grace.* Alresford, Hampshire: Earth Books.

Reiman, J. (2013). *The story of purpose: The path to creating a brighter brand, a greater company and a lasting legacy.* London: John Wiley & Sons Ltd.

Renshaw, B. (2018). *Purpose: The extraordinary benefits of focusing on what matters most.* London: LID Publishing.

Revans, R. (1982). *The origin and growth of action learning.* Bromley: Chartwell Bratt.

Rimanoczy, I. and Brown, C. (2008). Bringing action reflection learning into action learning. *Action Learning: Research and Practice,* 5(2), 185–192.

Roberts, D. (2012). Climate change is simple. Tedx talk, The Evergreen State College. Retrieved 1st November 2019 from https://youtu.be/A7ktYbVwr90

Rogers, C. (1951). *Client-centered therapy: Its current practice, implications and theory.* London: Constable.

Rogers, J. (2008). *Coaching skills: A handbook.* 2nd edition. Maidenhead: Open University Press.

Rooke, D., Siegel, D., Poelmans, S.A.Y. and Payne, J. (2012). The healthy mind platter. *NeuroLeadership Journal* (4).

Rooke, D. and Torbert, W. (2005). Seven transformations of leadership. *Harvard Business Review,* April, 66–76.

RSA. (1995). *Tomorrow's company.* London: RSA.

Ryde, J. (2009). *Being White in the helping professions.* London: Jessica Kingsley.

Ryde, J. (2019). *White privilege unmasked.* London: Jessica Kingsley.

Ryde, J., Seto, L. and Goldvarg, D. (2019). Diversity and inclusion in supervision. In E. Turner and S. Palmer (Eds.) *The heart of coaching supervision: Working with reflection and self-care.* Abingdon: Routledge.

Scharmer, O. (2008). *Theory U: Leading from the future as it emerges.* San Francisco, CA; Berrett-Koehler Publishers.

Scharmer, O. and Kaufer, K. (2013). *Leading from the emerging future: From ego-system to eco-system economies.* San Francisco, CA: Berrett-Koehler Publishers, Inc.

Schon, D. (1983). *The reflective practitioner: How professionals think in action.* London: Temple Smith.

Schwab, K. (2016). *The fourth industrial revolution.* Cologne, Geneva: World Economic Forum.

Scotton, N. (2019). "The Earth was feverous and did shake . . ." Retrieved 1st November 2019 from www.enablingcatalysts.com/the-earth-was-feverous-and-did-shake/

Scoular, A. (2011). *Business coaching.* Harlow: Pearson Education Ltd.

Searles, H.F. (1955). The informational value of the supervisor's emotional experience. In *Collected papers of schizophrenia and related subjects.* London: Hogarth Press.

Seligman, M.E.P. and Csikszentmihalyi, M. (2000). Positive psychology: An introduction. *American Psychologist,* 55(1), 5–14. http://dx.doi.org/10.1037/0003-066X.55.1.5

Seligman, M. (2011). *Flourish – A visionary new understanding of happiness and well-being.* New York, NY: Free Press.

Senge, P. (1990). *The fifth discipline.* London: Random Books.

Senge, P. and Kofman, F. (1993) Communities of commissions: The heart of learning organizations, *Organizational Dynamics* (Autumn), 5–23.

Senge, P. (2008). *The Necessary Revolution: How individuals and organizations are working together to create a sustainable world.* New York, NY: Doubleday.

Senge, P.M., Flowers, B., Scharmer, O. and Jaworski, J. (2005). *Presence: An exploration of profound change in people, organizations, and society*. New York, NY: Doubleday Publishing.

Senge, Peter. (2014). Systems thinking for a better world. Talk at the Aalto Systems Forum, Finland, 2014.

Sharpe, B. (2013). *Three horizons: The patterning of hope*. Axminster: Triarchy Press.

Siegel, D. (2010). *Mindsight transform your brain with the new science of kindness*. New York, NY: One World, Random House.

Sisodia, R., Wolfe, D. and Sheth, J.N. (2007). *Firms of endearment: How world-class companies profit from passion and purpose*. London: Financial Times/Prentice Hall.

Solzhenitsyn, A. (1973). *Gulag Archipelego 1918–1956*. Vol. 1. London: Harper and Row.

Soska, T.L. and Conger, J. (2010). The shifting paradigm of executive leadership development: Moving the focus to the impact of the collective. In K.A. Bunker, D.T. Hall and K.E. Kram (Eds.) *Extraordinary leadership: Addressing the gaps in senior executive development*. San Francisco, CA: Jossey-Bass.

Spence, G.B., Stout-Rostron, S., Van Reenen, M. and Glashoff, B. (2019). Exploring the delayed effects of leadership coaching: A pilot study. *Coaching: An International Journal of Theory, Research and Practice*. doi:10.1080/17521882.2019.1574308

St John-Brooks, K. (2014). *Internal coaching: The inside story*. London: Karnac Books Ltd.

Stewart, I. and Joines, V. (1987). *TA Today: A new introduction to transactional analysis*. Nottingham: Lifespace Publishing.

Stiglitz, J.E. (2015). *The great divide: Unequal societies and what we can do about them*. New York, NY: W.W. Norton & Company.

Stolorow, R.D. and Atwood, G.E. (1992). *Context of being: The intersubjective foundations of psychological life*. Hilldale, NJ: The Analytic Press.

Stolorow, R.G., Atwood, G.E. and Orange, D. (2002). *Worlds of experience: Interweaving philosophical and clinical dimensions in psychoanalysis*. New York, NY: Basic Books.

Stout-Rostron, S. (2013). *Business coaching: Wisdom and practice*. Knowres Publishing. Retrieved 1st November 2019 from ProQuest Ebook Central, https://ebookcentral.proquest.com/lib/soton-ebooks/detail.action?docID=3544778

Talboom, A.M. (1999). *The welfare sector hits hard: Exploratory research after the role of coaching and counselling within organizations*. Nijmegen Business School.

Thornton, C. (2016). *Group and team coaching: The secret life of groups*. 2nd edition. Abingdon: Routledge.

Thunberg, G., Taylor, A., Neubauer, L., Gantois, K., De Wever, A., Charlier, A., Gillibrand, H. and Villasenor, A. (2019). Think we should be at school? Today's climate strike is the biggest lesson of all. *The Guardian*, 15 March. Retrieved 1st November 2019 from www.theguardian.com/commentisfree/2019/mar/15/school-climate-strike-greta-thunberg

Torbert, B. (2004). *Action inquiry: The secret of timely and transforming leadership*. San Francisco, CA: Berrett-Koehler Publishers.

Turner, E. (2012). Confidentiality and CPD opportunities top internal coaches' wishlist. *Coaching at Work*, 7(4), 8.

Turner, E. (2019). The horns of the dilemma. *Coaching at Work*, 14(2), 48–51.

Turner, E. and Clutterbuck, D. (2019). All in the small print: A brief study of contracting issues in coaching and supervision. Presentation to the 8th international coaching supervision conference, 11 May, Oxford.

Turner, E. and Clutterbuck, D. (2019). *All in the small print: A brief study of contracting issues in coaching and supervision.* Presentation to 8th international coaching supervision conference, Oxford Brookes University, May 11th, 2019.

Turner, E. and Hawkins, P. (2017). Coming of age: The development of coaching supervision 2006–2014. *Coaching at Work*, 11(2), 30–35.

Turner, E. and Hawkins, P. (2016). Multi-stakeholder contracting in executive/business coaching: An analysis of practice and recommendations for gaining maximum value. *International Journal of Evidence Based Coaching and Mentoring*, 14(2), 48–65. Retrieved 1st November 2019 from https://radar.brookes.ac.uk/radar/items/299b7998-8bae-4cd2-b66c-5bcc01bdff59/1/

Turner, E. and Hawkins, P. (2019). Mastering contracting. In J. Passmore, B. Underhill and M. Goldsmith (Eds.) *Mastering executive coaching.* Abingdon: Routledge.

Turner, E. and Palmer, S. (2019) (Eds). *The heart of coaching supervision: Working with reflection and self-care.* Abingdon: Routledge.

Turner, E. and Passmore, J. (2017). The trusting kind. *Coaching at Work*, 12(6), 34–39.

Turner, E. and Passmore, J. (2018). Ethical dilemmas and tricky decisions: A global perspective of coaching supervisors' practices in coach decision-making. *International Journal of Evidence Based Coaching and Mentoring*, 16(1), 126–142. Retrieved 1st November 2019 from https://radar.brookes.ac.uk/radar/items/da4e8785-60aa-4867-8aa7-caebf259a94f/1/

Turner, E. and Passmore, J. (2019). Mastering ethics. In J. Passmore, B. Underhill and M. Goldsmith (Eds.) *Mastering executive coaching.* Abingdon: Routledge.

Turner, E. and Woods, D. (2015). When the police come knocking. *Coaching at Work*, 10(6), 28–34.

Turner, T., Lucas, M. and Whitaker, C. (2018). *Peer supervision in coaching and mentoring paperback.* Abingdon: Routledge.

Wageman, R., Hackman, J.R. and Lehman, E. (2005). Team diagnostic survey: Development of an instrument. *The Journal of Applied Behavioral Science*, 41(4), December, 373–398.

Wahl, D.C. (2016). *Designing regenerative cultures.* Axminster: Triarchy Press.

Walsh, B. (2014). *Contracting for value: Contributing factors for the ethical alignment of confidentiality and stakeholder needs in executive coaching.* Dissertation for Henley Business School MSc, unpublished. Retrieved 1st November 2019 from https://www.metaco.co.za/articles/Contracting%20for%20Value.pdf

Wampold, B.E. (2001). *The great psychotherapy debate: Models, methods and findings.* Mahwah, NJ: Lawrence Erlbaum Associates.

Ware, B. (2011). *The top five regrets of the dying.* Bloomington, IN: Balboa Press.

Wasylyshyn, K.M. (2003). Executive coaching: An outcome study. *Consulting Psychology Journal: Practice and Research*, 55(2), 94–106. http://dx.doi.org/10.1037/1061-4087.55.2.94

Watkins, J.M. and Mohr, B.J. (2001). *Appreciative enquiry: Change at the speed of imagination.* San Francisco, CA: Jossey-Bass/Pfeiffer.

Weintrobe, S. (Ed.) (2012). *Engaging with climate change: Psychoanalytic and interdisciplinary perspectives.* Hove: Routledge.

Wells, S. and McLean, J. (2013). One way forward to beat the Newtonian habit with a complexity perspective on organisational change. *Systems*, 1(4), 66–84.

Wells, S. and McLean, J. (in press). Emergent organizational change: A living systems perspective. In G. Metcalf, K. Kijima and H. Deguchi (Eds.) *Springer handbook of systems science*. Singapore: Springer Nature.

West, M.A. (2013). Developing cultures of high-quality care. Talk at the Kings Fund London, March 2013. Retrieved 1st November, 2019 from www.kingsfund.org.uk/audio-video/michael-west-developing-cultures-high-quality-care

West, M.A. and Dawson, J.F. (2012). *Employee engagement and NHS performance: Research report*. London: The King's Fund.

West, M.A., Guthrie, J.P., Dawson, J.F., Borrill, C.S. and Carter, M.R. (2006). Reducing patient mortality in hospitals: The role of human resource management. *Journal of Organizational Behaviour*, 27, 983–1002.

Whitmore, J. (2017). *Coaching for performance*. 5th edition. London: Nicholas Brealey Publishing.

Whitmore, J. and Einzig, H. (2016). Transpersonal coaching. In J. Passmore (Ed.) *Excellence in coaching*. 3rd edition. London: Kogan Page.

Whittington, J. (2016). *Systemic coaching & constellations*. 2nd edition. London: Kogan Page.

Wilber, K. (1993). *The spectrum of consciousness*. Wheaton: Theosophical Publishing House.

Wilber, K. (2006). *Integral spirituality*. Boston, MA: Shambhala.

Wilkinson, R. and Pickett, K. (2010). *The spirit level: Why equality is better for everyone*. London: Penguin Books.

World Population clock. (2019). Retrieved 1st November 2019 from www.worldometers.info/world-population/

Yalom, I. (2008). *Staring at the sun: Overcoming the terror of death*. San Francisco, CA: Jossey-Bass.

Zenger, J.H., Folkman, J.R. and Edinger, S.K. (2011). Making yourself indispensable. *Harvard Business Review*, 89(10), 84–90, 92, 153

Index